Advanced Methodology and Pedagogical Practices of Social Science Education

Advanced Methodology and Pedagogical Practices of Social Science Education

Dr Ismail Thamarasseri

Deepthy Baby

GenNext Publication

Published by

GenNext Publication
5, Ansari Road
Daryaganj, New Delhi-110002
Phone: 011-47034999, 9811692060
E-mail: gennextpublication@hotmail.com

Distribution Network
gyanbooks.com
India, USA, Canada, UK, Australia, France

ISBN: 978-93-5663-771-9

First Published, 2024

Printed at: Gyan Press, Delhi.

Advanced Methodology and Pedagogical Practices of Social Science Education

Author: Dr Ismail Thamarasseri & Deepthy Baby

Contents

Preface

Welcome to "Advanced Methodology and Pedagogical Practices of Social Science Education." This comprehensive book delves into the intricate realms of social science education, offering a rich tapestry of insights, methodologies, and pedagogical practices designed to enhance the teaching and learning experience in this dynamic field. This book develops an understanding about the Epistemological Frames of Social Science, Componential Convergence in Social Science and Assessment in Social Science Education.

Unit 1, "Epistemological Frames of Social Science," initiates the journey by exploring the foundational aspects of social science knowledge. This section examines the various epistemological frames that underpin the discipline, providing readers with a nuanced understanding of how knowledge is constructed and interpreted in the context of social science.

Unit 2, "Componential Convergence in Social Science," takes a closer look at the interdisciplinary nature of social science. It elucidates the convergence of components from different disciplines within the broader field of social science, emphasizing the interconnectedness that shapes a holistic understanding of societal phenomena.

Moving to Unit 3, "Pedagogical Applications of Social Science Discipline," the focus shifts to practical applications in teaching. This section provides educators with innovative and effective pedagogical approaches to engage students in the study of social science, fostering a deeper appreciation for the subject matter.

Unit 4, "Strategies for Social Science Instruction," builds upon the pedagogical foundation, offering a diverse array of strategies to enhance instruction. Educators will find valuable insights into creating dynamic and student-centred learning environments that promote critical thinking, collaboration, and a lifelong passion for social science.

Unit 5, "Social Science Teacher Educator," is dedicated to the professionals shaping the next generation of educators. It explores the role of social science teacher educators and provides guidance on cultivating the skills and knowledge necessary to excel in this pivotal position.

Finally, Unit 6, "Assessment in Social Science Education," concludes the journey by addressing the crucial aspect of evaluating student learning. This section explores effective assessment practices, ensuring that educators can gauge the effectiveness of their teaching methods and tailor their approaches to meet the diverse needs of learners.

Expected Course Outcomes

- Discuss the meaning, nature, theoretical imperatives, and componential convergence of the concept of social science in relation with education and curriculum.
- Deliberate on the aims and objectives of teaching social science in the relevance of knowledge of objectives in formulating appropriate methodology of teaching.
- Explain the principles and techniques of organisation of social science curriculum.
- Explore the nature and importance of inter-disciplinary approaches to teaching social science.
- Examine the psychological considerations of social science instruction.
- Use modern instructional strategies and models in the teaching and learning of social science.
- Debate on the nature, scope and use of technology in Social Science education.
- Identify various resources for learning social science and use the different media, materials, and resources for teaching Social Science.
- Construct and administer appropriate assessment tools of evaluation and interpret results.
- Identify priority areas of research and experimentation in Social Science education.
- Take part in actual classroom teaching to become an effective teacher educator in social science.

Throughout this book, we aim to provide a comprehensive resource for educators, teacher educators, and anyone interested in advancing their understanding of social science education. Each unit is crafted with care, drawing on the expertise of seasoned educators and scholars in the field. We invite you to embark on this enlightening exploration of advanced methodologies and pedagogical practices that will undoubtedly enrich the landscape of social science education.

The authors express their sincere gratitude to all faculty members and administrative staff of School of Pedagogical Sciences, Mahatma Gandhi University for their valuable support and facilities given during the course of the study. The authors are grateful to their friends and colleagues for their emotional support and valuable ideas, which greatly helped in the completion of the study. In preparation of this book the authors had to refer to the works of other authors and information sources. The authors extremely indebted to various authors, editors, educationists and scholars whose views and opinions are integrated in this book. The authors shall ever remain obliged to their parents, teachers, friends, and family members for their kind guidance and assistance. Above all, the authors humbly solicit the God Almighty's blessings and is always thankful for the strength and presence of mind showered up on them for completing the work successfully. To them all, the authors offer their grateful thanks to **M/s. Gyan Books Private Limited New Delhi** who came forward willingly undertakes the publishing of this book.

DR. ISMAIL THAMARASSERI

DEEPTHY BABY

March 2024
Kottayam, Kerala

UNIT - 1

EPISTEMOLOGICAL FRAMES OF SOCIAL SCIENCE

INTRODUCTION

Epistemology traditionally has been defined as the division of philosophy that investigates the nature and origin of knowledge. More specifically, epistemology usually is said to be concerned with either the development of common bodies of knowledge or the establishment of personal knowledge. In recent years, epistemology also has come to be used to encompass how people learn coupled with the term "constructivism," it signifies learning as an active process that occurs as each person constructs his or her own portrayal of reality. This unit is concerned with the implications of epistemology for social science education. There is a general lack of thought among educators about how what teachers bring to their teaching-for example, their frames of reference, including their beliefs about subject matter and how children learn-affects the purpose behind their teaching. Epistemology as knowledge-building and epistemology as learning are both relevant to the education of social science teachers. It is important to help social science teachers to be thoughtful about the epistemological elements in the frames of reference they bring to their teacher education programmes, about the varying epistemological orientations within and across the social sciences, and about their assumptions as to how students best learn. (Shaver, 1992)

The social sciences are the disciplines that study individual and group behaviour, and include anthropology, economics, geography, history, political sciences, psychology, social studies, and sociology. While each discipline within social science customizes its methodologies, the epistemological basis for each methodology remains largely unchanged.

The epistemology of the social sciences is a sub-topic of the philosophy of social science. By a study of epistemology, it means the study of what is knowledge in social science, how knowledge is acquired in social science, how knowledge is justified, and how social scientists come to know what they know. (Griffiths, 2010)

Epistemologically-balanced social research is neither the dispassionate gathering of factual information, nor the elaboration of universal assessments formed on the basis of armchair speculation. It involves engaging in inquiry in an independent manner and being aware of the perspectival character of the claims being made in the attempt to shed new light on social phenomena. The calibre of social science can be elevated when researchers recognize the symbolic nature of their work and the significance of their conclusions in the larger social order. (Gattone, 2020)

PHENOMENOLOGY AND SOCIAL SCIENCE

Phenomenology has its roots in a 20th century philosophical movement based on the work of the philosopher **Edmund Husserl** (1859-1938). As research tool, phenomenology is based on the academic disciplines of philosophy and psychology and has become a widely accepted method for describing human experiences. Phenomenology is a qualitative research method that is used to describe how human beings experience a certain phenomenon. A phenomenological study attempts to set aside biases and preconceived assumptions about human experiences, feelings, and responses to a particular situation. It allows the researcher to delve into the perceptions, perspectives, understandings, and feelings of those people who have actually experienced or lived the phenomenon or situation of interest. Therefore, phenomenology can be defined as the direct investigation and description of phenomena as consciously experienced by people living those experiences. Phenomenological research is typically conducted through the use of in-depth interviews of small samples of participants. By studying the perspectives of multiple participants, a researcher can begin to make generalizations regarding what it is like to experience a certain phenomenon from the perspective of those that have lived the experience.

Phenomenology is the philosophical study of the structures of experience and consciousness. As a philosophical movement it was founded in the early years of the 20th century by Edmund Husserl and was later expanded upon by a circle of his followers at the universities of Göttingen and Munich in Germany. Phenomenology is a term used in social science to refer to the philosophical underpinnings of a variety of approaches that tend to concentrate on the essential nature of the social world.

The relation between phenomenology and social sciences has gone through various stages. In phenomenological philosophy, its outstanding landmarks can be found in:

(a) the counterpoint that Husserl posited for the different sciences and his mounting interest in social sciences,

(b) the reinforcement of this line of thought by his followers - Alfred Schutz and Merleau-Ponty, for example-, and

(c) the radicalization of "non-intentional phenomenology" produced by Levinas and Henry.

In the ambit of social sciences, Schutz has been acknowledged to have been first in trying to establish the connection between both disciplines by broaching the phenomenology of the natural attitude understood as phenomenological psychology, thus freeing social sciences from the rule of philosophy because. From this perspective, they do not stem from it but from the life-world, a space that can be accessed by the methodology of social research, however restrictedly because it ends subdued to methodological deliberations. As a result, the relation between phenomenology and ontology remains unaccounted for.

The relationship between social science and social reality seems infinitely more complex than that between tool and object of analysis. In our time, the subterranean linkages of knowledge and experience have been vividly exposed: the crisis features of social reality have produced, or at least are accompanied by, an identity crisis in many academic disciplines - notably in social science. The manifestations of this malaise are familiar; they range from scholarly reassessments of specific research procedures to dramatic confrontations at professional meetings and in the context of professional organizations. Of late, such agonies have even surfaced in official pronouncements. In his recent presidential address to the political science fraternity, David Easton diagnosed professional unrest as a "new revolution" following closely on the heels of the behavioural or scientific renovation. As he pointed out, the preceding behavioural transformation had scarcely run its course before it was "overtaken by the increasing social and political crises of our time." Although not diametrically opposed to its predecessor, the new insurgency involved a profound challenge to professional orthodoxy: "The essence of the post-behavioural revolution is not hard to identify. It consists of a deep dissatisfaction with political research and teaching, especially of the kind that is striving to convert the study of politics into a more rigorously scientific discipline modelled on the methodology of the natural sciences."

KARL POPPER'S EVOLUTIONARY EPISTEMOLOGY

Evolutionary epistemology is an epistemological approach that is biologically oriented. It applies Charles Darwin's principle of natural selection to scientific theories and to other forms of knowledge. Actually, this contrasts with most theories of knowledge that are concerned with the foundations of belief or the probability of theories. Sir Karl Raimund Popper (1902-1994) revived this approach of evolutionary epistemology and applied to all form's knowledge development. It is involved with problem-solving and error elimination under different forms of selective pressure. According to Karl Popper, knowledge grows by trial and error, furthermore, by conjectures and refutations.

Karl Popper was an Austrian-British philosopher, academic and social commentator. One of the 20th century's most influential philosophers of science, Popper is known for his rejection of the classical inductivist views on the scientific method in favour of empirical falsification. He accepted this theory to explain all forms of learning and problem solving, which also includes the evolution of life on earth. That is, in the plant and animal world this involves the production of new reactions, new organs, new forms of life. And it involves the production of new ideas in human beings. When these new forms of life or theories appear, they confront selective pressures. They may arise from the biological environment or from competing forms of life. Thereby, ideas meet the competition of alternative theories, critical arguments and experimental tests.

Evolutionary epistemology is the effort to confront epistemological questions from the evolutionary point of view. Popper revived this approach to knowledge called evolutionary epistemology. Evolutionary epistemology applies Darwin's principle of natural selection to scientific theories and to other forms of knowledge. Actually, this contrasts with most theories of knowledge that are concerned with the foundations of belief or the probability of theories.

According to Popper, all knowledge grows by the method of variation and selection found in living organisms. Human knowledge is adaptive and increases by conjecture (blind variation of untested, new theories) and refutation (selective retention). The new approach from the standpoint of biology is not incremental, i.e., it unifies Karl Popper's whole philosophy of critical rationalism. The way in which Popper's philosophy of biology contributes to the integration of thought can be seen in the new expression of the main problem of epistemology. The important function of the theory of knowledge is to apprehend it as continuous with animal knowledge and to grasp also its discontinuity, if any, from animal knowledge. Moreover, Popper stated that the origin and the evolution of knowledge might be said to coincide with the origin and evolution of life and to be closely linked with the origin and evolution of the planet earth. Evolution theory bonds knowledge with it and human beings with the cosmos, so the problem of knowledge becomes a problem of cosmology. As Popper earlier compared the content of competing theories and assessed their verisimilitude, later he examined the whole realm of cognitive structures found in the animal kingdom, and compared the 'fit' between the organic system and its environment. Thus, Popper significantly generalizes the earlier approach, i.e., the experience is theory impregnated and structure-impregnated. It is the outcome of Popper's understanding and analysis of the process by which knowledge, be it human or animal grows. (Popper & Notturno, 2000) With regard to this view, the term 'knowledge' alludes to the objective end products of certain evolutionary processes, ranging from the emergence of organs such as the eyes to the most sophisticated scientific theories which man has propounded. Every knowledge attaining process must be considered as a succession of casual conjectures and continuous refutations that is similar to the evolutionary process.

Beginning with Sir Karl Popper's (1963) ideas concerning conjectures and refutations (also called trials and errors), the following position is defended within traditional evolutionary epistemology: there is a growth of (scientific) knowledge which is comparable with the succession of adaptations in evolution. The task of evolutionary epistemology thus becomes explaining this growth.

Karl Popper argued that at no stage during evolution does an organism receive knowledge from the outer world. Bold conjectures are made about the outer world and if these hypotheses are not falsified by experiments performed by the scientific community, they survive. In the long run, unfit theories are eliminated by the process of falsification, and there is a growth in knowledge. Theories that survive longer than others are understood to tentatively corroborate the truth. The analogy with biological evolution is clear: a selectionist account is preferred over an instructionist one. This means that at no point does an organism choose its genetic endowment. However, if this organism, with the genetic endowment that it is born with, stands the test of the environment, that is, if it survives long enough so that it can reproduce, then the organism's genetic traits survive, and it is said that it is adapted to its environment. In the long run, only the fit survives; maladaptive organisms are not able to survive long enough to reproduce and spread their genes in the gene pool again, and therefore die out.

Thus, just as the Modern Synthesis stresses that an organism can by no means directly receive instructions from the environment, Popper (1963) emphasizes that we force our interpretations upon the world prior to our observations: "Without waiting, passively, for repetitions to impress regularities upon us, we actively try to impose regularities upon the world." These are the conjectures that are put forward for trial, to be selected or eliminated according to the test-results. Scientific theories are thus not the result of observations, but of wild hypotheses. Although Popper himself is not part of the field of evolutionary epistemology, his work on conjectures and refutations is often regarded as a first account on evolutionary epistemology.

KRESS'S MULTI-MODALITY THEORY

Multimodality is the application of multiple literacies within one medium. For example, understanding a televised weather forecast (medium) involves understanding spoken language, written language, weather specific language (such as temperature scales), geography, and symbols (clouds, sun, rain, etc.). Multiple literacies or "modes" contribute to an audience's understanding of a composition. Everything from the placement of images to the organization of the content to the method of delivery creates meaning. This is the result of a shift from isolated text being relied on as the primary source of communication, to the image being utilized more frequently in the digital age. Multimodality describes communication practices in terms of the textual, aural, linguistic, spatial, and visual resources used to compose messages.

While all communication, literacy, and composing practices are and always have been multimodal, academic and scientific attention to the phenomenon only started gaining momentum in the 1960s. Inspiring scholar, linguist and semiotician, **Gunther Kress** (1940-2019) is one of the main developers of social semiotics who continue to contribute and investigate the common principles behind multimodal communication. In their work, the authors outline an approach to a theory of semiotics relevant to contemporary semiotic practice. Throughout their collaborative and individual work, Kress and van Leeuwen (2005) discuss semiotic principles in respect to multimodal meaning, dimensions of semiotic analysis, e.g., discourse, genre, style, modality, and, all in all, the use of communicative modes and media in instances of communicative practice. The authors investigate texts in regard to socially formed and changeable sets of options that have meaning potential in particular contexts of use. Gunther Kress was an Australian semiotician who was Chair of Semiotics and Education in the Department of Culture, Communication and Media within the Institute of Education of University College London. Kress was born in Nuremberg Germany and trained as a linguist in Australia and London under MAK Halliday.

Gunther Kress's scholarship on multimodality is canonical within social semiotic approaches and has a considerable influence in many other approaches as well (writing studies). Kress defines mode in two ways. In the first, a mode "is a socially and culturally shaped resource for making meaning. Image, writing, layout, speech, moving images are examples of different modes." In the second, "semiotic modes, similarly, are shaped by both the intrinsic characteristics and potentialities of the medium and by the requirements, histories and values of societies and their cultures."

In the book, *Multimodality: A Social Semiotic Approach to Contemporary Communication* (2010), Kress pursues his lifelong interest in the pedagogic dimensions of multimodality. The book titled *Multimodal Discourse* (2001) Gunther Kress and Theo Van Leeuwen outlines a new theory of communication for the age of interactive media. The book provide students with a wide-ranging analysis of the various communication styles and the ways by which text is now understood as the interaction of sound, music, vision, colour and language.

Multimodality is a theory which looks at how people communicate and interact with each other, not just through writing (which is one mode) but also through speaking, gesture, gaze, and visual forms (which are many modes). Multimodality is a theory which looks at the many different modes that people use to communicate with each other and to express themselves. This theory is relevant as an increase in technology tools, and associated access to multimedia composing software, has led to people being able to easily use many modes in art, writing, music, and dance and every-day interactions with each other. A **mode** is generally defined as a communication channel that a culture recognizes. Examples of modes are writing, gesture, posture, gaze, font choice and colour, images, video, and even the interactions between them.

While many of these modes have always existed, they have not always been recognized as a legitimate or culturally accepted form of communication or expression. Learning theorists who advocate for multimodality emphasize that people communicate in a variety of ways, and that in order to completely understand someone, the many modes they use to communicate must be observed and recognized. The theory of multimodality can be found in writings and discussions related to communication theory, linguistics, media literacy, visual literacy, anthropological studies, and design studies.

MAX WEBER'S SOCIAL ACTION

Max Weber (1864-1920) was one of the founding fathers of Sociology. Weber saw both structural and action approaches as necessary to developing a full understanding of society and social change. The three key points of Max Weber's thoughts is as under:

- Firstly, he argued that 'Verstehen' or empathetic understanding is crucial to understanding human action and social change, a point which he emphasised in his classic study 'The Protestant Ethic and the Spirit of Capitalism';
- Secondly, he believed we could make generalisations about the basic types of motivation for human action (there are four basic types) and
- Thirdly, he still argued that structure shaped human action, because certain societies or groups encourage certain general types of motivation (but within these general types, there is a lot of variation possible). This final point can be illustrated by a quote from one of his most important works 'Economy and Society', first published in the 1920s, in which he said 'Sociology is a science concerning itself with interpretive understanding of social action and thereby with a causal explanation of its course and consequences.'

Max Weber defines social action as "action is social in so far as by virtue of the subjective meaning attached to it by acting individual it takes account of the behaviour of others and is thereby oriented in its course it includes all human behaviour when and insofar as the acting individual attaches a subjective meaning to it". Max Weber defined four types of ideal actions. But what did he mean by ideal actions? He meant that these actions might not occur similarly in the real world as they have been explained in the Weber theory. However, they may exist as a mixture of a contaminated form of social action.

Max Weber did not just believe that individuals shape society – societies encourage certain types of motive for action – for example, the religion of Calvinism encouraged people to save money, which eventually led to capitalism. Weber believes that there are **four ideal types of social actions**. Ideal types are used as a tool to look at real cases and compare them to the ideal types to see where they fall. No social action is purely just one of the four types.

- **Traditional Social Action**: actions controlled by traditions, "the way it has always been done".

- **Affective Social Action**: actions determined by one's specific affections and emotional state, you do not think about the consequences.
- **Value Rational Social Action**: actions that are determined by a conscious belief in the inherent value of a type of behaviour (for example, religion).
- **Instrumental-Rational Social Action**: actions that are carried out to achieve a certain goal, you do something because it leads to a result.

To illustrate these different types of action, consider someone "going to school" in terms of these four ideal types: Traditionally, one may attend college because her grandparents, parents, aunts, and uncles have as well. They wish to continue the family tradition and continue with college as well. When relating to affective, one may go to school just because they enjoy learning. They love going to college whether or not it will make them broke. With value rational, one may attend college because it's a part of his/her religion that everyone must receive the proper education. Therefore, this person attends college for that reason only. Finally, one may go to college because he/she may want an amazing job in the future and in order to get that job, he/she needs a college degree.

Max Weber was particularly interested in the later of these – he believed that modern societies encouraged 'Instrumental-Action' – that is we are encouraged to do things in the most efficient way (e.g., driving to work) rather than thinking about whether driving to work is the right thing to do (which would be value-rational action). Weber believed that modern societies were obsessed with efficiency – modernizing and getting things done, such that questions of ethics, affection and tradition were brushed to one side – this has the consequence of making people miserable and leading to enormous social problems. Weber was actually very depressed about this and had a mental breakdown towards the end of his life.

SCOTT AND PRELL'S SOCIAL NETWORK ANALYSIS

Christina Prell (Department o Sociological Studies, University of Sheffield) and John Scott (Department of Sociology, University of Plymouth) are contemporary educators who made significant academic contributions in the field of social network analysis.

The roots of social network thinking are to be found in relational or structural approaches to social analysis that developed in classical sociology. While some approaches to sociology and anthropology used the ideas of culture and cultural formation to explain social patterns of feeling, thought, and behaviour, and others stressed the material environment and the physicality of the body as crucial determinants, a particularly important strand of social thought focused its attention on the actual patterns of interaction and interconnection through which individuals and social groups are related to each other. In some cases, this involved a conception of the 'social organism', or social system, as a structure of institutions that constrain the subjectivity and actions of those who occupy positions within those institutions. For other theorists, however, greater attention was given to the immediate face-to-face encounters through which individuals relate to each other and that are constantly refigured through the actions of these individuals.

Social Network Analysis looks at how people within social networks (for example: families, clubs, Facebook groups) relate to each other and what these interactions say about both the individual actors and the entire social network.

Social network analysis looks at how people (actors) relate to each other across their social networks. It is based on network theory (from computer science), which explains that certain behaviours can be better understood by diagramming or mapping how people or groups share information, talk, or interact in other ways.

A social network can be a variety of sizes: from small (e.g., two-generational immediate family), to more mid-sized (e.g., school class, sports team, or club), to quite large (e.g., Facebook group, college/university alumni group). Social network analysis can include looking at people's actions in online social networks (e.g., Facebook, Google+, MySpace), in addition to the more traditional social networks that exist off of the Web, like families, clubs, hobby groups, political parties, and friend/acquaintance groups.

Social network analysis is useful in any research field which looks at how people relate to each other. These fields can span from anthropology to communications to sociology. There are mapping and visualization software available which can help researchers understand social networks from a more objective basis and explain their findings to others.

Interest in social network analysis has grown considerably in the last decade, following a long period of gradual expansion that began in the 1960s. There is a long history behind this growth of interest, with much of the key work in the second half of the twentieth century having been undertaken in the United States. Interest in continental Europe picked up somewhat earlier than in Britain and Ireland, reflecting the deep origins of social network analysis in German social theory, but it is now a world-wide specialism with a growing influence in many substantive research areas.

Social network analysis is based around the idea of seeing social relations in formal terms as patterns of points and lines in a mathematical space with formal properties that can be analysed with precision. This metaphor of the social network reflects an awareness of network ideas in electrical and transport engineering and in geographical views of networks as landscape features. However, the specific origins of the idea are firmly rooted in sociology itself. It was in classical German sociology that the idea of the social network was really established. In the various writings of Ferdinand Tonnies, Max Weber, and, above all, Georg Simmel there developed a sociological framework according to which large scale social structures had to be seen in terms of the social relations among individuals that resulted from their subjectively meaningful interactions. These theorists showed that interactions formed interweaving patterns of connection that comprise the warp and weft of social webs of connection. For many theorists, these webs of connection were to be analysed in formal terms, rather than in terms of their substantive contents. Social structures such as classes, states, and economies were envisaged as concatenations of these configurations. From the later 1960s, advances in computing began to make possible the investigation of large-scale social networks and an explosion in social network analysis took place. Whilst methodological and software developments have undoubtedly played a key role in stimulating the recent re-emergence of interest in network analysis, by making it both more sophisticated and more accessible, theoretical and substantive developments both within and outside of the social sciences have played a key role too.

GEORG SIMMEL'S CONFLICT THEORY

German sociologist **Georg Simmel** (1858–1918) believed that conflict can help integrate and stabilize a society. He said that the intensity of the conflict varies depending on the emotional involvement of the parties, the degree of solidarity within the opposing groups, and the clarity and limited nature of the goals. Georg Simmel is known to develop an approach of formal sociology by capturing the form of basic social processes. He does not view social structure as source of domination and subjugation but as inseparable mingling of associative and dissociative social processes.

Simmel views conflict as ubiquitous and inevitable in society, lies in the idea of 'organismic' view of the social world. It was a new and dominating idea of his time. This organismic view led Simmel to view consequences of conflict not for change but for bringing continuity of the system. Conflict, is designed to resolve dualism, is a way of achieving some kind of unity. Even it may be through annihilation of one of the conflicting parties.

Simmel postulates that the organismic whole is characterized by an innate hostile impulse or a need of hating and fighting among in the organismic whole. He says that conflict is reflection of not only of the interest but also of the hostile instincts. Such conflict is exacerbated by the conflict of interest or mitigated by harmonious relations as well as by the instinct of love. Simmel has devoted all his efforts to analyse positive consequences of the conflict for maintaining the whole and it unites. Georg Simmel has presented image of social organisation/social system, different from Karl Marx, as following.

- Social relationships occur within the social organisation/ social system can be typified as an organismic intermingling of associative and dissociative processes.
- Such processes are the reflection of both instinctual impulses of the actors and the imperatives dictated by various types of social relationships.
- Conflict is ubiquitous feature of the social system, but not necessarily led to the breakdown of the system.
- Conflict is the fundamental process operating to preserve the social whole.

Simmel has developed proposition of the conflict by direct observation of the events and processes occurring in the society. Conflict, is manifested in the different states of intensity and violence in society, is understood through polar ends of competition and fight. Competition is more regulated and parallel striving of parties and the fight denotes less regulation and more direct combating attitudes of the parties. He has proposed the following two sets of the proposition of the conflict- relating to the intensity and violence; and the functions; promoting solidarity, integration and orderly change of the system.

Conflict- Intensity and Violence

- If more conflict is considered as a means to clearly achieve the goals/ends then the conflict is less likely to be violent.
- The conflict is more violent when the greater degree of emotion of the conflicting parties is involved. The more emotional involvement and emotional arousal happens under the following.

(a) When greater is the solidarity of members of the conflicting parties, (b) When greater is the harmony of members of the conflicting parties.

Conflict- Functions- For the Conflicting Party

When conflict is more violent, then (a) The more despotic centralization of the conflicting parties/groups occur, (b) The greater will be the internal solidarity of the conflict groups, (c) If conflicting parties are small then lesser will be the tolerance of dissent and deviance, (d) If parties are in minority group, then greater will be the internal solidarity.

If more violent are the inter group hostility, then (a) The more frequent is the conflict, (2) The less group boundaries to disappear.

Functions of Conflict for the systemic whole

- If conflicting groups have different degree of the power in the system, then the conflict will be less violent, it has integrative consequences for the whole.
- If more frequent is the conflict, then it is less violent and has integrative consequences because of the following. (a) The more members may release their hostilities, (b) The more norms of regulation of the conflict are created, (3) The conflict promotes more functional interdependence.
- If conflict is more violent and more prolonged then the more coalition among the previously unrelated groups in the system is observed.
- If more prolonged is the threat of the violence, then more enduring is the coalition of the conflicting parties.

DAISAKU IKEDA'S PEACE EDUCATION

Daisaku Ikeda (2nd January 1928 – 15th November 2023) is a contemporary Japanese Buddhist philosopher, educator, author, and nuclear disarmament advocate. He has served as the third president and then honorary president of the Soka Gakkai, the largest of Japan's new religious movements.

Daisaku Ikeda, founder of the Ikeda Centre for Peace, Learning, and Dialogue, is a Buddhist thinker and leader, peace builder, prolific writer and poet, educator, and proponent and practitioner of wide-ranging dialogue. Ikeda's dialogue partners have included Arnold Toynbee, Mikhail Gorbachev, Nelson Mandela, Rosa Parks, Linus Pauling and other influential figures in the worldwide shift to a culture of peace and mutual understanding. Many of these dialogues have been published in book form.

Born in Tokyo in 1928, Ikeda experienced first-hand the tragic reality of war and militarism. In the chaos of post-war Japan, he came to embrace Buddhism through an encounter with the educator and pacifist Josei Toda, who had been imprisoned for his beliefs during World War II, and who later became the second president of the Buddhist lay organization Soka Gakkai.

As third president of the Soka Gakkai and founder of the Soka Gakkai International, Mr. Ikeda has developed and inspired the largest, most diverse international lay Buddhist association in the world. Based on the 700-year-old tradition of Nichiren Buddhism, a form of Mahayana Buddhism, the movement is characterized by its emphasis on value creation (soka): each individual finding value in their unique path while contributing value to humanity.

Mr. Ikeda has founded a number of cultural, educational, and peace research institutions around the world, including the Boston Research Centre for the 21st Century in 1993 (renamed the Ikeda Centre for Peace, Learning, and Dialogue in 2009), the Toda Institute for Global Peace and Policy Research in 1996, and Soka University of America in 2001. All of these institutions share a commitment to soka-inspired values of peace and humanism, but function as independent organizations.

Ikeda is a Buddhist leader, peacebuilder, school founder, and prolific author whose six decades of contributions to peace education have had a global impact in practice but have remained unexamined in the extant, particularly Anglophone, literature. Using excerpts and bilingual discourse analysis of the Ikeda corpus, the authors focus on five aspects to trace the past, present, and future of Ikeda's contributions to peace education: first, they trace the biographical roots of Ikeda's contributions to his early educational experiences and encounter with Josei Toda (1900–1958). Second, they outline the Nichiren Buddhist philosophy informing Ikeda's approach to peace education. Third, they explicate in the context of peace and peace education Ikeda's concept of value-creating, or Soka education (soka kyoiku) relative to value-creating pedagogy (soka kyoikugaku) theorized by Tsunesaburo Makiguchi (1871–1944). In light of this relation, they also trace the origin of the Soka Gakkai International, of which Ikeda is founding president. Fifth, they clarify Ikeda's educational proposals made explicitly under the label of 'peace education,' namely, cultural exchange, a United Nations for Education, and education for disarmament and human rights (including anti-bullying, sustainability, and global citizenship).

Ikeda's perspectives, proposals, and practices of Soka education and 'peace education' can be viewed as a tripartite ontological model of a process of becoming, moving from inner transformation by means of dialogue to global citizenship.

Daisaku Ikeda (2002) says, "Education must cultivate the wisdom to reject and resist violence in all its forms. It must foster people who intuitively understand and know–in their minds, in their hearts, with their entire being–the irreplaceable value of human beings and the natural world. I believe such education embodies the timeless struggle of human civilization to create an unerring path to peace."

Since 26 January 1983, Ikeda has submitted annual peace proposals to the United Nations, addressing such areas as building a culture of peace, gender equality in education, empowerment of women, UN reform and universal human rights with a view on global civilization.

Ikeda's proposals for nuclear disarmament and abolishing nuclear weapons submitted to the special session of the UN General Assembly in 1978, 1982 and 1988 built on his mentor Josei Toda's 1957 declaration condemning such weapons of mass destruction as "an absolute evil that threatens the people's right of existence." Calling for human security and sustainability in his 2012 peace proposal, he advocated for a transition away from nuclear-powered energy. In his 2015 peace proposal, he called on the international community for concerted multilateral action - "shared action" - for protecting human rights of displaced persons including refugees and migrants, ridding the world of nuclear weapons and constructing a global sustainable society. In his 2019 peace proposal, he advocated for multilateral support toward the entry into force of the Treaty on the Prohibition of nuclear weapons (TPNW), renewed efforts based on Article 6 of the Non-Proliferation Treaty to de-escalate tensions, and an international framework to ban lethal autonomous weapons (LAWs). In his 2020 peace proposal, "Towards Our Shared Future: Constructing an Era of Human Solidarity", Ikeda urges nations to collaborate to confront issues like natural disasters and climate change. In his 2021 peace proposal, Ikeda welcomed the entry into force of the TPNW and called for the "deterrent force" not of nuclear weapons but of "joint action and solidarity ... brought to bear against" the critical impacts of climate change and the COVID-19 pandemic.

NATIONAL CURRICULUM FRAMEWORK FOR TEACHER EDUCATION (NCFTE 2009)

The National Council for Teacher Education (NCTE) has prepared the National Curriculum Framework for Teacher Education, which was circulated in March 2009. The Framework has been prepared in the background of the National Curriculum Framework (NCF), 2005 and the principles laid down in the Right of Children to Free and Compulsory Education Act, 2009 which advocates for a transformed framework on teacher education. The framework which would be consistent with the changed philosophy of school curriculum recommended in the NCF, 2005. While clearing the vision of teacher education in India, the framework has some important dimensions of the new approach to teacher education.

Important Dimensions of the Framework NCFTE 2009

- Reflective practices are considered to be the chief aim of teacher education.
- Pupil-teachers should be provided opportunities for self-learning, reflection, integration and expression of new ideas.
- Developing competencies for self-directed learning and ability to think, be critical and to work collectively.
- Providing adequate opportunities to student-teachers for observing and engaging with children, communicate with and get linked to children.
- The Framework has pointed out the centre of attention, objectives and broad areas of study in terms of academic and practical learning.
- To well execute the curricular operations and assessment related strategies for the various preliminary teacher education programmes.
- The sketch also outlines the elementary issues that should direct formulation of all programmes of these courses.
- The Framework has emphasized on the approach and methodology of in-service teacher training programmes.
- It has also pin pointed the strategy for implementation of the Framework.

Six Chapters of NCFTE 2009: The National Curriculum Framework for Teacher Education of 2009 contains the following six chapters, viz:

1. Context, Concerns and Vision of Teacher Education
2. Curricular Areas of Initial Teacher Preparation
3. Transacting the Curriculum and Evaluating the Developing Teacher

4. Continuing Professional Development and Support for In-Service Teachers
5. Preparing Teacher Educators
6. Implementation Strategies

The NCTE has put all efforts to frame a vision document for teacher education in India. All the

stakeholders were consulted to give their views on the qualitative and quantitative improvements that could be achieved in educating teachers at various levels like school, graduate, post-graduate, doctoral and post-doctoral levels. The NCFTE, 2009 is broader policy document and have many good implications for Indian teacher education.

POSITIVISM, ANTI POSITIVISM AND POST POSITIVISM

Positivism, in Western philosophy, generally, any system that confines itself to the data of experience and excludes a priori or metaphysical speculations. More narrowly, the term designates the thought of the French philosopher Auguste Comte (1798–1857).

As a philosophical ideology and movement, positivism first assumed its distinctive features in the work of Comte, who also named and systematized the science of sociology. It then developed through several stages known by various names, such as empirio-criticism, logical positivism, and logical empiricism, finally merging, in the mid-20th century, into the already existing tradition known as analytic philosophy.

Positivism is the name for the scientific study of the social world. Its goal is to formulate abstract and universal laws on the operative dynamics of the social universe. A law is a statement about relationships among forces in the universe. In positivism, laws are to be tested against collected data systematically. Auguste Comte - who saw Newton's law of gravity as the exemplar - advocated positivism as a means to legitimate the new discipline of sociology. Herbert Spencer and Emile Durkheim executed this advocacy in formulating laws that were assessed by data. Positivism however, has, never gone unchallenged, particularly in sociology and anthropology; and as a consequence, it has been subject to intense epistemological debate. The debate was, for much of the first half of the twentieth century, framed by the Vienna Circle, a group of intellectuals in Vienna who debated the nature of thought and logic on the one side, and their relations to empirical data on the other. This debate continues in many different guises at the beginning of the twenty-first century.

Positivism is a term with widely use in social science and philosophy. In general, it can be defined as an approach which applies scientific method of natural science to study human activity using objective enquiry and thereby presupposes the unity of the sciences. Positivism entails the view that scientific knowledge can be positively verifiable and foundation of knowledge is built on the discovery of general laws (Delanty, 2005). Moreover, Marsh and Smith (2001) argue that Positivism is obviously foundationalist, which is the idea believe that there is a real world out there and it is independent from agent's knowledge of it. Therefore, the essay can offer the main features of Positivism which are including, first, empiricism; second, scientific explanation; third, scientific method and the attempt to predict the case study.

Anti-positivism includes a high involvement on the part of the researcher and a low number of respondents. Anti-positivism came about in the 19th century, when scientists Wilhelm Dilthey and Heinrich Rickert began to question sociological positivism and sociological naturalism because they argued that the world of nature is not the same as the world of society, as human societies have unique aspects like meanings, symbols, rules, norms, and values - all that can be described as the culture. This view was further developed by Max Weber, who introduced the term 'Anti-positivism' (also known as Humanistic Sociology). According to this view, the sociological research conducted must concentrate on humans and their cultural values. There has been controversy on how a line between subjective and objective research can be drawn.

- In 1948, Weber, an 'Interactionist', stated that complete value-freedom or scientific objectivity is not possible within sociology
- In 1962, Kuhn, an 'anti-positivist', stated that sociology cannot be a science as sociologists do not agree on one accepted paradigm
- In 1971, Gouldner, like Kuhn an 'anti-positivist, stated that all sociologists commit themselves and are directed by a particular set of 'domain assumptions'

Max Weber and Georg Simmel introduced interpretive understanding (Verstehen) into sociology and is a systematic interpretive process in which an outside observer such as a sociologist relates to an indigenous people or sub-cultural group on their own terms and from their own point-of-view, rather than interpreting them in terms of his or her own concepts. This concept has been both expanded and criticized by later social scientists. Other sociologists have argued that this way only allows a person from one culture to analyse another. Verstehen was introduced into the practice of sociology in the United States by Talcott Parsons, an American follower of Max Weber. Parsons incorporated this concept into his 1937 work 'The Structure of Social Action'.

What is 'Verstehen'? Verstehen can mean either a kind of empathic or participatory understanding of social phenomena. In anthropological terms this is sometimes described as cultural relativism. In sociology it is an aspect of the comparative-historical approach. It relates to how people in life give meaning to the social world around them and how the social scientist accesses and evaluates this "first-person perspective". Critics of 'Verstehen' argue that there is no methodological unity of science, i.e., that we cannot use the same tools to study natural and social sciences.

Anti-positivists then add that positivism is restricted to phenomena i.e., that it is impossible to study freedom, irrationality and various unpredictable actions that are common in individual human behaviour. They also argue that knowledge can never be neutral, as it directly translates into power and that positivists attempt to draw an artificial line between observer and the subject. Finally, anti-positivists argue that positivism's three goals – description, control, and prediction – are incomplete, since they lack the goal of understanding.

Post positivism or post empiricism is a metatheoretical stance that critiques and amends positivism and has impacted theories and practices across philosophy, social sciences, and various models of scientific inquiry. While positivists emphasize independence between the researcher and the researched person (or object), post positivists argue that theories, hypotheses, background knowledge and values of the researcher can influence what is observed. Post positivists pursue objectivity by recognizing the possible effects of biases. While positivists emphasize quantitative methods, post positivists consider both quantitative and qualitative methods to be valid approaches.

Post positivists believe that human knowledge is based not on a priori assessments from an objective individual, but rather upon human conjectures. As human knowledge is thus unavoidably conjectural, the assertion of these conjectures is warranted, or more specifically, justified by a set of warrants, which can be modified or withdrawn in the light of further investigation. However, post positivism is not a form of relativism, and generally retains the idea of objective truth.

Post positivists assume that any attempt to ground knowledge outside human consciousness is futile. While post positivists do not, of course, deny the existence of a physical world, they argue that all knowledge about that world is constructed by human consciousness through language.

While positivism dominated research in the 19th century, by the early 20th century knowledge-makers in several academic fields were becoming disillusioned with this approach. The positivistic methods that had been so successful in advancing knowledge in the natural sciences - physics, chemistry, biology - were proving to be much less successful in social science research. Particularly in the fields of anthropology and psychology, researchers were frustrated in their attempts to identify universal patterns and construct paradigms that could adequately account for the complexities of human behaviour. In the first half of the 20th century, two intellectual movements swept across Europe and eventually made their way to America, changing the way knowledge is defined and produced.

CONSTRUCTION, DE-CONSTRUCTION AND RE-CONSTRUCTION

Every theory needs to follow specific rules – its logic – to draw relations between its objects; such a logic indicates a particular understanding of cause and effect. Theories need also to have entry points from where they start developing.

As suggested by Luhmann (1993), deconstruction of a theory can only happen through higher-order observations. This implies that the self-reference issues discussed before shall be resolved in this way. If I accept my theory about theory, then it must be assessed following its own guidelines without recurring in unsolvable paradoxes. Therefore, second-order (or eventually higher-order) observations of the proposed theory shall provide the tools for its own meta-analysis, solving possible paradoxes from self-reference and guaranteeing its consistence. Nevertheless, the subjectivity constitution of all observers, which synchronizes their acts (as to be discussed next), keeps playing a role in the theory (de)construction processes and an explicit methodology may alleviate issues arisen therefrom.

Theories may evolve in different ways – some may be used in solving problems external to them, while other may specialize in their own self-reproduction. The use of a theory depends on its structural coupling with the environment. Theories are constitutive parts of disciplines. But disciplines are not only clusters of theories; they in fact have structural effects on their future. For instance, anyone who wants to contribute to a given theory within a discipline cannot isolate herself from what has been already established. If a given person was educated in a specific discipline, her decisions have little chance to be revolutionary. The established structures have conditioned her education beforehand. Everyone trained in a given discipline is constituted by its established norms, relations, theories etc. The research in a given field is nowadays further constrained by strongly coupled processes of reviewing and funding, which are usually carried out by people with similar constitution.

By being a construction, theories are always subject to deconstructions by second order observers taking into account such particularities. If the deconstructed theory is planned to be reused, the deconstruction process shall be designed under the logic and the objects of the newly proposed theory. The framework used to build the transdisciplinary methodology shall map any theory from its previously established domain to a new one through the following steps:

- **Construction**: Understanding how theories as systems have evolved and constitute the individual researchers, and how the theories have been constructed from their entry-points, objects and internal logic. This part is about second-order observation and reflexivity.
- **Deconstruction**: By understanding the theories' construction processes, deconstruction may be done by questioning the soundness of entry-points, objects and logic given their historical and contextual moments.
- **Reconstruction**: From the critical analysis done through the deconstruction process, different researchers constituted by different disciplines shall find the common, transdisciplinary, ground between their individual theories looking at the totality of the phenomenon to be assessed. The new interdisciplinary theories and methods shall be built therefrom.

By looking theory as a system, a group activity might be used to develop a shared, transdisciplinary, methodology. Such a methodology shall have the strength to combat the structural effects of disciplines on the individual researchers. In this way, effects of ideology can be alleviated and researchers emancipated to carry out true interdisciplinary research.

GROWTH, DEVELOPMENT AND DE-GROWTH

Social growth is a development of an individual's knowledge and ability in dealing with other individuals and groups. Social growth is not limited to conformity; much social growth can lie outside the range of cultural expectations. A peaceful society worth living in is based on basic social policy values, such as equality of opportunity, solidarity and participation. Long term social policy investments in society promote sustainable development and economic growth. Education, health and social protection systems provide people with an opportunity to develop from their own resources and live independently. More – education and health are human rights.

- **Education is a powerful driver of development**. We promote formal and informal education in preschool, basic education and university education. To make optimal use of the potential of young people, we develop concepts for economic and social integration and empowerment of youth. Social development is about improving the well-being of every individual in society so they can reach their full potential. The success of society is linked to the well-being of each and every citizen.
- **Social development means investing in people**. It requires the removal of barriers so that all citizens can journey toward their dreams with confidence and dignity. It is about refusing to accept that people who live in poverty will always be poor. It is about helping people so they can move forward on their path to self-sufficiency. Every child must have the opportunity to grow, develop their own skills and contribute to their families and communities in a meaningful way. If they are healthy, well-educated and trained to enter the workforce and are able to make a decent wage they are better equipped to meet their basic needs and be successful. Their families will also do well and the whole of society will benefit.
- **Learning must start early in life**. By investing in early learning initiatives, we can ensure a greater degree of success amongst our citizens. Making sure that children get a good start in their education goes a long way to increasing their success later in life. An affordable, high-quality child-care system is also needed for society to succeed. When people know that their children are being well taken care of, they can be more productive in their jobs. When employers have good employees, their business is more likely to succeed. When businesses succeed, the economic situation of a community is improved. An investment today in good child care programmes can provide many long-term economic benefits for society. In addition, a safe affordable place to live is very important in helping people achieve self-sufficiency. It is the focus of family life; where families can live safely, nurture their children, build community relationships and care for aging parents. Without a decent place to live, it is difficult to function as a productive member of society.

Other investments in people that contribute to the economic prosperity of society include youth programs and services, post-secondary education, job creation, promotion of healthy, active living and safe and secure communities.

To reduce poverty, we need to take a social development approach and invest in our people. By investing in people, we can reduce poverty. We need to go beyond looking at government to find ways to develop our most valuable resources, our people. We need to share responsibility with community organizations, businesses, universities and municipalities in the task of improving the well-being of all New Brunswickers and preventing and reducing poverty.

The term degrowth refers to an economic situation during which the economic wealth produced does not increase or even decrease. This concept is to be distinguished from the recession, a simple observation of a negative growth rate in the context of a productivist economy. The concept of degrowth is a voluntary process and not a reality. It is based on the principle of awareness of a finite world, with limited resources, and on the idea that only a reduction in global production and consumption can ensure the future of humanity and the preservation of the planet.

In fact, the ideology of degrowth implies a principle of balance at all levels, and in particular a readjustment of disparities. This means, on one hand, the reduction of natural resources withdrawn by rich countries. On the other hand, poorer, "developing" countries should be able to experience, at least to a reasonable level, the developments that have already taken place in rich countries. From the comfort of a home and having basic hygienic conditions to education, healthcare services and all the other positive consequences of the latest developments already experienced in "developed" countries.

Some of the first ideas regarding preserving the environment and the excessive exploitation of natural resources emerged at the end of the Second World War. However, it was in the early 1970s that the concept of degrowth took off, with the publication of *The Entropy Law and the Economic Process*, a book by Nicholas Georgescu-Roegen that was quickly followed by the work of the *Club of Rome* with the *Limits To Growth* Report in 1972.

The ideas that came out of both these pieces were subject to further theories, developments and debate by many thinkers of different backgrounds (from economists to ecologists and philosophers). As a result, a couple of intangible principles were found and grounded:

- A large part of the resource's humans uses and rely on are dependent of ecosystem services and are limited;

- Each withdrawal of non-renewable resources has the potential to jeopardize the long-term survival chances of humanity;
- Infinite growth (demographic, economic …) in a finite world is impossible.
- Today, despite the absence of a total agreement and action on the most radical perspective that the idea of degrowth supports, many of the ideas put forward are reinforced by the undeniable reality of global warming as a result of human actions.

This is even more the case as the use of the Gross Domestic Product (GDP) as a tool for measuring growth is increasingly questioned. Indeed, as an answer to its inefficiency, distinguished economists are working on more relevant and comprehensive alternative indicators, such as the Human Development Index (HDI), the ecological footprint or the social health index.

De-growth is a shadow concept that's doesn't come up often at discussions taking place in the economic sphere. However, it still shows up in many discussions, especially those related to sustainable development. In fact, when it comes to ecology and sustainable development, the idea that the current economic model based on growth is the root of the environmental problems we are facing is becoming widespread.

Indeed, it is to support economic growth GDP progress that the world's economic system is constantly pushing towards the consumption of natural resources, damaging ecosystems and polluting them by burning fossil fuels. It is mainly due to the preponderance of these economic activities and their externalities on the environment that global warming is the hot topic on the agenda today, together with other environmental issues such as the degradation of biodiversity or air pollution.

CONCLUSION

In conclusion, Unit one, "Epistemological Frames of Social Science," has provided a comprehensive exploration of diverse epistemological perspectives that shape the foundations of social science. From the introspective lens of phenomenology to Karl Popper's evolutionary epistemology, Kress's multi-modality theory, and Max Weber's emphasis on social action, the unit delves into a rich tapestry of theoretical frameworks. The inclusion of Scott and Prell's social network analysis, Georg Simmel's conflict theory, and Daisaku Ikeda's peace education further contributes to a nuanced understanding of societal dynamics. Additionally, the examination of the National Curriculum Framework for

Teacher Education (NCFTE 2009) highlights the importance of educational paradigms in shaping social knowledge. The discourse on positivism, anti-positivism, and post-positivism, as well as the concepts of construction, de-construction, and re-construction, underscore the evolving nature of social science methodologies. The unit concludes with a reflection on growth, development, and de-growth, prompting critical thinking about the route's societies follow. Overall, this unit serves as a valuable foundation for navigating the epistemological landscapes that underpin the study of social phenomena.

UNIT - 2

COMPONENTIAL CONVERGENCE IN SOCIAL SCIENCE

INTRODUCTION

In the ever-evolving landscape of the social sciences, the intricate interplay of various components becomes the focal point of understanding the complex tapestry of human societies. Welcome to the intellectual journey of "Componential Convergence in Social Science," where we embark on a comprehensive exploration of essential topics that form the bedrock of societal dynamics. From critical geo-political inquiry and economic restructuring to the nuances of culture, ecology, and human rights, this book unit delves into the interwoven fabric that defines contemporary social structures.

Our first port of call is the realm of geo-politics, unravelling critical inquiries into the geopolitical understanding of society and the intricate dance between nations, economies, and power. With a particular emphasis on geo-political economy, this chapter sets the stage for a deeper comprehension of how global forces shape the societies we inhabit. Moving forward, we navigate the waters of social adaptation and community living, exploring the transformative impact of economic restructuring on living standards. As we probe into the intricate web of values and culture, we uncover the threads that bind communities together and give them a unique identity.

Eco-habitation emerges as a critical theme, inviting readers to contemplate the principles of eco-friendly living, the effective utilization of resources, and the challenges posed by issues of scarcity and population. Citizenship and obligations to the state follow, guiding us through the responsibilities that individuals bear within the societal framework. The exploration extends to the realms of human rights, education, and the dignity of the human being – foundational elements that contribute to the ethical fabric of societies. Language mediation surfaces as a potent force in shaping societal narratives, acting as a bridge and, at times, a barrier in communication.

As we traverse through the chapters, historico-pedagogic sources of knowledge generation become a focal point, unravelling the historical and educational underpinnings that have shaped our understanding of society. Finally, we delve into the resource base for social science, investigating the wellsprings from which knowledge in this field is drawn. This unit invites you to embark on a multidimensional journey, challenging preconceived notions and fostering a holistic understanding of the myriad factors that converge to shape the societies we inhabit. Join us in unravelling the intricate layers that define the contemporary social landscape.

GEOPOLITICAL UNDERSTANDING ABOUT SOCIETY

Geopolitics explains how countries, businesses, extremist groups, etc. try to reach their political goals by controlling geographic features of the world. We call these features geographical entities. Geographical entities are the places, regions, territories, scales, and networks that make up the world. Geopolitics looks at a particular use of power: how countries and other groups compete to control these entities within the international community. Controlling these entities is seen to help countries and groups reach their goals. Geopolitics is always looked at with an international and global dimension, meaning that the issues being looked at are connected to the global scale.

Geopolitical understanding about society involves analysing the complex interplay between politics, geography, and society on a global scale. It seeks to understand how geopolitical factors such as borders, resources, and power dynamics influence the structure, behaviour, and development of societies. Here are some key aspects of geopolitical understanding about society

- **Geopolitical Borders**: Geopolitics often begins with the study of borders and boundaries. A geopolitical border can be grasped as a zone of confluence of perceptions with a particular area. The environment takes on the consequences of a world that turns on economic priorities
- Resources and Economic Development: Access to natural resources, such as oil, minerals, and arable land, plays a crucial role

in a society's economic development and geopolitical influence. Resource geopolitics is all about who gets what when where and how. Resources have provided some of the key means and motives of global European power expansion. They have also been the focus of inter-state rivalry. Western geopolitical thinking about resources has been dominated by the relationship of trade war and power at the core of which were overseas resources and maritime navigation. The global economy relied on oil for much of the 20th century as a portable and indispensable fuel. The immense wealth associated with oil generates political struggles to control it.

- **Security and Conflict**: Geopolitical factors heavily influence the security landscape of societies. The geopolitical conflicts can shape the social fabric of a nation, affecting everything from government policies to individual daily life. Some examples of geopolitical risks are cross-border or international conflicts, hybrid warfare and cyberattacks, de-dollarization dynamics, shifting trade relations, sovereign debt exposures, critical mineral competition.
- **Migration and Refugees**: Geopolitical conflicts and economic disparities often lead to population movements, including immigration and refugee flows. So geopolitical factors shape the movement of people and migration patterns.
- **International Organizations**: Geopolitics also involves the study of international organizations like the UNO, NATO, and the European Union. These institutions can impact societies by promoting diplomacy, peacekeeping, and the development of international norms and agreements.
- **Ideological and Cultural Influences**: Geopolitics can influence the spread of ideologies, religions, and cultural norms, values and practices across our society. The global competition between different ideologies, such as democracy and authoritarianism, can shape the political and social systems of individual nations.
- **Soft Power and Diplomacy**: Soft power is the capacity to influence other nations through the use of persuasion and attraction rather than coercion or force. Soft power relies on culture, arts, and science. In the diplomatic field, soft power is built via, among others, education diplomacy, science diplomacy, public diplomacy, and diplomacy. Geopolitics isn't just about military and economic power; it also encompasses the use of soft power and diplomacy to influence societies.

- **Globalization**: Globalisation can be defined as the process of change, increasing interconnectedness and interdependence among countries and economies, bringing the world closer through better world-wide communication, transport and trade links. This process is changing the world dramatically and quickly, affecting economic, social, political and cultural aspects of life and bringing both opportunities and challenges. Geopolitical understanding must take into account the forces of globalization, which have interconnected societies and economies more than ever before.

Human Rights and Global Governance: Geopolitics intersects with issues of human rights, international law, and global governance. Governance as a concept has emerged as an important theme in discussions of post-Cold War politics at the global scale. Often used as either a supplement to, or as a critique of, international organizations involved in contemporary globalization, it suggests that governance is not just a matter of state authority and international organization but also a matter of authority and legitimacy in other social arrangements. In its mode of critique governance can be used to challenge the geographical specifications of politics at the largest of scales and in particular the traditional preoccupations of geopolitics with territorial control and power politics. But likewise, these geopolitical themes can also be used to illuminate the modern territorial assumptions that often continue to constrain the conceptualizations of global governance.

Climate Change and Environmental Challenges: Climate change acts as a powerful force multiplier of geopolitical risk. Accelerated by population growth and declining water resources, climate change can drive rapid and radical structural changes in affected countries' economies and demographics. Environmental issues, such as climate change, resource scarcity, and environmental degradation, are increasingly important in geopolitics. These challenges can lead to competition for resources and increase social and political consequences.

In summary, geopolitical understanding about society involves recognizing that societies do not exist in isolation but are deeply interconnected with the geopolitical forces that shape the world. It requires analysing how geographical factors and power dynamics at the global level influence the development, security, and identity of individual societies.

CRITICAL GEO POLITICAL ENQUIRY

A critical geopolitical inquiry is an exploration and analysis of global political topics, events, and processes from an often interdisciplinary and critical perspective. Geopolitics is the study of how geography, politics, economy, and culture interact to influence how people behave and how other countries interact. When studied critically, this field of study entails challenging presumptions, power dynamics, and the influence of many elements on geopolitics.

- **Multidisciplinary Approach**: Political science, geography, economics, sociology, history, and cultural studies are just a few of the academic fields that critical geopolitical inquiries frequently draw upon. A more thorough grasp of the intricate dynamics affecting international relations is made possible by this multidisciplinary approach.
- **Critical Theory**: Critical geopolitical analysis includes critical theories including poststructuralism, feminism, Marxism, and postcolonialism.
- **Globalization and Economic Factors:** The critical approach recognizes the impact of globalization on geopolitics, including the role of multinational corporations, global supply chains, and economic inequality in shaping international relations.
- **Environmental Issues:** Critical geopolitical analysis is becoming more and more relevant to environmental concerns like resource shortages and climate change. These problems are considered to be important catalysts for international conflict and cooperation.
- **Postcolonial viewpoint:** Critical geopolitics frequently adopts a postcolonial viewpoint, recognizing colonialism's historical legacy and its ongoing influence on the world's power systems.
- **Agency of non-state players:** In addition to traditional state players, this approach takes into account the agency of non-state actors, such as NGOs, global social movements, and businesses.
- **Ethical and Normative Considerations:** Critical geopolitical research examines concerns pertaining to justice, human rights, and international governance.

GEOPOLITICAL ECONOMY

An interdisciplinary topic called geopolitical economy combines aspects of geopolitics and economics to study how political and economic factors interact on a global scale. It aims to comprehend how political choices and the balance of power among different countries affect economic systems and vice versa. The following are some crucial elements and ideas in geopolitical economy:

- **Geopolitics:** The study of how geographic elements like location, resources, and territory affect political choices and global interactions is referred to as geopolitics. The development of a nation's foreign policy and economic plan frequently depends heavily on geopolitical factors.
- **International Relations**: Geopolitical economy and international relations are closely related fields of study because they both focus on how nations interact with one another on a global scale. Analysing alliances, conflicts, trade agreements, and the application of military force to pursue economic and political objectives are all part of this.
- **Globalisation:** Geopolitical economy's main focus is the process of globalisation, which is characterised by the growing transnational connectivity of economies and societies. Economic and political aspects of globalisation have changed how countries interact and compete on the global stage.
- **Resource Geopolitics**: Control of and access to important natural resources, such as water, minerals, and oil, can have profound geopolitical and economic repercussions. International conflicts and the development of economic strategies are frequently fuelled by competition for these resources.
- **Trade and Economic Alliances:** The development of trade agreements and economic alliances is influenced by geopolitical factors. In response to geopolitical problems, nations frequently enter into such accords to strengthen their economic might and security.
- **Geopolitical risks:** Businesses and investors functioning in the global economy must take geopolitical risks into account. These risks can include political unrest, trade tensions, sanctions, and the possibility of armed conflict. Markets and investment opportunities may be significantly impacted by these hazards.
- **Development and powershifts**: Geopolitical economy also analyse the rise and fall of major powers as well as how changes in the global political and economic landscape might transform the international system. The development of developing economies and the relative waning of traditional powers are examples of this.
- **International Organisations**: Organisations like the World Bank, International Monetary Fund (IMF), World Trade Organisation (WTO), and United Nations all have a big impact on the global

economy. They support the regulation of trade, finance, and international relations.

- **Soft power and Economic Diplomacy**: Geopolitical economics acknowledges the value of soft power, which includes diplomatic influence, economic assistance, and cultural influence, that influencing international relations and furthering a nation's objectives.
- **Security and Defence Economics**: A country's geopolitical standing and economic potential are directly related to its military spending and defence plans. The study of geopolitical economy reveals the connections between these elements.

Geopolitical economy is a dynamic area that varies along with shifts in the political and economic climate of the world. These linkages are investigated by experts in the field to provide light on the intricate relationships that exist between geopolitics and the world economy. Governments, organisations, and individuals must navigate these dynamics in order to take advantage of the opportunities and overcome the obstacles of the modern world.

SOCIAL ADAPTATION AND COMMUNITY LIVING

Social adaptation

Social adaptation, also known as social adjustment or social integration, is the process by which individuals learn to function effectively within a specific social environment or society. It involves acquiring the necessary skills, behaviours, and attitudes to fit into and interact successfully with the people and institutions within that social context. Social adaptation is a fundamental aspect of human development and is essential for building relationships, gaining social acceptance, and thriving in various social settings. Here are some key aspects of social adaptation:

- **Learning Social Norms and Values**: Individuals learn the cultural norms, values, and customs of their society through socialization processes that begin in childhood. This includes understanding acceptable behaviours, beliefs, and ways of interacting with others.
- **Acquiring Social Skills**: Social adaptation involves acquiring the necessary social skills to communicate effectively, resolve conflicts, and build relationships. These skills can encompass verbal and non-verbal communication, empathy, active listening, and problem-solving.

- **Navigating Social Roles**: In a society, people frequently fill a variety of social roles, such as those in the family, workplace, or community. Understanding and performing these responsibilities well are necessary for adaptation.
- **Coping with Change**: As people go through life's stages and experience new social conditions, social adaptation is a lifelong process. This continual process includes adjusting to significant life changes like moving to a new city or starting a new job.
- **Overcoming Obstacles**: Some people may have trouble adjusting to social situations because they are hesitant, anxious around people, or have trouble making connections. Interventions, therapy, or support networks may be beneficial in certain situations.
- **Cultural Sensitivity**: In multicultural society, social adaptation also entails sensitivity to and respect for various cultural perspectives and backgrounds. This includes being aware of and respecting cultural variations.
- **Peer and Social Group Dynamics**: Integrating into peer groups, social networks, or communities is a common aspect of social adaptation. To feel a sense of belonging, one may need to comprehend group dynamics and abide by group rules.
- **Emotional and psychological well-being**: Emotional and psychological well-being are crucial for successful social adaption. Positive social connections and a strong social support system can improve mental health and general life satisfaction.
- **Identity Development**: A person's sense of self and identity can be influenced through social adaption. Different facets of an individual's identity may change depending on the social setting, such as how they behave at work versus with friends.

Social adaptation is a dynamic and ongoing process, as societies and individuals continuously evolve and respond to changing circumstances. It is influenced by factors such as culture, environment, education, and personal experiences. Successful social adaptation is often associated with positive outcomes, such as a sense of belonging, social cohesion, and overall well-being, while challenges in adaptation can lead to feelings of alienation, conflict, or stress.

Community Living

Community living within society refers to the practice of individuals or families residing in organized, cooperative, or shared living arrangements within the broader context of a larger community or neighbourhood. It emphasises the value of creating social networks, sharing resources, and encouraging a feeling of community among locals while making a constructive contribution to the community at large. Here are some key aspects of community living within society:

- **Shared Resources**: As part of community living, it's usual to pool resources and utilise shared amenities or services. This may include common dining areas, outdoor spaces, laundry facilities and transport choices. It also helps the Residents to lessen their own expenses and environmental impact.
- **Social Interaction**: Community living fosters increased social interaction among residents. Neighbours in such settings are more likely to interact with one another, build friendships, and support one another. This social connectivity can reduce feelings of isolation and loneliness.
- **Collaborative Decision-Making**: Many community living arrangements involve collective decision-making processes. Residents come together to discuss and decide on various aspects of their shared living environment, such as rules, responsibilities, and community projects. This collaborative approach empowers individuals and creates a sense of ownership.
- **Sustainability**: Eco-friendly practises and sustainability are given top priority in several community living concepts. To lessen their environmental impact and encourage sustainable living, residents could participate in community gardens, recycling campaigns, or renewable energy projects.
- **Cultural Diversity**: In larger communities, residents may come from diverse cultural backgrounds, creating opportunities for cultural exchange and learning. This can lead to a richer, more inclusive community experience.
- **Support Systems**: Community living often provides a built-in support system. In times of need, such as illness or emergencies, residents can rely on their neighbours for assistance, which can be especially valuable for older adults or individuals with limited mobility.
- **Community Engagement**: Many community living arrangements encourage residents to engage with the broader society through volunteer work, community service, or participation in local events. This helps residents remain connected to the larger community and contribute positively to it.

- **Conflict Resolution**: Community living may require effective conflict resolution mechanisms to address disputes or disagreements among residents. Establishing clear protocols for conflict resolution can help maintain harmony within the community.
- **Advocacy and Networking**: Residents of community living arrangements may collectively advocate for local issues or collaborate with other similar communities to address shared concerns or promote common goals.
- **Community Identity**: Over time, community living can lead to the development of a unique community identity and culture that distinguishes it within the larger society.

While community living can offer numerous benefits, it also comes with its own challenges, such as the need for effective communication, shared decision-making, and conflict resolution skills. Success in community living within society relies on a commitment to the principles of cooperation, mutual respect, and shared responsibility, ultimately contributing to a more interconnected and vibrant society.

ECONOMIC RESTRUCTURING AND LIVING STANDARDS

Economic restructuring can have a significant impact on living standards within a society. This process typically involves changes in the composition and organization of an economy, often driven by factors such as technological advancements, shifts in global markets, government policies, and changes in consumer preferences. The effects of economic restructuring on living standards can vary depending on several factors, including the nature of the restructuring and the policy environment in which it occurs. Here are some key points to consider:

- **Employment Opportunities**: Economic restructuring may lead to job creation in some sectors while reducing employment opportunities in others. For example, the transition from a manufacturing-based economy to a service-based economy can result in job displacement for some workers, but it can also create new opportunities in service industries like technology, healthcare, and finance.
- **Income Inequality**: Economic restructuring can contribute to income inequality. As certain industries and occupations become more profitable, individuals with the skills and resources to participate in those sectors tend to benefit the most. This can lead to disparities in income and living standards between different groups in society.

- **Skill Requirements**: As industries evolve, the demand for specific skills may change. Workers who lack the necessary skills may experience lower living standards if they are unable to adapt to the new job market. Access to education and training programmes can play a critical role in helping individuals acquire the skills needed for higher-paying jobs.
- **Geographic Disparities**: Economic restructuring can also create geographic disparities in living standards. For example, regions heavily reliant on declining industries may experience economic decline and lower living standards, while areas with growing industries may see increased prosperity.
- **Social Safety Nets**: Government policies and social safety nets can mitigate some of the negative effects of economic restructuring on living standards. Programs such as unemployment benefits, job training, and income support can help individuals and communities' weather economic transitions.
- **Consumer Benefits**: Economic restructuring can lead to improved living standards for consumers if it results in the availability of more innovative and affordable goods and services. Technological advancements, for example, can lead to the development of new products that enhance the quality of life.
- **Environmental Considerations**: Economic restructuring can also have environmental implications. Shifting toward more sustainable and environmentally friendly industries and practices can contribute to higher living standards in the long run by preserving natural resources and reducing pollution.
- **Globalization**: Economic restructuring is often intertwined with globalization, which can impact living standards in various ways. While globalization can lead to increased trade and economic growth, it can also result in job displacement and wage pressure, particularly for low-skilled workers. Managing the effects of globalization through trade policies and social safety nets is essential.
- **Regional Disparities**: Economic restructuring can also lead to regional disparities in living standards. Areas heavily reliant on declining industries may experience economic decline, while regions with a strong presence in emerging sectors may thrive. Governments often need to address these regional disparities through targeted policies and investments.

- **Infrastructure and Public Services**: The quality of infrastructure and public services, such as healthcare, education, and transportation, plays a significant role in determining living standards. Investments in these areas are essential to support economic growth and enhance the well-being of citizens.

In summary, the impact of economic restructuring on living standards is complex and multifaceted. While it can lead to opportunities for economic growth and improved living standards, it can also result in challenges such as income inequality and job displacement. Effective government policies, education and training programs, and a focus on inclusive growth can help mitigate the negative effects and ensure that economic restructuring benefits a broad segment of the population.

VALUES AND CULTURE

Values and culture are interconnected aspects of human society that shape individuals' beliefs, behaviours, and social norms. Values are the core principles and beliefs that guide an individual's or a group's behaviour and decision-making. They represent what is considered important, desirable, or morally right within a society. Values are beliefs and principles that guide and inform our attitudes, behaviours, and decisions. They serve as a foundation for what individuals and societies consider important and desirable. Values can be both individual and collective, and they are often shaped by a variety of factors, including upbringing, education, religion, and personal experiences.

Values are an integral part of culture. They often underpin cultural norms and behaviours. A culture's values influence how individuals within that culture perceive and respond to various situations. For example, a culture that places a high value on individualism may encourage self-expression and independence, while a collectivist culture may prioritize group harmony and cooperation.

Conversely, culture can shape an individual's values. Growing up within a specific culture can lead to the internalization of that culture's values and belief systems. However, individuals can also challenge or adapt these values over time, particularly when exposed to different cultures and perspectives.

Values are fundamental beliefs and principles that guide individuals and groups in making decisions and judgments about what is right and wrong, important and unimportant. These beliefs are deeply ingrained and often form the basis of one's moral and ethical framework. Values can be both individual and societal, and they can vary widely from one person to another and from one culture to another. Some common examples of values include:

- **Honesty**: Valuing truthfulness and integrity in one's actions and communication.
- **Respect**: Treating others with dignity and consideration, regardless of differences.
- **Responsibility**: Taking ownership of one's actions and obligations.
- **Equality**: Believing in the fair treatment and opportunity for all individuals.
- **Compassion**: Demonstrating empathy and concern for the well-being of others.
- **Freedom**: Valuing personal autonomy and the right to make choices.

Culture refers to the shared beliefs, customs, practices, language, art, and social norms of a particular group of people. It encompasses the way people live, their traditions, and their collective identity. Culture is not limited to nationality or ethnicity; it can also be associated with various subcultures, such as religious, regional, or organizational cultures. Key aspects of culture include:

- **Language**: The way people communicate and express themselves is a fundamental part of culture.
- **Traditions and Rituals**: Ceremonies, holidays, and customary practices unique to a culture.
- **Social Norms**: The unwritten rules that govern behaviour and interactions within a society or group.
- **Art and Creativity**: Cultural expressions through music, dance, literature, visual arts, and more.
- **Values and Beliefs**: The shared moral and ethical principles that guide a culture's behaviour.

The Relationship between Values and Culture

Values are often a core component of a culture. They influence the norms, customs, and traditions within a society. Additionally, culture can shape and reinforce the values held by its members. For example, a culture that places a high value on collectivism may promote community-oriented values, while a culture emphasizing individualism may prioritize personal achievement and autonomy. It's important to recognize that values and culture can evolve over time and may be subject to change through various influences, including globalization, technological advancements, and generational shifts. Understanding the values and culture of a group or society is crucial for effective communication, social cohesion, and respectful interactions. It also plays a significant role in shaping individual identity and worldview.

In summary, values are the guiding principles that influence individual and collective behaviour, while culture encompasses the broader context in which these values are situated. Together, they shape the identity and actions of individuals and societies, and they play a crucial role in how we navigate the complex world we live in. Here's a deeper exploration of the interconnection between values and culture:

- **Shaping and Reflecting Culture**: Values play a significant role in shaping a culture. They influence how people within a society perceive right and wrong, what they prioritize, and how they make decisions. Conversely, culture also influences the formation of values. People tend to adopt the values of the culture in which they are raised and from which they derive their identity.
- **Cultural Norms**: Values are the foundation of cultural norms. Norms are the shared expectations and behaviours that are considered acceptable within a specific culture. These norms often reflect the underlying values of that culture. For example, if a culture highly values punctuality, the cultural norm may be to arrive on time for appointments and meetings.
- **Socialization and Transmission**: Culture serves as a vehicle for transmitting values from one generation to the next. Children learn the values of their society through socialization, including interactions with family, peers, and educational institutions. Cultural institutions, such as religious organizations or community groups, often reinforce and transmit specific values.
- **Decision-Making and Behaviour**: Values guide individual and collective decision-making and behaviour within a culture. They help people prioritize goals, make ethical judgments, and determine how to interact with others. For instance, a culture that values honesty may discourage lying and encourage truthfulness in personal and professional interactions.
- **Diversity and Variation**: Different cultures can have distinct sets of values, and these values can lead to diverse customs, traditions, and social norms. What is considered virtuous or taboo can vary significantly from one culture to another. This diversity can lead

to cross-cultural misunderstandings or conflicts when people from different cultural backgrounds interact.

- **Change and Adaptation**: Values can change over time as societies evolve and adapt to new circumstances. Cultural values can shift in response to technological advancements, globalization, and other social, economic, or political factors. Cultural change often involves a negotiation between traditional values and emerging values, leading to cultural evolution.

Values and culture are influenced by a wide range of factors, both internal and external. These factors contribute to the complexity and diversity of cultural systems and the values held by individuals and societies. Here are some of the key factors that influence values and culture:

- **Historical Context**: Historical events, such as wars, colonization, revolutions, and social movements, can profoundly shape the values and cultural norms of a society. These events can lead to the adoption of new values or the preservation of traditional ones.
- **Geography and Environment**: The physical environment in which a culture develops can impact its values and way of life. For example, cultures in arid regions may value water conservation, while those in fertile areas may emphasize agriculture.
- **Religion and Spirituality**: Religious beliefs and practices often play a central role in shaping values and cultural norms. Different religions have their own moral codes and principles that guide behaviour and shape cultural identity.
- **Economic Factors**: Economic systems and conditions can influence cultural values. Capitalist societies, for instance, may prioritize individualism and competition, while more collectivist cultures may emphasize communal values and cooperation.
- **Social and Political Systems**: The structure of government, laws, and political ideologies can influence cultural values. Democracies may prioritize individual rights and freedoms, while authoritarian regimes may emphasize obedience and conformity.
- **Technology and Innovation**: Advances in technology can introduce new values and behaviours. The internet and social media, for example, have transformed communication and social interactions, influencing cultural norms and values related to privacy, connectivity, and information sharing.
- **Globalization**: Increased global interconnectedness through trade, travel, and communication has led to the exchange of ideas,

values, and cultural practices between societies. This can both preserve and change traditional values.

- **Demographics**: The composition of a population, including factors like age, gender, ethnicity, and socioeconomic status, can impact cultural values. Different demographic groups may hold varying values and worldviews.
- **Education and Media**: Educational systems and media play a crucial role in shaping values and cultural norms by transmitting information, narratives, and ideologies. They can promote certain values and challenge others.
- **Cultural Contact**: Interactions with other cultures, through trade, migration, or conquest, can lead to the exchange of values and the blending of cultural elements. This can result in the emergence of hybrid cultures.
- **Crisis and Change**: Crises, such as natural disasters or economic downturns, can lead to shifts in cultural values as societies adapt to new challenges and circumstances.
- **Family and Socialization**: The family is often the primary agent of socialization, where individuals learn cultural values and norms from a young age. Socialization within peer groups and communities also reinforces these values.
- **Psychological and Individual Factors**: Personal experiences, temperament, and personality traits can influence an individual's interpretation and adoption of cultural values.

ECO-HABITATION: ECO-FRIENDLY LIVING, EFFECTIVE USE OF RESOURCES, SCARCITY ISSUES, POPULATION RELATED ISSUES

Eco-habitation, or eco-friendly living, refers to a way of life that focuses on minimizing environmental impact and maximizing the sustainable use of resources. It involves adopting practices and making choices that reduce energy consumption, waste generation, and overall ecological footprint. Here are some key aspects related to eco-habitation:

- **Effective Use of Resources**: Eco-habitation emphasizes the efficient and responsible use of resources such as water, energy, and materials. This includes practices like water conservation through low-flow fixtures and rainwater harvesting, energy efficiency through the use of renewable energy sources and energy-saving appliances, and waste reduction through recycling, composting, and minimal use of disposable items.

- **Scarcity Issues**: Eco-habitation recognizes the challenges posed by resource scarcity. It encourages strategies like sustainable agriculture, which focuses on minimizing water usage, reducing chemical inputs, and conserving soil fertility. It also promotes responsible consumption patterns that prioritize long-lasting, durable, and repairable products over disposable ones.
- **Population-Related Issues**: The concept of eco-habitation acknowledges the impact of population growth on resource availability and environmental sustainability. It encourages family planning and education to promote smaller family sizes and ensure access to reproductive health services. Additionally, eco-habitation emphasizes the need for sustainable urban planning and design, including compact and walkable communities, efficient public transportation systems, and green spaces.
- **Sustainable Building Practices**: Eco-habitation often involves sustainable building practices that minimize the environmental impact of construction and reduce energy consumption in buildings. This includes using eco-friendly materials, implementing efficient insulation and ventilation systems, incorporating renewable energy sources, and adopting green building certifications like LEED (Leadership in Energy and Environmental Design) or BREEAM (Building Research Establishment Environmental Assessment Method).
- **Eco-Housing Communities**: Eco-habitation promotes the development of eco-housing communities where like-minded individuals or families live together, sharing resources, and implementing sustainable practices on a larger scale. These communities often include features like shared gardens, community composting, renewable energy generation, and collective decision-making processes.

By adopting eco-habitation practices, individuals and communities can contribute to mitigating environmental challenges, conserving resources, and creating a more sustainable future. It requires a holistic approach that considers the interconnectedness of environmental, social, and economic aspects to foster a balanced and environmentally conscious way of life.

Role of Education

Education plays a vital role in promoting and facilitating eco-habitation, which is the practice of sustainable and environmentally friendly living. Here are some ways in which education contributes to eco-habitation:

- **Environmental awareness and knowledge**: Education creates environmental awareness and provides individuals with knowledge about the importance of sustainable living, conservation of natural resources, and the impacts of human activities on the environment. It helps individuals understand the interconnectedness between human actions and the health of the planet.
- **Sustainable practices**: Education equips individuals with the skills and understanding necessary to adopt sustainable practices in their daily lives. It teaches concepts such as energy conservation, water efficiency, waste reduction, recycling, and the use of environmentally friendly products. Through education, individuals learn about the environmental benefits of sustainable practices and how to implement them effectively.
- **Ecological literacy**: Education fosters ecological literacy by teaching individuals about ecosystems, biodiversity, and the delicate balance of nature. It helps individuals understand the importance of protecting and preserving natural habitats, biodiversity, and ecosystem services. This knowledge encourages individuals to make choices that minimize their ecological footprint and contribute to the well-being of the environment.
- **Sustainable consumption and production**: Education promotes sustainable consumption and production patterns. It raises awareness about the impacts of overconsumption, resource depletion, and waste generation. By educating individuals about the concept of a circular economy, resource conservation, and responsible consumption, education encourages individuals to make informed choices that minimize waste and promote sustainable production and consumption practices.
- **Sustainable technologies and innovations**: Education plays a crucial role in introducing individuals to sustainable technologies and innovations. It familiarizes individuals with renewable energy sources, energy-efficient technologies, green building practices, and other sustainable innovations. Education equips individuals with the knowledge and skills to adopt and implement these technologies in their homes, workplaces, and communities.
- **Policy advocacy and engagement**: Education empowers individuals to become informed and engaged citizens who can advocate for sustainable policies and practices. It provides individuals with the understanding of environmental issues, policy frameworks, and the tools for effective advocacy. Education

encourages individuals to participate in community initiatives, environmental campaigns, and policy discussions to promote eco-friendly living and advocate for sustainable practices.

- **Next-generation environmental leaders**: Education prepares the next generation to become environmental leaders and change agents. By integrating environmental education into school curricula, educational institutions foster a sense of environmental responsibility and equip students with the knowledge, skills, and values needed to address environmental challenges. Education cultivates a sense of agency, inspiring students to become environmental stewards and actively contribute to eco-habitation efforts.

In summary, education plays a crucial role in promoting eco-habitation by raising awareness, providing knowledge and skills, promoting sustainable practices, fostering ecological literacy, encouraging sustainable consumption and production, introducing sustainable technologies, facilitating policy advocacy, and preparing future environmental leaders. By integrating environmental education across various educational settings, individuals can make informed choices and actively contribute to creating a more sustainable and eco-friendly future.

CITIZENSHIP AND OBLIGATIONS TO THE STATE

Traditions and approaches to citizenship vary throughout history and across the world according to different countries, histories, societies, cultures and ideologies, resulting in many different understandings of the concept of citizenship. The concept of citizenship is reflected in today's most common understanding of citizenship as well, which relates to a legal relationship between the individual and the state. Most people in the world are legal citizens of one or another nation state, and this entitles them to certain privileges or rights. Being a citizen also imposes certain duties in terms of what the state expects from individuals under its jurisdiction. Thus, citizens fulfil certain obligations to their state and in return they may expect protection of their vital interests. However, the concept of citizenship has far more layers of meaning than legal citizenship. Nowadays "citizenship" is much more than a legal construction and relates – amongst other things – to one's personal sense of belonging, for instance the sense of belonging to a community which you can shape and influence directly. Such a community can be defined through a variety of elements, for example a shared moral code, an identical set of rights and obligations, loyalty to a commonly owned civilisation, or a sense of identity. In the geographical sense, "community" is usually defined at two main levels, differentiating between the local community, in which the person lives, and the state, to which the person belongs. In the relationship between the individual and society we can distinguish four dimensions which correlate with the four subsystems which one may recognise in a society, and which are essential for its existence: the political / legal dimension, the social dimension, the cultural dimension and the economic dimension.

- The **political** dimension of citizenship refers to political rights and responsibilities vis à vis the political system. The development of this dimension should come through knowledge of the political system and the promotion of democratic attitudes and participatory skills.
- The **social** dimension of citizenship has to do with the behaviour between individuals in a society and requires some measure of loyalty and solidarity. Social skills and the knowledge of social relations in society are necessary for the development of this dimension.
- The **cultural** dimension of citizenship refers to the consciousness of a common cultural heritage. This cultural dimension should be developed through the knowledge of cultural heritage, and of history and basic skills (language competence, reading and writing).
- The **economic** dimension of citizenship concerns the relationship between an individual and the labour and consumer market. It implies the right to work and to a minimum subsistence level. Economic skills (for job-related and other economic activities) and vocational training play a key role in the fulfilment of this economic dimension.

Citizenship is a legal status that conveys certain rights, privileges, and responsibilities upon individuals within a specific political community or nation. While the rights and privileges associated with citizenship may vary from country to country, there are some common obligations that citizens typically have toward the state. It's important to note that the specifics can differ significantly based on the legal and political systems of different nations. Here are some general obligations that citizens may have:

- **Allegiance and Loyalty:** Citizens are often expected to be loyal to their country. This loyalty may manifest in various forms, such as showing respect for national symbols, participating in civic activities, and, in some cases, serving in the military when required.

- **Legal Compliance:** Citizens are generally expected to abide by the laws and regulations of their country. This includes respecting property rights, paying taxes, and obeying other legal mandates.
- **Voting:** Many democratic countries encourage or mandate citizens to participate in the political process through voting. Voting is seen as a fundamental way for citizens to express their preferences and contribute to the functioning of a representative government.
- **Civic Engagement:** Citizens are often encouraged to be actively engaged in their communities. This can involve volunteering, participating in local governance, or contributing to the well-being of the community in various ways.
- **Jury Duty:** In many legal systems, citizens may be called upon to serve on a jury when required. This is considered a civic duty and is crucial for the functioning of the justice system.
- **National Service:** Some countries have mandatory military service or alternative forms of national service for citizens. This is seen as a way for individuals to contribute to the defense or well-being of the nation.
- **Respect for Others:** Citizens are often expected to respect the rights and dignity of other citizens. This includes respecting diversity, treating others fairly, and avoiding discriminatory behaviour.
- **Education:** Many societies emphasize the importance of education, and citizens may be encouraged or required to ensure that themselves and their children receive a certain level of education.
- **Environmental Stewardship**: As members of a state, citizens have a responsibility to protect and preserve the environment. This can involve adopting sustainable practices, supporting environmental policies, and actively participating in efforts to combat climate change and protect natural resources
- **Military Service and National Defense**: Many countries require their citizens to serve in the military or perform mandatory national service, particularly during times of war or when national security is at stake. This obligation is crucial for protecting the country's sovereignty and ensuring its defense.
- **Payment of Taxes**: Citizens are obligated to pay taxes on their income, property, and goods in accordance with the tax laws of their country. These tax revenues contribute to funding public

services, infrastructure development, and various government programs.

- **Social Responsibilities**: Citizens are expected to adhere to ethical and moral principles that promote social harmony, respect for diversity, and the well-being of others. This includes treating fellow citizens with respect, practicing tolerance, and promoting social cohesion.

It's important to note that the specific obligations of citizenship can vary between countries, as they are determined by the legal and political frameworks of each nation-state. Furthermore, the rights and obligations of citizenship are generally reciprocal, as the state isexpected to protect the rights of its citizens in return for their fulfilment of obligations.

Role of Education

Education plays a significant role in fostering good citizenship and promoting an understanding of obligations to the state. Here are some ways in which education contributes to citizenship and obligations to the state:

- **Civic education**: Education provides individuals with knowledge and understanding of the political system, governance structures, and the rights and responsibilities of citizens. Civic education teaches individuals about the principles of democracy, the rule of law, human rights, and the importance of active participation in civic life. It helps individuals understand their role as citizens and their obligations to the state.
- **Awareness of rights and responsibilities**: Education equips individuals with an understanding of their rights as citizens, such as freedom of speech, assembly, and expression, as well as their corresponding responsibilities. It emphasizes the importance of respecting the rights of others and the need to uphold democratic values. Education fosters a sense of civic duty, encouraging individuals to contribute positively to their communities and the state.
- **Political literacy and engagement**: Education promotes political literacy by providing individuals with an understanding of political processes, elections, and the importance of informed decision-making. It encourages individuals to engage in political discussions, analyse diverse perspectives, and participate in democratic processes, such as voting and advocacy. Education empowers individuals to actively engage with their representatives and institutions, promoting responsible citizenship.

- **Ethical and moral development**: Education plays a role in nurturing ethical and moral development, which is essential for responsible citizenship. It teaches values such as honesty, integrity, fairness, empathy, and respect for others. Education helps individuals develop a sense of moral responsibility towards their fellow citizens and the broader society, encouraging them to make ethical choices and contribute positively to the state.
- **Social cohesion and diversity appreciation**: Education promotes social cohesion by fostering understanding, respect, and appreciation for diversity within the state. It encourages individuals to learn about different cultures, religions, and perspectives, fostering a sense of unity and shared identity. Education helps individuals recognize and challenge discrimination, prejudice, and inequality, promoting inclusivity and social cohesion.
- **Critical thinking and active citizenship**: Education cultivates critical thinking skills, enabling individuals to question and analyse information critically. It encourages individuals to be active and engaged citizens who can contribute to the development of the state. Education empowers individuals to identify societal challenges, seek solutions, and work collaboratively to address them, thereby fulfilling their obligations to the state.
- **Environmental and global citizenship**: Education promotes environmental and global citizenship by raising awareness about environmental issues, sustainable development, and global challenges. It helps individuals understand the interconnectedness of the world and their role in protecting the environment and promoting global well-being. Education fosters a sense of responsibility towards the planet and encourages individuals to act as global citizens, working towards a more sustainable and just world.

In summary, education plays a vital role in fostering good citizenship and promoting obligations to the state. By providing civic education, promoting political literacy and engagement, nurturing ethical development, fostering social cohesion, cultivating critical thinking skills, and encouraging environmental and global citizenship, education equips individuals to become responsible, informed, and engaged citizens who contribute positively to their communities and fulfil their obligations to the state.

HUMAN RIGHTS EDUCATION

Human rights education (HRE) is the learning process that seeks to build up knowledge, values, and proficiency in the rights that each person is entitled to. This education teaches students to examine their own experiences from a point of view that enables them to integrate these concepts into their values, decision-making, and daily situations. According to Amnesty International, HRE is a way to empower people, training them so their skills and behaviours will promote dignity and equality within their communities, societies, and throughout the world.

Human Rights Education is all about equipping people with the knowledge, skills and values to recognize, claim and defend their rights. Various Human Rights organizations and representatives have defined human rights education in their own ways. Here are some of the most prominent definitions:

- "Education, training and information aimed at building a universal culture of human rights. A comprehensive education in human rights not only provides knowledge about human rights and the mechanisms that protect them, but also imparts the skills needed to promote, defend and apply human rights in daily life. Human rights education fosters the attitudes and behaviours needed to uphold human rights for all members of society." (UNO)
- Navi Pillay, former United Nations High Commissioner for Human Rights said that, "Human rights education builds knowledge, skills and attitudes prompting behaviour that upholds human rights. It is a process of empowerment which helps identify human rights problems and seek solutions in line with human rights principles. It is based on the understanding of our own responsibility to make human rights a reality in our community and society at large."
- "Human rights education means education, training, dissemination, information, practices and activities which aim, by equipping learners with knowledge, skills and understanding and moulding their attitudes and behaviour, to empower them to contribute to the building and defence of a universal culture of human rights in society, with a view to the promotion and protection of human rights and fundamental freedoms." (Council of Europe)

The "Universal Declaration of Human Rights" is acknowledged as a landmark document in human rights history. It states that basic human rights require protection and that every person is entitled to a certain base number of rights and freedoms through it. This is believed to be the most influential document used to determine what qualifies as human rights and how to implement these ideas and rights into everyday life. It was translated into more than 500 languages worldwide and was drafted by representatives from various countries and regions with varying legal and cultural experiences. The declaration was adopted by the United Nations General Assembly on 10th December, 1948, making this annual Human Rights Day ever since. To this day, the 30-article compilation stands and states that this document is, "a common standard of achievement for all peoples and all nations".

Education on these ideals was addressed in 1953 with the UNESCO Associated Schools Programme, which served as an "initial attempt to teach human rights in formal school settings". The emphasis on educating the next generations progressed in 1995 with the beginning of the United Nations' Decade for HRE. The first formal request though came about in UNESCO's 1974 article "Recommendation concerning Education for International Understanding, Cooperation and Peace, and Education relating to Human Rights and Fundamental Freedoms." The participants of the International Congress on the Teaching of Humans Rights eventually met in 1978 to form a specific definition of what would be required in formal curriculum. The aims that Congress agreed on included the encouragement of tolerant attitudes with a focus on respect, providing knowledge of human rights in the context of national and international dimensions as well as their implementations, and finally developing awareness of human rights translating into reality whether social or political on national and international levels. Human Rights Education became an official international concern after the World Conference on Human Rights in 1993. This conference brought the issue of formally educating to many countries,' and eventually the United Nations, attention. In 1995, the UN approved the Decade for HRE, which reformed the aims of the application once again. Since this development by the UN, the incorporation of HRE into formal school curriculum has been developed and diversified with the assistance of nongovernmental organizations, intergovernmental organizations, and individuals dedicated to spreading the topic through formal education.

The Asia-Pacific Centre for Education for International Understanding (APCEIU) and the United Nations Academic Impact mutually organized the 2018 United Nations Global Citizenship Education Seminar at the UN Headquarters in New York City. These seminars help progress HRE by bringing people together to form new ideas and concepts to improve the movement. Advocates for HRE believe it is crucial because it imparts and spreads out the human rights vocabulary and provides students with the ability to take a critical approach towards human rights.

Objectives of Human Rights Education

- Human Rights education promotes respect for human rights of all individuals.
- It develops the knowledge, skills, and values of human rights.
- It develops the socio-psychological, human personality.
- It helps people and policy makers to evolve the ways and means to overcome the problems of each nation and that of the international community.
- It helps to foster understanding, tolerance, gender equality
- It develops friendships among all nations and eliminates racial, ethnic, religious, and linguistic differences.

Why is Human Rights Education Important?

- Human Rights Education is important for many reasons. Below are some of the most frequently mentioned reasons why human rights education is important.
- Human Rights Education is crucial for building and advancing societies
- Human Rights Education empowers people to know, claim and defend their rights
- Human Rights Education promotes participation in decision making and the peaceful resolution of conflicts
- Human Rights Education encourages empathy, inclusion and non-discrimination

Here are some more reasons why human rights education is important:

- **It enables people to claim their rights:** This is the most obvious benefit of HRE. In the "Declaration on the Right and Responsibility of Individuals, Groups, and Organs of Society to Promote and Protect Universally Recognized Human Rights and Fundamental Freedoms," Article 6 states that everyone has the right to know about their rights. By receiving that education, people can identify when rights are being violated and stand up to defend them.
- **It teaches young people to respect diversity:** When young people are exposed to human rights education, it teaches them to respect diversity from an early age. This is because no matter the differences between people – race, gender, wealth, ethnicity, language, religion, etc. – we all still deserve certain rights. Human

rights also protect diversity. The earlier people learn about this, the better it is for society.

- **It teaches history:** Understanding history through a human rights lens is critical to a good education. If human rights weren't included, lessons would be incomplete. Learning about human rights through history challenges simple and biased narratives. It teaches students the origins of human rights, different historical perspectives, and how they evolved too today. With this foundation in history, students better understand modern human rights.
- **It teaches people to recognize the root causes of human rights issues:** By recognizing the roots of problems, people are better equipped to change things. As an example, it isn't enough to know that homelessness is a human rights issue. To effectively address it, people need to know what causes homelessness, like low-paying jobs and a lack of affordable housing. Studying history is an important part of identifying the roots of human rights issues.
- **It fosters critical thinking and analytical skills:** HRE doesn't only provide information about human rights. It also trains people to use critical thinking and analyse information. Many human rights issues are complicated, so one of HRE's goals is to teach people how to think. Students learn how to identify reliable sources, challenge biases, and build arguments. This makes human rights discussions more productive and meaningful. Critical thinking and analysis are important skills in every area of life, not just human rights.
- **It encourages empathy and solidarity:** An important piece of human rights education is recognizing that human rights are universal. When people realize that and then hear that rights are being violated elsewhere, they are more likely to feel empathy and solidarity. The violation of one person's rights is a violation of everyone's rights. This belief unites people – even those very different from each other – and provokes action.
- **It encourages people to value human rights:** When people receive human rights education, what they learn can shape their values. They will realize how important human rights are and that they are something worth defending. People who've received human rights education are more likely to stand up when they believe their rights (and the rights of others) are being threatened. They'll act even when it's risky.

- **It fuels social justice activities:** If people didn't know anything about human rights, positive change would be rare. When people are educated and equipped with the necessary skills, they will work for social justice in their communities. This includes raising awareness for the most vulnerable members of society and establishing/supporting organizations that serve basic needs. With HRE, people feel a stronger sense of responsibility to care for each other. Believing in social justice and equality is an important first step, but it often doesn't move far beyond a desire. HRE provides the knowledge and tools necessary for real change.
- **It helps people support organizations that uphold human rights:** Knowing more about human rights and activism helps people identify organizations that stand up for human rights. It also helps them avoid organizations (e.g. corrupt corporations) that directly or indirectly disrespect rights. These organizations are then forced to change their practices to survive.
- **It keeps governments accountable:** Human rights education doesn't only encourage people to hold organizations accountable. It encourages them to hold governments accountable, as well. Human rights experts say that HRE is critical to government accountability. Armed with knowledge, skills, and passion, citizens have the power to challenge their governments on issues and demand change. HRE also helps provide activists with resources and connections to the global human rights community.

DIGNITY OF HUMAN BEING

"Dignity" is defined as "the state of being worthy of honour or respect" (Oxford Encyclopaedic

English Dictionary). When this concept is associated with the adjective human, it is used to denote that all human beings possess equal and inherent worth and therefore ought to be accorded the highest respect and care, regardless of age, sex, socioeconomic status, health condition, ethnic origin, political ideas, or religion. Inherent human dignity should be distinguished from moral dignity, which is a synonym of "honour." While the former plays a central role in the legal instruments relating to bioethics, the latter has less relevance in this field. On the one hand, the inherent dignity, as it is inseparable from the human condition, is the same for all, cannot be gained or lost, and does not allow for any degree. Even the worst criminal cannot be stripped of his or her inherent dignity and has therefore the right not been subjected to inhuman or degrading treatments or punishments. On the other hand, moral dignity does not relate to the existence itself of persons but to their behaviour; it is the result of a virtuous life, that is, of a life lived-in accordance with moral principles. This is why moral dignity is not possessed by all individuals to the same degree (e.g., an honest citizen has more dignity than a pickpocket). While this is a kind of dignity that people may occasionally exhibit, lack, or lose, the dignity in which all humans are said to be equal is a characteristic that belongs permanently and inherently to every human as such.

The concept of intrinsic human dignity operates in modern times as the bedrock of the international human rights system that emerged in the aftermath of the Second World War. It plays also a key role in the international policy documents relating to bioethics that have been adopted since the end of the 1990s. Human dignity can be characterized as the "shaping principle" of international bioethics or as the "overarching principle" of the global norms governing biomedical issues). Far from representing a shift merely in style, the higher profile accorded to human dignity in bioethics is seen as a true shift in substance that deserves to be carefully considered.

Types of Human Dignity

- The Dignity of Merit: It is depending on social rank and position. It can come and go.
- The Dignity of Moral or Existential Stature: The Dignity of Moral stature is the result of the moral deeds of the subject.
- The Dignity of Identity: The Dignity of Identity is tied to the integrity of the subject's body and mind, and in many instances, although not always, also dependent on the subject's self-image.
- The Universal Human Dignity: All human beings are born free and equal in dignity and rights.

LANGUAGE MEDIATION IN SOCIETY

Mediation is a structured, interactive process where an impartial third party neutrally assists disputing parties in resolving conflict through the use of specialized communication and negotiation techniques. All participants in mediation are encouraged to actively participate in the process. Mediation is a "party-centred" process in that it is focused primarily upon the needs, rights, and interests of the parties. The mediator uses a wide variety of techniques to guide the process in a constructive direction and to help the parties find their optimal solution. A mediator is facilitative in that they manage the interaction between parties and facilitates open communication.

Language mediation in society refers to the role that language plays in facilitating communication and understanding among individuals or groups who speak different languages. This process involves the use of a mediator or mediation tools to bridge the linguistic gap and enable effective communication. Effective language mediation is essential for building bridges between people and fostering inclusivity in diverse societies. It promotes understanding, collaboration, and harmony by breaking down barriers created by linguistic and cultural differences. Language is central to social interaction in every society, regardless of location and time period.

Language and social interaction have a reciprocal relationship: language shapes social interaction and social interactions shape language. Language is a crucial means for communication and interaction. Language not only reflects and expresses facts and observations; it also influences attitudes and behaviour. It thus constitutes a vital component of the cultural prerequisites underlying societal development. The linguistic strategies that mediators use to adapt their language to various mediation situations is the focus of this current study. There are several strategies involved in this research which mediators are taught during mediation training. These strategies are often discussed in books on mediation as "methods for communication". However, these strategies are not well defined or are explained but only taught by giving examples and retelling individual experiences. Consequently, there is a need for a better linguistic explanation of the various strategies actually used in mediation.

In order to better teach mediation strategies to mediators from all different positions in life, a linguistic analysis of the methods used by mediators is necessary. Focusing on a linguistic analysis for teaching mediation would make the mediation strategies more accessible to trainees from non-law-oriented backgrounds and would give better explanations of the actual techniques used rather than focusing on learning through mediation examples. To identify and analyse the linguistic procedures, steps and definitions that are used by mediators, linguistic methods from Conversation Analysis will be applied in order to analyse the different linguistic phenomena that occur in the speech of mediators. Conversation analysis emphasizes looking into the natural formation of language especially in a back-and-forth conversational context. Since mediation is based on real-time language production, it is very important to view it as a conversation rather than a semi-scripted court procedure. Although certain parts of mediation can be scripted, such as a mediator's introduction and explanation of the guidelines of the mediation, the large majority of the process is focused on unscripted questioning, answering, expanding, explaining interests and negotiating. The parties do not typically have prepared statements but they informally discuss the situation, particularly their wants and interests in the conflict. Because of this specific focus in mediation, as well as mediation's emphasis on naturally produced, informal and nonspecific language, Conversation Analysis is an appropriate linguistic analysis for looking into the language of mediation.

Types of Language Mediation: There are two types of mediation that can be used to do this:

- Intra-linguistic mediation which is carried out within the same language, for example English to English,
- Interlinguistic mediation which is carried out between two different languages, for example Spanish to English

Here are several aspects of language mediation in society:

- **Interpretation and Translation:** Interpretation involves oral translation of spoken language. Interpreters help people who speak different languages to communicate in real-time, such as in meetings, conferences, or legal proceedings. Translation involves written conversion of text from one language to another. Translators work with written documents, such as books, articles, legal texts, and more.
- **Cultural Mediation:** Beyond linguistic differences, cultural nuances can also impact communication. Cultural mediators help individuals navigate cultural differences and understand each other's perspectives, behaviours, and customs.
- **Technology as a Mediator:** Technology, such as language translation apps, plays a growing role in mediating language barriers. These tools can facilitate written and spoken communication between individuals who speak different languages.
- **Education and Language Mediation:** Educational institutions often serve as mediators by offering language programs and courses to help individuals learn new languages. This contributes to better communication and understanding in multicultural societies.
- **Community Interpreting:** In community settings, interpreters play a crucial role in healthcare, social services, and legal environments. They help individuals who may not be proficient in the dominant language of the community to access essential services.

- **Legal and Judicial Mediation:** In legal contexts, language mediation is crucial for ensuring fair and accurate communication during court proceedings. This may involve interpreters, translators, or legal professionals with language expertise.
- **Diplomatic and International Relations:** In the realm of diplomacy and international relations, language mediation is essential for fostering cooperation and understanding between countries with different native languages.
- **Media and Language Mediation:** Media outlets often play a role in mediating language by providing news and information in multiple languages. This can contribute to a more informed and connected global society.
- **Accessible Communication:** Language mediation is crucial for ensuring that information is accessible to diverse audiences, including those with language-related disabilities. This includes providing sign language interpretation and other forms of communication support.
- **Mediation in Conflict Resolution**: In conflict resolution or mediation processes, language mediation involves ensuring that all parties can understand and communicate effectively. Mediators may need to work with interpreters or translators to facilitate dialogue between individuals or groups that speak different languages.
- **Cultural Mediation:** Language is closely tied to culture, and misunderstandings can arise due to cultural differences. Cultural mediators help individuals or groups navigate these differences, promoting cross-cultural understanding and effective communication.
- **Technology in Language Mediation:** With advancements in technology, there are now tools and platforms that can assist in language mediation. For example, machine translation services, language learning apps, and communication platforms with built-in translation features can aid in overcoming language barriers.
- **Educational Settings:** Language mediation is essential in multicultural and multilingual educational environments. Teachers and educators may use various strategies and resources to ensure that students who speak different languages can fully participate in the learning process.
- **Community and Social Services:** Language mediation is often required in community and social service settings to ensure that individuals with limited proficiency in the local language can

access necessary services. This may include healthcare, legal services, and social support.

HISTORIC-PEDAGOGIC SOURCES OF KNOWLEDGE GENERATION

Man needs knowledge and generates it for the purpose of his life activities. Without going into the theory of knowledge (epistemology), it may be considered that what we call 'Knowledge' is the product of knowing, perceiving, thinking, guessing, being mistaken, remembering, finding out, inferring, proving, reflecting, imagining and so on. Knowledge may be in the form of fact, belief or judgement. A fact is anything that exists or can be conceived of; what we claim to know is belief or judgement. Human knowledge takes the form of belief or judgement about a particular phenomenon. Some beliefs may be supported by evidence, may be based on our perceptions and experiences.

The beliefs, which are supported by evidence are called justified beliefs. Only justified beliefs are knowledge. Knowledge includes what we know about matters of fact as well as the principles and processes of inference. It has three elements: (i) there is a system of ideas; (ii) the ideas correspond to things actually existing; and (iii) there is belief in such correspondence.

If we look at the historical perspective it will be evident that efforts of centuries were required by man to improve his capacity and readiness to obtain reliable knowledge. To gain some insight into the tortuous pathway he traversed, the following discussions briefly examine the various sources of knowledge he has drawn upon to solve problems. These are: (i) Life experiences, (ii) Authority, (iii) Customs and tradition, (iv) Deductive reasoning, (v) Inductive reasoning, and (vi) Scientific Method.

Life Experiences

The process of knowledge generation is dynamic and influenced by a variety of factors, including individual experiences, cultural contexts, education, and societal advancements. Here are some key life experiences that contribute to knowledge generation:

- **Education:** Formal education plays a crucial role in shaping an individual's understanding of the world. Schools, colleges, and universities provide structured learning environments that expose individuals to a wide range of subjects and perspectives.
- **Curiosity and Exploration:** The innate human curiosity drives individuals to explore and seek new information. Whether

through travel, reading, or experimentation, the desire to learn and discover contributes significantly to knowledge generation.

- **Personal Challenges:** Overcoming personal challenges often leads to valuable insights and knowledge. Facing adversity forces individuals to adapt, learn new skills, and develop a deeper understanding of themselves and the world around them.
- **Interpersonal Relationships:** Interactions with others, including friends, family, colleagues, and mentors, play a crucial role in knowledge generation. Social dynamics and communication contribute to the exchange of ideas and the development of a more nuanced understanding of various subjects.
- **Cultural Influences:** Cultural background and exposure to diverse perspectives shape one's worldview and contribute to knowledge diversity. Exposure to different cultural practices, traditions, and belief systems enriches an individual's understanding of the complexities of the world.
- **Technology and Innovation:** Living in an era of rapid technological advancement provides unique opportunities for knowledge generation. Access to information through the internet, collaboration through digital platforms, and exposure to cutting-edge technologies contribute to a continuously evolving knowledge landscape.
- **Critical Thinking and Reflection:** Developing critical thinking skills and the ability to reflect on one's experiences and beliefs are crucial aspects of knowledge generation. Questioning assumptions and seeking evidence-based conclusions contribute to a deeper understanding of various subjects.
- **Failure and Success:** Experiencing both failure and success provides valuable lessons. Failures offer opportunities for learning and growth, while success validates and reinforces knowledge. Both outcomes contribute to a more nuanced understanding of one's capabilities and the world.
- **Scientific Inquiry and Research:** Engaging in scientific inquiry and research is a structured way of generating knowledge. The scientific method involves observation, hypothesis formation, experimentation, and analysis, contributing to the accumulation of systematic knowledge.
- **Environmental Impact:** The physical environment, including nature and the external world, influences knowledge generation.

Environmental changes and challenges can spark innovation and a deeper understanding of the interconnectedness of various systems.

Authority

Seeking and consulting the authorities is a well-established method of getting knowledge and solving problems encountered in the environment. When one has not had personal experience with a phenomenon, the obvious recourse is to consult their parents, their teachers, or even their older siblings for answers to problems with which they are not familiar. Rather than attempting to determine truth independently, people often seek the advice of experts who, because of their intellect, training, experience, or aptitudes, are better informed than other people. Experts are necessary in a complicated culture such as ours where knowledge is expanding so rapidly that no one can be an expert at everything. And obviously certain individuals have such a wide experience and deep insight that their advice can be of immense benefit. But it should never be forgotten that as sources of knowledge, authorities have limitations. Authorities cannot be infallible.

Customs and Traditions

Customs and traditions play a significant role in knowledge generation, shaping the way societies accumulate, transmit, and preserve information. Here are several ways in which customs and traditions contribute to knowledge generation:

- **Cultural Knowledge Transmission:** Customs and traditions are powerful vehicles for transmitting cultural knowledge from one generation to another. Through rituals, ceremonies, and oral traditions, societies pass down information about their history, values, and ways of life.
- **Preservation of Wisdom:** Many customs and traditions are rooted in historical experiences and lessons learned by past generations. They serve as repositories of wisdom, encapsulating practical knowledge that has been tested and refined over time.
- **Social Norms and Ethics:** Customs and traditions often establish social norms and ethical guidelines. They provide a framework for understanding what is acceptable behaviour within a community, thereby influencing the creation and dissemination of knowledge within that context.
- **Ritualized Learning:** Rituals and ceremonies associated with customs often involve specific actions, words, or symbols. These

rituals can serve as mnemonic devices, aiding in the retention and recall of knowledge. The repetitive nature of rituals reinforces key cultural and societal knowledge.

- **Cultural Identity and Worldview:** Customs and traditions shape the cultural identity and worldview of a community. The values and beliefs embedded in these practices influence how individuals perceive and interpret the world around them, affecting the knowledge they generate and accept.
- **Problem-Solving Frameworks:** Traditional customs often contain problem-solving approaches that have been developed over time. These approaches are based on the collective wisdom of a community and may offer unique perspectives and solutions to challenges.
- **Innovation and Adaptation:** While customs and traditions are often associated with the preservation of existing knowledge, they also play a role in innovation and adaptation. As societies encounter new challenges, traditional practices may evolve to address these challenges, contributing to the generation of new knowledge.
- **Community-Based Research:** Some customs involve community-based research methods, where knowledge is generated collectively through observation, experimentation, and shared experiences. This collaborative approach to knowledge generation is deeply ingrained in certain cultural practices.

It's important to note that while customs and traditions can be valuable sources of knowledge, they can also present challenges when they resist change or hinder the adoption of new ideas. Striking a balance between preserving cultural heritage and embracing new knowledge is crucial for the continued development of societies.

Deductive Reasoning

Deductive reasoning is a logical process in which a conclusion is drawn from a set of premises or statements. It is a method of reasoning that moves from general principles or premises to specific instances. The process typically follows a structured and systematic approach. Here's a breakdown of deductive reasoning:

- **Premises:** Deductive reasoning starts with one or more general premises or statements that are assumed to be true. These premises serve as the foundation for the argument.

- **Logic:** Using deductive logic, specific conclusions are drawn from the given premises. This involves applying established rules of inference or logical principles to derive a new statement.
- **Conclusion:** The conclusion reached through deductive reasoning is necessarily true if the premises are true and the logic is valid. The goal is to ensure that the conclusion follows logically from the given information.
- **Validity:** Deductive reasoning emphasizes the concept of validity. A deductive argument is considered valid if the conclusion logically follows from the premises. If the premises are true and the logic is valid, the conclusion must also be true.
- **Syllogism:** Syllogism is a common form of deductive reasoning involving three statements: a major premise, a minor premise, and a conclusion. The conclusion is inferred from the major and minor premises.

Example of deductive reasoning using a syllogism:

- Major Premise: All humans are mortal.
- Minor Premise: Socrates is a human.
- Conclusion: Therefore, Socrates is mortal.

In this example, the conclusion is derived from the general premise that all humans are mortal and the specific premise that Socrates is a human. Deductive reasoning is often contrasted with inductive reasoning, where conclusions are drawn from specific observations or cases to establish general principles. Deductive reasoning is a fundamental aspect of formal logic and plays a crucial role in mathematics, philosophy, and various scientific disciplines.

Limitations of Deductive Reasoning

Deductive reasoning has obviously its own limitation. Deductive conclusion depends upon pre-existing knowledge; it does not enable scholars to gain new knowledge or to make new discoveries. Deductive reasoning stresses on the forms of argument and not on the truth or falsity of the statements. According to the deductive mode of reasoning if the form of argument is sound, then even a false premise will not matter. Of course, this does not mean that deductive reasoning has no role in the knowledge generation process. Rather it has its own use in formulating and proposing hypotheses from the general truth (theory), this helps knowledge generation through enquiry by the use of hypothesizing. Deductive reasoning can systematize what is already known and can identify new relationships as one proceeds from known to unknown, but it cannot be relied upon as a self-sufficient method for securing reliable knowledge Top of Form

Inductive Reasoning

Inductive reasoning is a type of logical thinking that involves making generalizations based on specific observations. Unlike deductive reasoning, which starts with a general premise and applies it to specific cases, inductive reasoning begins with specific observations and uses them to make broader generalizations. The process of inductive reasoning typically involves:

- **Observation**: Gathering data, facts, or evidence through observations or experiences.
- **Pattern Recognition**: Identifying patterns or regularities in the observed data.
- **Hypothesis Formation**: Formulating a tentative generalization or hypothesis based on the observed patterns.
- **Prediction**: Using the generalization to make predictions about future events or observations.
- **Testing**: Verifying the validity of the generalization through further observations or experiments.

One key aspect of inductive reasoning is that the conclusions reached are not certain but are instead probabilistic. The strength of an inductive argument depends on the reliability of the observations and the degree to which the generalization fits the observed patterns. An example of inductive reasoning could be observing that the sun has risen every morning in the past, leading to the generalization that the sun will rise tomorrow. While this is a reasonable assumption based on past observations, it doesn't guarantee that the sun will always rise in the future. Inductive reasoning is used in various fields, including science, where hypotheses are often formed based on observed patterns and then tested through experiments.

Limitations of Inductive Reasoning

Inductive reasoning has inherent limitations. Just as in the case of deductive reasoning, inductive reasoning also, only by itself, does not lead to much advancement of knowledge. Its basic limitation is that it can be applied to only as many events as can be observed, and hence the conclusions arrived at cannot really be infallible. The conclusions reached by imperfect inductive reasoning do contain information that is not present, even implicitly, in one of the premises (the observed instances). If all the premises (observed instances) are true, the probability of conclusions arrived at may be of varying degrees.

Historically, knowledge generation and pedagogy (the method and practice of teaching) have been shaped by various sources. Here are some key historic pedagogic sources of knowledge generation:

- **Oral Tradition**: In ancient times, knowledge was often transmitted orally from one generation to another. Elders, priests, and storytellers played a crucial role in passing down information, traditions, and cultural practices through spoken words.
- **Ancient Texts and Manuscripts**: Many ancient civilizations, such as Mesopotamia, Egypt, China, India, and Greece, produced written texts and manuscripts that served as educational resources. These texts covered a wide range of subjects, including philosophy, science, mathematics, and literature.
- **Philosophical Dialogues**: In ancient Greece, philosophers like Socrates, Plato, and Aristotle engaged in philosophical dialogues. These discussions were not only a method of seeking truth but also a form of teaching and knowledge dissemination.
- **Religious Texts and Institutions**: Religious texts and institutions have played a significant role in shaping education and knowledge. Religious scriptures often contain moral and ethical teachings, and religious institutions have historically been centres of learning.
- **Medieval Universities**: During the Middle Ages, universities emerged in Europe as centres of learning. The curriculum included subjects like theology, philosophy, medicine, and law. Latin was the language of instruction, and manuscripts were copied and studied.
- **The Renaissance and Humanism**: The Renaissance saw a revival of interest in classical learning, humanism, and the arts. The emphasis shifted from religious studies to a more balanced education, including literature, history, and the sciences.
- **Scientific Revolution**: The Scientific Revolution in the 16th and 17th centuries led to a transformation in the way knowledge was generated and disseminated. Observation, experimentation, and empirical evidence became central to the scientific method.
- **Enlightenment Thinkers:** Enlightenment thinkers, such as John Locke, Jean-Jacques Rousseau, and Voltaire, emphasized reason, individual rights, and education. Their ideas contributed to the development of modern educational philosophy.

- **Industrial Revolution and Formal Education:** The Industrial Revolution brought about changes in society and the economy, leading to the establishment of formal educational systems. Schools and universities became more structured and accessible.
- **Print Culture and Mass Education:** The invention of the printing press facilitated the mass production of books, making knowledge more widely available. This contributed to the democratization of education.
- **Digital Revolution:** In the modern era, the digital revolution has transformed the way knowledge is accessed and shared. The internet, online resources, and digital technologies have revolutionized education and learning methodologies.

These historic pedagogic sources highlight the evolution of educational practices and the diverse ways in which knowledge has been generated and transmitted over time. Today, a combination of traditional and modern methods continues to shape the field of education.

RESOURCE BASE FOR SOCIAL SCIENCE

TEXTBOOK

Textbook is a specially written book which contains selective and systematic knowledge. It is not a bare statement of knowledge but is armed with various teaching- learning devices to fulfil the desired instructional role. According to Bacon Paul, a textbook is a "book designed for classroom use, carefully prepared by experts in the field and equipped with the usual teaching devices". There are three different types of history textbooks listed by Johnson: (i) **Precise Textbook** - it represents a skeleton or framework of facts with essential explanations, in-text questions and activities. (ii) **Manuals** - these develop the outline but leave some room for further development. The function of the history textbook is that in the lower classes it can be relied on for essential information, so organised as to show order and continuity and so presented as to be clear, interesting and attractive; and in the senior classes, it should contain well- arranged comprehensive knowledge and should expand its scope and size to meet the changing concept of what is considered educationally sound and desirable. Apart from textbooks, there are supplementary readers in history. They contain important information and facts which could not be given in the textbook.

MUSEUM

Museums are institutions that collect, preserve, and exhibit objects and artifacts of artistic, cultural, historical, or scientific significance. These institutions play a crucial role in educating the public and preserving our collective heritage. Museum is a place that provides information, education and enjoyment. Museums which preserve historical and cultural objects impart wholesome education at all levels and provide new impetus to teaching methods. Schools can have a history museum with sections on Local history, National history, and international history. The section on Local history can contain local relics like statues of kings and rulers, carvings on bricks or stones, pottery pieces, ancient books, ancient coins, costumes, etc. It stimulates interest in the students to study history with a sense of reality. The section on National history can be built up with the help of models according to the topic as it may not be possible for each school to get original relics. Similarly, flags, world history, curios from different countries, stamps, coins, dolls, etc. can be kept in the section on international history. Museums can focus on various themes, including art, history, science, technology, natural history, and more. Here are some key points about museums:

Types of Museums

- **Art Museums:** Display and preserve visual art, including paintings, sculptures, and other art forms.
- **History Museums:** Showcase historical artifacts and provide information about past events and cultures.
- **Science Museums:** Explore scientific principles and discoveries through interactive exhibits and displays.
- **Natural History Museums:** Feature exhibits on the natural world, including fossils, minerals, and biological specimens.
- **Technology Museums:** Highlight technological advancements and innovations throughout history.
- **Specialized Museums:** Cover specific topics such as aviation, maritime, music, and more.

Functions of Museums

- **Education:** Museums serve as educational institutions, providing information and context for their collections.
- **Preservation:** They play a crucial role in preserving cultural and historical artifacts for future generations.
- **Research:** Museums often support research activities, contributing to academic and scientific knowledge.

- **Cultural Enrichment:** Museums enhance cultural understanding and appreciation by showcasing diverse perspectives.
- **Exhibits and Collections:** Museums organize exhibits to display their collections in a way that engages and educates visitors. Collections may include paintings, sculptures, historical documents, fossils, scientific instruments, and more.
- **Interactive and Digital Experiences:** Many modern museums incorporate interactive exhibits and digital technologies to enhance the visitor experience. Virtual tours and online platforms provide access to museum collections for a global audience.
- **Global Importance:** Museums contribute to tourism and local economies by attracting visitors from around the world. They participate in cultural exchange programs, lending and borrowing artifacts for international exhibitions.

CHARTS

Charts are combinations of graphic and pictorial media designed for the orderly and logical visualising of relationship between key facts and ideas. The main function of the charts is always to show relationships such as comparisons, developments, processes, classification organisation, etc. Charts should be simple in their form and design. They should be accurate. They should be the brief summary of some historical events. Most commonly used charts in history are:

- **Genealogy charts**: These charts are used to represent the growth and development of an empire or dynasty.
- **Flow charts**: These are used to show sequence and the functional relationships.
- **Chronology charts**: They provide a chronological framework within which events and development may be recorded.
- **Tabulation charts**: They present the historical data in a tabular form. They enable students to gain a comprehensive view of the facts at sight

FIELD TRIPS

Field trips are educational excursions that take students out of the classroom and into real-world environments to enhance their learning experiences. These trips can be to a variety of locations, such as museums, historical sites, science centres, nature reserves, businesses, or cultural institutions. Field trips to historical places can provide unparallel learning experiences, particularly, in the teaching of history. They can provide first hand observation and new information to enable students to understand the history, which is not merely a story, but is very useful for developing appreciation of architecture, sculpture, painting, etc. There can be various kinds of trips such as:

- Trips within the school or trips within a walking distance.
- Longer trips to historical spots in the community.
- Day trips to a state capital, college, historical spot, etc.
- Trips during vacations for a week or so to Delhi, Mumbai, Kolkata, Ajanta or Ellora caves or other places of historical interest.

Field trips offer several benefits for students, including:

- **Real-world application:** Field trips provide students with the opportunity to see the practical applications of what they are learning in the classroom. This hands-on experience can deepen their understanding of a subject.
- **Engagement:** Being in a different environment can make learning more engaging and memorable. Students often find field trips to be a refreshing break from routine classroom activities.
- **Social interaction:** Field trips can promote social interaction and teamwork among students. They offer a chance for students to bond with their peers and teachers in a less formal setting.
- **Cultural exposure:** Visiting museums, historical sites, or cultural institutions exposes students to different cultures, histories, and ways of life, fostering a broader perspective and understanding.
- **Inspiration:** Field trips can inspire students by exposing them to new ideas, concepts, and potential career paths. Seeing professionals in action or witnessing real-world applications of knowledge can spark interest and motivation.
- **Critical thinking:** Encountering new environments and situations during field trips can stimulate critical thinking skills. Students may be prompted to analyse, evaluate, and problem-solve in real-world contexts.
- **Memory retention:** Experiencing information through multiple senses during a field trip can contribute to better retention of knowledge. The multisensory experience enhances the learning process.
- **Life skills:** Field trips often involve navigating public spaces, following guidelines, and behaving responsibly outside of the

school environment. These experiences can help students develop life skills such as independence and responsibility.

ARCHIVES

An archive is a place where people can go to gather first hand facts, data, and evidence from letters, reports, notes, memos, photographs, and other primary sources. Archives provide a classroom where students from lower grade through college can study and learn history by using manuscripts, photographs, oral history transcripts, audio-visual tapes, and other archival material. Using archives in teaching requires cooperation between the archivist and the teacher. The archivist needs an awareness of the goals and content of the course being offered. The teacher must be informed of the documents and items available in local archives, historical societies, or, museums that are relevant to the course. Teaching students through archives would be difficult; however, it is important to involve them through some presentations. Frequent class tours and field trips to local archives, historical societies or museums are an effective way for using archives successfully. Lectures through archive would make the learning more meaningful rather than imparted inside the classroom. Visual images and sound recordings hold the attention of students and leave a lasting impression. Therefore, teachers and archivist can use photographs and tapes that narrate a story or particular historical events. Providing students an opportunity to prepare a brief write-up about the presentations or some aspects of the archives is an additional way to reflect on the relationship between archives and history.

DOCUMENT

The term document is generally associated with written or printed record as evidence of historical facts. In this method the old records are depicted before students as documentary proofs or evidences. They can be presented as cinema or TV films showing some of the human or social activities in historical times. The important documents that can be used for teaching of history includes: letters, diaries, constitutions, proclamations, court decisions, official minutes, certificates, magazines, newspapers, transcriptions, wills, autobiographies, etc. Documentary evidences provide the exact picture of historical events.

ARTIFACTS

Artifacts are objects made by human beings, especially with a view to using them at a later stage. It may be a handmade object, a tool, or the remains of one, as a shard of pottery, characteristic of an earlier time or cultural stage, especially such an object found at an archaeological excavation. The manmade objects or realia include food, clothing and adornment, tools and weapons, housing, transportation, personal possessions, household items, fine arts, and objects from everyday life. By using artifacts, students get chance for inquiry and investigation. If you present artifacts in an interesting way, students get chance to understand things clearly, observe facts, express their observations, etc. Artifacts are representative of cultures, historical eras, and geographic location. They make history learning meaningful because children have opportunities to construct understanding and build knowledge. And students consider the practical use and personal value of objects over time and within particular cultures. Learning of history becomes challenging because students get opportunity for inquiry, collaborative learning, risk taking, thinking fluently and flexibly, and arriving at valuable solutions. Students become active by engaging in hands-on explorations.

INFORMATION AND COMMUNICATION TECHNOLOGY

Information and Communication Technology (ICT) refers to the use of technology to manage and process information, and facilitate communication. It encompasses a broad range of technologies and tools that are used to store, transmit, process, and retrieve information. ICT plays a crucial role in various aspects of our personal and professional lives, as well as in the functioning of societies and economies. Here are key components and concepts related to ICT:

- **Information Technology (IT):** This includes the hardware, software, and networks used for the processing and management of information. Computers, servers, storage devices, and software applications fall under the umbrella of IT.
- **Telecommunications:** This involves the transmission of information over distances using technologies like telephone networks, internet, and wireless communication. Telecommunications is a vital aspect of ICT, enabling the exchange of data and facilitating real-time communication.
- **Internet:** The internet is a global network that connects millions of computers and networks worldwide. It provides a platform for communication, collaboration, and access to information through services like email, websites, social media, and online applications.

- **Software:** Software applications, including operating systems, productivity tools, databases, and specialized applications, are essential components of ICT. They enable users to perform various tasks and manipulate data.
- **Hardware:** ICT hardware includes devices like computers, servers, routers, switches, smartphones, and other electronic equipment used for processing and transmitting information.
- **Networks:** Networks are the infrastructure that allows different devices to communicate with each other. Local Area Networks (LANs), Wide Area Networks (WANs), and the internet are examples of networking technologies that facilitate data exchange.
- **Data Management:** ICT involves the collection, storage, retrieval, and processing of data. Databases and data management systems are used to organize and manage large volumes of information.
- **Cybersecurity:** With the increasing reliance on digital technologies, ensuring the security of information and communication has become critical. Cybersecurity measures aim to protect systems, networks, and data from unauthorized access, attacks, and data breaches.
- **E-Government:** Many governments use ICT to provide online services to citizens, making government operations more efficient and accessible. This includes services like online tax filing, permit applications, and public information portals.
- **E-Commerce:** ICT plays a crucial role in electronic commerce, enabling online buying and selling of goods and services. E-commerce platforms, online payment systems, and digital marketing are examples of ICT applications in business.
- **Digital Transformation:** Organizations and industries are undergoing digital transformation by integrating ICT into their processes, operations, and business models to improve efficiency, innovation, and competitiveness.
- **Cloud Computing:** Cloud computing involves the delivery of computing services, including storage, processing power, and applications, over the internet. It provides scalable and flexible solutions for businesses and individuals.

CONCLUSION

In conclusion, the exploration of unit two on Componential Convergence in Social Science has provided a comprehensive understanding of the intricate web that constitutes our societal fabric. Through a lens of geopolitical understanding, critical inquiry, and an exploration of geopolitical economy, we have delved into the nuanced dimensions of social adaptation, community living, economic restructuring, and living standards. Values and culture, as well as the crucial aspects of eco-habitation, have emerged as pivotal considerations in the contemporary landscape, emphasizing the need for eco-friendly living, judicious resource utilization, and addressing issues of scarcity and population. Citizenship and obligations to the state, coupled with human rights education and the recognition of the dignity of every individual, underscore the importance of responsible societal participation. Language mediation acts as a vital tool in shaping social dynamics, and historic-pedagogic sources serve as the bedrock for knowledge generation. The unit has, therefore, laid a robust foundation by elucidating the multifaceted aspects of social science, offering insights into the intricate interplay of diverse elements that shape our collective human experience.

UNIT - 3

PEDAGOGICAL APPLICATIONS OF SOCIAL SCIENCE DISCIPLINE

INTRODUCTION

Welcome to Unit 3: "Pedagogical Applications of Social Science Discipline." In this unit, we delve into the intricate realm of social science pedagogy, exploring the conceptual foundations that underpin effective teaching in this multifaceted discipline. The journey begins with an in-depth analysis of the pedagogical landscape of social science, unravelling its unique characteristics and challenges. We then navigate through essential pedagogical principles that guide educators in fostering a dynamic and engaging learning environment. The unit further explores diverse pedagogical approaches, including Fusion, Integration, and Correlation approaches, offering insights into how these methodologies can enhance the teaching and learning experience. Lastly, we examine the contrasting dynamics of an integrated versus disciplinary emphasis within the realm of social science, providing a comprehensive understanding of the varied instructional strategies employed in this vibrant field. Join us as we embark on a comprehensive exploration of the pedagogical applications that elevate the teaching and learning experience in social science education.

CONCEPTUAL BACKGROUND OF SOCIAL SCIENCE PEDAGOGY

Social science pedagogy refers to the theory and practice of teaching social sciences, which encompass a wide range of disciplines like sociology, psychology, anthropology, economics, political science, history, and more. It involves the use of various instructional strategies, methods, and approaches to help students develop a deep understanding of social phenomena, human behaviour, and the structures and systems that shape societies. Here is a conceptual background of social science pedagogy:

- **Interdisciplinary Nature**: Social science pedagogy recognizes that social sciences are inherently interdisciplinary. It emphasizes the importance of integrating knowledge and methodologies from different social science disciplines to provide a holistic understanding of human societies and their complexities.
- **Active Learning**: Social science pedagogy promotes active learning strategies to engage students in critical thinking, problem-solving, and analysis. This includes class discussions, debates, case studies, role-playing, and simulations to foster a deeper understanding of social issues.
- **Critical Thinking and Analytical Skills**: The pedagogical approach emphasizes the development of critical thinking and analytical skills. Students are encouraged to question assumptions, evaluate evidence, and make informed judgments about social phenomena.
- **Real-World Application**: Social science pedagogy often incorporates real-world examples and current events to demonstrate the practical relevance of social science concepts. This helps students connect theory to the world around them.
- **Inquiry-Based Learning**: Social science pedagogy encourages students to formulate research questions, design studies, and conduct empirical research when applicable. This helps students develop research skills and apply them to address social issues.
- **Multicultural Perspective**: Recognizing the diversity of societies and cultures around the world, social science pedagogy promotes a multicultural perspective. It encourages students to understand and appreciate different worldviews and social practices.
- **Ethical Considerations**: Ethical considerations are a significant part of social science pedagogy. It encourages students to think about the ethical implications of social research and social policies, fostering a sense of social responsibility.
- **Case Studies and Problem-Based Learning**: Case studies and problem-based learning approaches are often used to explore complex social issues in depth. These methods allow students to grapple with real-world problems and develop solutions.
- **Critical Pedagogy**: Some educators employ critical pedagogy in social science teaching, which involves examining power

dynamics, social inequalities, and the impact of social structures on individuals and communities. It encourages students to challenge the status quo and work towards social justice.

- **Technology Integration**: The integration of technology is increasingly common in social science pedagogy. It includes using online resources, simulations, and data analysis tools to enhance the learning experience and develop digital literacy skills.
- **Assessment and Feedback**: Social science pedagogy emphasizes the importance of assessment and feedback to gauge students' progress and understanding. Formative and summative assessments are used to measure learning outcomes.
- **Inclusive and Diverse Classrooms**: Creating inclusive and diverse classrooms is a key consideration. Educators strive to ensure that students from all backgrounds feel valued and included, and they incorporate diverse perspectives into the curriculum.

Social science pedagogy is dynamic and adaptable, evolving in response to changes in society, technology, and educational research. It seeks to equip students with the knowledge and skills needed to analyse and address the complex social issues of our time.

PEDAGOGICAL ANALYSIS OF SOCIAL SCIENCE

Pedagogy is a method of teaching in which teachers teach, both in theory and in practice. Pedagogy is shaped by educator's teaching beliefs and involves their understanding of culture and different learning styles. It is essential for students to have meaningful classroom relationships in order to build on prior learning. Pedagogy refers to the way of teaching students, whether it is the theory or practice of educating. It is a relationship between the culture and techniques of learning. The main aim of pedagogy is to build on previous learning of the students and work on the development of skills and attitudes of the learners. Pedagogy enables the students to get a thorough understanding of the subject and helps them in applying those learning in their daily lives outside of the classroom. Pedagogy in teaching can be referred to as an educator's understanding of how the students learn. The teachers are focused on presenting the syllabus to the students in such a way that it is relevant to their needs. Pedagogy demands classroom interactions between the teacher and students which create a significant impact on the learner's mind. Pedagogy enables teachers to understand the best suitable practices for a classroom setting. It helps them to know how different students learn and grasp information so that they can tailor their lessons to satisfy those needs. It is likely to improve the quality of teaching and the way it is received by the students. Pedagogy plays an important role to help teachers understand the best ways to conduct a classroom. It gives them insights into how students learn differently in different topics so that they can conduct lessons to suit these needs. It aims to improve the quality of education for students.

Importance of Pedagogy in Teaching

- **Improves quality of teaching:** If a well-thought pedagogy is implemented in the classrooms, the quality of education can show a drastic improvement. This will benefit the students by helping them thoroughly understand the education material, thereby improving the learning outcomes.
- **Encourage cooperative learning environment:** The implementation of pedagogy in education encourages the students to work together towards completing a task and learn together. This increases their perceptions by understanding and taking views from the other students, thereby adapting the cooperative learning environments making them better leaders in the future.
- **Eliminates monotonous learning:** Pedagogy and child development work hand in hand. It helps the student to think in different ways and move beyond the traditional methods of memorization and comprehension for learning. It invokes complex processes of learning among the students such as analysing, creative thinking, and evaluation. Further, it makes students more receptive to what the teacher is teaching.
- **Student can follow their ways of learning:** A well thought pedagogy can help the students to grasp education in various ways. It caters to the learning abilities of different students. Students can follow their preferred ways of learning and stick to them. In this way, the students develop a better understanding of the subject, which eventually improves their skills and learning outcomes.
- **Convenient learning approach for all**: Students with special needs require different ways of learning and teaching in the institutes. Implementation of a suitable pedagogical approach will help them learn better and encourage them to be a part of the mainstream learning community.
- **Improves teacher-student communication:** The teacher understands the student in a better way which helps them to focus on the student's weaknesses and guide them.

A pedagogical analysis of social science involves examining how the subject of social science is taught and learned, focusing on the methods, strategies, and approaches used in the teaching and learning of social science concepts and content. In its simple meaning the term pedagogical analysis (a composition of two words pedagogy and analysis) stands for a type of analysis based on pedagogy. Analysis as a term stands for a process of breaking or separating a thing into its smaller parts, elements or constituents. We break a teaching unit into its constituents –subunit, topics or single concepts etc. through the process of unit analysis. In addition, we can break the contents of the prescribed course in a subject into its various constituents – major and minor sections, sub-sections, units and sub- units, major concept and minor concepts, topics etc by carrying out a process of content analysis.

Here are some key aspects of such an analysis:

- **Learning Objectives**: Identify the learning objectives of social science education. What specific knowledge, skills, and attitudes are students expected to acquire?
- **Curriculum Design**: Analyse the curriculum to determine how social science topics are organized and sequenced. Consider the inclusion of various sub-disciplines within social science, such as sociology, psychology, economics, political science, and anthropology. Assess whether the curriculum reflects a balanced and comprehensive approach to social science.
- **Teaching Methods**: Examine the instructional methods employed in social science education. Are lectures, discussions, case studies, simulations, or experiential learning utilized? Evaluate the use of technology and multimedia resources in teaching social science.
- **Assessment**: Analyse the assessment strategies used in social science education. Are there a variety of assessment types, such as exams, essays, projects, presentations, and group work? Consider the alignment of assessments with the stated learning objectives.
- **Teaching Materials**: Review the textbooks, reading materials, and online resources used in social science courses. Are they up-to-date and diverse in perspectives? Consider the availability of primary sources, case studies, and real-world examples to make the subject matter more engaging.
- **Pedagogical Approaches**: Explore the pedagogical approaches employed, such as problem-based learning, inquiry-based learning, or critical thinking exercises. Assess whether interdisciplinary or

transdisciplinary approaches are encouraged to address complex societal issues.

- **Inclusivity and Diversity**: Evaluate how social science education incorporates diverse perspectives, voices, and cultures. Consider the inclusion of underrepresented groups in social science content.
- **Critical Thinking and Analytical Skills**: Analyse how social science courses promote critical thinking, data analysis, and research skills. Assess whether students are encouraged to question assumptions and evaluate evidence.
- **Student Engagement**: Investigate the level of student engagement in social science courses. Are students actively participating in discussions and activities? Consider the incorporation of current events and contemporary issues to make the subject matter relevant.
- **Teacher Training**: Examine the training and professional development opportunities provided to social science educators. Assess whether teachers have access to resources and support to enhance their pedagogical skills.
- **Classroom Environment**: Evaluate the classroom environment, both physical and virtual, and how it supports social science learning. Consider the use of classroom discussions, group work, and collaborative projects.
- **Ethical Considerations**: Analyse how ethics and social responsibility are integrated into the curriculum. Assess whether students are encouraged to consider the ethical implications of social science research and decision-making. A pedagogical analysis of social science should ultimately aim to improve the teaching and learning of the subject, fostering critical thinking, active citizenship, and a deeper understanding of human societies and their complexities.

Needs of Pedagogical Analysis

Pedagogy i.e. the science of teaching is a master plan that includes a detail of what is to be done by a teacher, the instructional strategies, instructional equipment and the cardinal objectives of instruction. Depending on what can actually learn and what are the expectation sets for learners of a particular stage of development, specific instructional objectives are determined and appropriate set of activities provided. The teacher decides instructional objectives, equipment and strategies with every aspect of learning conditions to be created. Favourable conditions for positive learning cell for knowledge of various factors operating in different conditions. Pedagogical analysis is appropriate objectives and strategies in various instructional situations and assess the levels the level of actual learning at the end. A comprehensive vision of required tasks, strategies for realization of specific goals facilitates effective teaching. So, pedagogical analysis offers enormous potential for improving the delivery of information in all form of education. It involves various logical steps to arrive at logical inference. It also helps the students to understand concepts, principles or phenomena.

Components and Operations Involved in the task of Pedagogical Analysis

Looking in the way, by the term pedagogical Analysis of any subject content we certainly aim to carry out the task of the analysing the prescribed course material or a particular unit/sub-unit/topic/single concept of the subject being taught to a particular class by systematically executing the following four operations in a close interactive style.

- Content analysis of the unit/topic/single concept being taught by the teacher in the subject.
- Setting of the teaching or instructional objectives of the content material of the topic in hand by writing them in specific behavioural terms.
- Suggesting methods, techniques, teaching learning activities, aids and equipment helpful for the teaching learning of the topic in hand quite in tune with the realization of the set instructional objectives.
- Suggesting appropriate evaluation devices in the form of oral, written or practical activities and test questions etc for evaluating the outcomes of the teaching learning process carried in relation to the teaching of the topic in hand.

Objectives of Pedagogic Analysis

Pedagogic analysis is a process used in education to evaluate and improve teaching and learning methods. Its objectives include:

- **Enhancing Learning Outcomes**: Pedagogic analysis aims to identify the most effective teaching methods and materials to optimize student learning and understanding of the subject matter.
- **Tailoring Instruction**: It helps educators customize their teaching approaches to meet the specific needs and learning styles of individual students or groups.

- **Curriculum Development**: By analysing the pedagogical aspects of a curriculum, educators can refine and adapt it to ensure it aligns with educational goals and standards.
- **Assessing Learning Progress**: Pedagogic analysis provides a means to continuously assess student progress, allowing educators to adjust their instruction as needed.
- **Identifying Barriers to Learning**: It helps in recognizing obstacles to learning, such as student misconceptions or difficulties, and finding strategies to address them effectively.
- **Innovating Teaching Methods**: Pedagogic analysis encourages the exploration of new teaching strategies and technologies that can enhance the teaching and learning process.
- **Teacher Professional Development**: It supports the growth and development of educators by providing feedback and insights into their teaching practices, helping them refine their skills.
- **Quality Assurance**: In institutional settings, pedagogic analysis can be used to ensure the quality of education by evaluating the effectiveness of teaching methods and materials.
- **Research and Scholarship**: Pedagogic analysis can contribute to the field of education by generating research that helps in understanding the best practices in teaching and learning.
- **Student-Centred Learning**: It promotes a student-centred approach, emphasizing active learning, critical thinking, and problem-solving skills.
- **Cultural Sensitivity**: Pedagogic analysis can help educators be culturally responsive, considering the diversity of the student population and adapting teaching methods accordingly.
- **Continuous Improvement**: It fosters a culture of continuous improvement, where educators are committed to refining their teaching methods and students are encouraged to reflect on their own learning.

Pedagogic analysis refers to the systematic examination and evaluation of teaching and learning processes. The scope of pedagogic analysis is broad and encompasses various aspects of education and instruction. Here are some key areas within the scope of pedagogic analysis:

- **Curriculum Analysis**: Examining the content and structure of educational programs and curricula to ensure they align with educational goals and objectives.

- **Instructional Design Analysis**: Evaluating the design and development of educational materials, lesson plans, and teaching strategies to enhance their effectiveness.
- **Assessment Analysis**: Assessing the methods and tools used for evaluating students' learning outcomes and their alignment with learning objectives.
- **Learning Environment Analysis**: Analysing the physical and digital environments in which teaching and learning occur to optimize conditions for learning.
- **Pedagogical Strategies Analysis**: Evaluating the techniques, methods, and approaches used by educators to facilitate learning, including pedagogical innovations.
- **Educational Technology Analysis**: Assessing the integration of technology in education, including the selection of appropriate tools and platforms, and their impact on learning outcomes.
- **Learning Styles and Individual Differences Analysis**: Considering the diverse needs and preferences of learners and adapting teaching methods accordingly.
- **Classroom Management Analysis**: Examining strategies for creating a positive and productive classroom atmosphere to support effective teaching and learning.
- **Teacher Competence Analysis**: Assessing the qualifications, skills, and professional development of educators to ensure they are well-prepared to deliver quality education.
- **Student Engagement and Motivation Analysis**: Investigating methods to keep students engaged, motivated, and enthusiastic about learning.
- **Feedback and Assessment Analysis**: Evaluating the processes of providing feedback to students and how assessment results are used to inform instruction.
- **Inclusive Education Analysis**: Examining strategies and policies that promote inclusivity and accommodate diverse learners, including those with special needs.
- **Lifelong Learning Analysis**: Analysing approaches to encourage continuous learning beyond formal education and promote a culture of lifelong learning.
- **Policy and Regulatory Analysis**: Evaluating educational policies, regulations, and reforms that impact the quality and accessibility of education.

- **Research in Pedagogy**: Investigating and contributing to the body of knowledge in the field of pedagogy through research and data analysis.

Advantages of Pedagogic Analysis

Pedagogic analysis refers to the systematic examination and evaluation of teaching and learning processes. The scope of pedagogic analysis is broad and encompasses various aspects of education and instruction. Here are some key areas within the scope of pedagogic analysis:

- *Curriculum Analysis*: Examining the content and structure of educational programmes and curricula to ensure they align with educational goals and objectives.
- *Instructional Design Analysis*: Evaluating the design and development of educational materials, lesson plans, and teaching strategies to enhance their effectiveness.
- *Assessment Analysis*: Assessing the methods and tools used for evaluating students' learning outcomes and their alignment with learning objectives.
- *Learning Environment Analysis*: Analysing the physical and digital environments in which teaching and learning occur to optimize conditions for learning.
- *Pedagogical Strategies Analysis*: Evaluating the techniques, methods, and approaches used by educators to facilitate learning, including pedagogical innovations.
- *Educational Technology Analysis*: Assessing the integration of technology in education, including the selection of appropriate tools and platforms, and their impact on learning outcomes.
- *Learning Styles and Individual Differences Analysis*: Considering the diverse needs and preferences of learners and adapting teaching methods accordingly.
- *Classroom Management Analysis*: Examining strategies for creating a positive and productive classroom atmosphere to support effective teaching and learning.
- *Teacher Competence Analysis*: Assessing the qualifications, skills, and professional development of educators to ensure they are well-prepared to deliver quality education.
- *Student Engagement and Motivation Analysis*: Investigating methods to keep students engaged, motivated, and enthusiastic about learning.

- *Feedback and Assessment Analysis*: Evaluating the processes of providing feedback to students and how assessment results are used to inform instruction.
- *Inclusive Education Analysis*: Examining strategies and policies that promote inclusivity and accommodate diverse learners, including those with special needs.
- *Lifelong Learning Analysis*: Analysing approaches to encourage continuous learning beyond formal education and promote a culture of lifelong learning.
- *Policy and Regulatory Analysis*: Evaluating educational policies, regulations, and reforms that impact the quality and accessibility of education.
- *Research in Pedagogy*: Investigating and contributing to the body of knowledge in the field of pedagogy through research and data analysis.

PEDAGOGICAL PRINCIPLES

Pedagogical principles are fundamental ideas and guidelines that inform and shape the practice of teaching and learning. They provide a framework for educators to design effective instructional strategies and create a positive and productive learning environment. While there are many pedagogical principles, here are some of the most important ones:

- *Learner-Centred Approach*: Focus on the needs, interests, and abilities of the learners. Recognize that each student is unique and may have different learning styles and paces.
- *Active Learning*: Encourage students to actively engage with the material through discussions, problem-solving, hands-on activities, and critical thinking, rather than passively receiving information.
- *Constructivism*: Build on students' prior knowledge and encourage them to construct their own understanding through exploration, inquiry, and reflection.
- *Scaffolding*: Provide support and guidance to students as they progress in their learning, gradually reducing the level of support as they become more independent learners.
- *Authentic Learning*: Create real-world, meaningful tasks and activities that connect the curriculum to the students' lives, making learning relevant and practical.
- *Assessment for Learning*: Use a variety of formative assessment

methods to gauge students' progress and adjust instruction accordingly. Assessment should be seen as a tool for improvement rather than just a way to assign grades.

- *Diversity and Inclusion*: Recognize and respect the diverse backgrounds, cultures, and abilities of students. Adapt teaching methods to accommodate different learning needs.
- *Motivation*: Understand and address the motivation of students. Connect the curriculum to their interests and provide opportunities for autonomy and mastery.
- *Feedback*: Provide timely, constructive feedback that helps students understand their strengths and areas for improvement. Encourage self-assessment and reflection.
- *Clear Objectives and Expectations*: Communicate clear learning objectives and expectations to students. Make sure they understand what is expected of them and what they will achieve.
- *Technology Integration*: Use technology as a tool to enhance learning, but ensure that it is purposeful and aligns with the pedagogical goals.
- *Collaborative Learning*: Encourage students to work together, promoting social interaction, cooperation, and communication skills.
- *Reflection*: Encourage students to reflect on their learning experiences, helping them develop metacognitive skills and self-awareness.
- *Inquiry-Based Learning*: Encourage students to ask questions, explore topics, and discover answers through their own investigations.
- *Holistic Development*: Promote the development of not just academic knowledge but also social, emotional, and ethical aspects of a student's character.

These pedagogical principles can serve as a foundation for effective teaching and learning and can be adapted and combined to suit the specific needs of different educational contexts and age groups. Effective educators often employ a combination of these principles to create a rich and engaging learning experience for their students.

PEDAGOGICAL APPROACHES: FUSION, INTEGRATION AND CORRELATION APPROACH

The fusion, integration, and correlation approaches are pedagogical approaches that emphasize the connection and integration of different subjects or disciplines. These approaches aim to provide a holistic understanding of knowledge and promote interdisciplinary thinking. Here's an overview of each approach:

- **Fusion approach**: The fusion approach involves merging or blending different subjects or disciplines to create a unified and comprehensive understanding of a particular topic or theme. It goes beyond traditional subject boundaries and encourages students to explore connections and relationships among various disciplines. For example, in a fusion approach to education, a topic like climate change may be explored through the lenses of science, geography, economics, and social studies, allowing students to understand the complex nature of the issue from multiple perspectives.
- **Integration approach**: The integration approach involves the intentional and systematic integration of different subjects or disciplines to explore common themes or concepts. Instead of teaching subjects in isolation, educators seek to integrate related content and skills across multiple disciplines. This approach promotes a deeper understanding of the interconnectedness of knowledge and encourages students to apply their learning in meaningful ways. For instance, integrating literature, history, and art to study a specific historical period can provide students with a more comprehensive understanding of the cultural, social, and artistic aspects of that era.
- **Correlation approach**: The correlation approach focuses on identifying and emphasizing the connections and correlations between different subjects or disciplines. It highlights the interdependencies and relationships among various areas of knowledge. Educators using the correlation approach intentionally design learning experiences that highlight these connections, helping students see how different subjects complement and enrich each other. For example, when studying a novel in literature class, students might also explore the historical context in history class and the psychological aspects of the characters in psychology class, thus gaining a deeper understanding of the literary work.

All three approaches - fusion, integration, and correlation - encourage students to develop critical thinking skills, make interdisciplinary connections, and see the relevance of different subjects in real-world contexts. By adopting these approaches, educators can help students develop a more comprehensive and interconnected understanding of knowledge, fostering a broader perspective and promoting the application of learning across various disciplines.

INTEGRATED VS DISCIPLINARY EMPHASIS OF SOCIAL SCIENCE

The integrated and disciplinary emphasis of Social Science represent two different approaches to teaching and studying the subject. Here's a comparison between the two:

Disciplinary Emphasis	Integrated Emphasis
Focus: In a disciplinary emphasis, Social Science is taught as separate disciplines, such as sociology, psychology, anthropology, political science, economics, and history.	**Focus**: In an integrated emphasis, Social Science is taught in an interdisciplinary or multidisciplinary manner, focusing on the connections and interrelationships between different disciplines.
Siloed Approach: Each discipline is taught independently, with its own theories, methods, and content. Students study each discipline as a separate subject, often delving deep into the specific theories, concepts, and methodologies associated with each field.	**Holistic Perspective**: The integrated approach seeks to provide a broader and more holistic understanding of social phenomena. It emphasizes the interconnectedness of different social science disciplines and the importance of considering multiple perspectives.
Specialization: The disciplinary approach allows for specialization and in-depth exploration within each discipline. Students develop a focused understanding of the specific field they are studying.	**Problem-Solving Orientation**: The integrated approach encourages critical thinking and problem-solving skills by analysing social problems and phenomena from various angles. It helps students recognize that social issues are complex and require insights from multiple disciplines.
Expertise Development: This approach is beneficial for students who plan to pursue further studies or careers in specific social science disciplines. It provides a solid foundation and specialized knowledge within a particular field.	**Real-World Relevance**: Integrated teaching aligns with the real-world nature of social problems, which often require collaboration and the integration of different perspectives to address effectively.

The choice between an integrated and disciplinary emphasis depends on various factors, including educational goals, curriculum design, and learner needs. Both approaches have them advantages and considerations. Some educational institutions and programs may adopt a blended approach that incorporates elements of both disciplinary and integrated emphasis, striking a balance between specialization and interdisciplinary thinking. It's important to note that neither approach is inherently superior to the other. The choice should be based on the educational context and the desired outcomes for students. Ultimately, the goal is to provide a comprehensive and meaningful learning experience that equips students with the knowledge, skills, and perspectives needed to understand and navigate the complexities of the social world.

CONCLUSION

In conclusion, Unit three has provided a comprehensive exploration of the pedagogical applications within the realm of Social Science discipline. The conceptual background has laid the foundation for understanding the unique challenges and opportunities associated with teaching social sciences. The pedagogical analysis has offered insights into effective teaching methodologies, while the delineation of pedagogical principles has served as a guiding framework for educators. The discussion on fusion, integration, and correlation approaches has illuminated diverse instructional strategies, allowing teachers to tailor their methods to the specific needs of their students. Finally, the examination of integrated versus disciplinary emphasis has highlighted the importance of finding a balanced approach to ensure a holistic and meaningful learning experience for students. By delving into these topics, this unit equips educators with valuable tools to enhance their pedagogical practices in the dynamic field of Social Science education.

UNIT - 4

STRATEGIES FOR SOCIAL SCIENCE INSTRUCTION

INTRODUCTION

Welcome to Unit four, "Strategies for Social Science Instruction." This unit delves into a comprehensive exploration of effective teaching methodologies and strategies tailored specifically for the dynamic field of social science. We will embark on a journey through various psychological considerations, including behaviourist, cognitivist, constructivist, and humanistic theories that underpin social science instruction. The unit will also address the essentials of creating inclusive classrooms, emphasizing the diverse needs of learners. Additionally, we will navigate the terrain of skill development through micro-teaching, peer tutoring, macro-teaching, and team teaching. The integration of Information and Communication Technology (ICT) is a crucial aspect, with a focus on online learning, e-learning, m-learning, Open and Distance Learning (ODL), virtual learning, and teleconferencing. Scaffolding strategies will be explored to support learners effectively, and we will delve into modular explorations for developing learning packages. The unit will conclude with an examination of various models of teaching, including the Group Investigation Model and Social Inquiry Model, providing educators with a rich toolkit to enhance their social science instructional practices.

PSYCHOLOGICAL CONSIDERATIONS OF SOCIAL SCIENCE INSTRUCTION

The psychological considerations of social science instruction are crucial for creating effective and engaging learning experiences. Social science education encompasses a broad range of disciplines, including psychology, sociology, anthropology, political science, and economics. Here are several psychological considerations that educators should take into account when teaching social science:

- **Individual Differences:** (a) **Learning Styles:** Recognize and accommodate diverse learning styles among students. Some may learn better through visual aids, while others may prefer hands-on activities or discussions. Understanding these differences can enhance the effectiveness of instruction. (b) **Cognitive Abilities:** Consider variations in cognitive abilities and tailor instruction to accommodate students with different levels of analytical and critical thinking skills. (c) **Motivation:** Understand the individual motivations of students. Connecting social science concepts to real-world examples or personal experiences can enhance intrinsic motivation.
- **Cultural Sensitivity:** Acknowledge and respect cultural diversity within the classroom. Social science topics often involve discussions about different cultures, societies, and historical events. Be mindful of potential cultural biases in instructional materials and aim for inclusivity. Foster an inclusive learning environment where students feel comfortable expressing their perspectives and experiences. This can contribute to a richer understanding of social science concepts.
- **Relevance and Real-World Application:** Emphasize the practical applications of social science concepts to make the material more relevant to students' lives. Highlight how these concepts can be applied in real-world situations, fostering a deeper understanding and engagement. Provide examples that connect social science theories to contemporary issues. This helps students see the relevance of what they are learning and encourages critical thinking about current events.
- **Active Learning and Engagement:** Incorporate active learning strategies, such as group discussions, case studies, role-playing, and hands-on activities. Social science concepts are often better understood when students can apply them in interactive and meaningful ways. Use multimedia resources, including videos, simulations, and interactive technology, to cater to different learning preferences and maintain student interest.
- **Developmental Considerations:** Recognize the developmental stages of students and adjust the complexity of the material accordingly. Younger students may benefit from more concrete

examples, while older students can delve into more abstract and complex social science theories. Consider the socio-emotional development of students, addressing topics with sensitivity and providing a supportive environment for discussions on potentially sensitive subjects.

- **Feedback and Assessment:** Provide constructive feedback to help students understand their strengths and areas for improvement. Encourage self-reflection and critical analysis of their own learning. Use a variety of assessment methods, including formative and summative assessments, to gauge student understanding. This helps in adapting instruction to meet the needs of individual learners.

Incorporating these psychological considerations into social science instruction can create a more inclusive, engaging, and effective learning experience for students. By acknowledging and addressing the diverse needs of learners, educators can promote a deeper understanding of social science concepts and encourage lifelong learning.

BEHAVIOURISM IN TEACHING SOCIAL SCIENCE

Behaviourism is a psychological theory that focuses on observable behaviours, considering them as the result of conditioning and reinforcement. In the context of teaching social science, behaviourism can be applied in various ways to shape and modify students' behaviour and learning outcomes. Here are some key principles and strategies related to behaviourism in teaching social science

Behaviourism is a twentieth-century term, made popular by the psychologist John Watson (1878-1958) in 1913. Although Watson introduced psychological behaviourism, there is also a version called philosophical behaviourism. Psychological behaviourism is the view that psychology should study the behaviour of individual organisms. Psychology should be defined not as the study of the mind and internal mental processes via introspection, but as the science of behaviour. The most famous proponents of psychological behaviourism were John Watson and B.F. Skinner (1904-1990). Other notable behaviourists were Edwin Guthrie (1886-1959), Edward Tolman (1886-1959), Clark Hull (1884-1952), and Kenneth Spence (1907-1967).

Philosophical behaviourism, by contrast, is a research programme advanced primarily by philosophers of the twentieth century. This school is much more difficult to characterize, but in general, it is concerned with the philosophy of mind, the meaning of mentalistic terms, how we learn this meaning, and how we know when to use these terms. Besides these two generic versions of behaviourism, there are several subvarieties.

Methodological behaviourism is the view that it does not matter whether there is a mind or not; psychologists should just study behaviour. Logical behaviourism (also called analytic behaviourism or semantic behaviourism) is the view that all mentalistic terms or concepts can be defined or translated into behavioural terms or concepts. Epistemological behaviourism and evidential behaviourism hold roughly the view that the only way to know about a mental state is by observing behaviour.

John B Watson (1878-1958) was an American psychologist who became an ardent proponent of behaviourism. A graduate student at the university of Chicago, during formative years of functionalistic movement, he became interested in animal research and founded an animal laboratory. He emphasized study of behaviour by experiments. He explained his behaviourism in an article "psychology and the behaviourist" which was published in the psychological review (1913). He believed that concepts like 'mind- consciousness' and image have no place. He stated that, psychology was the science of behaviour. According to him behavioural acts are to be described objectively in "terms of stimulus and response, in terms of habit formation, habit integration and the like". Watson discarded mentalistic concepts such as consciousness and mind, etc. and proposed the four methods for behavioural research:

- Observation, with and without instrumental control.
- The conditioning reflex method.
- The verbal report method.
- Testing method.

The other notable psychologists of this school were Skinner, Pavlov, Tolman, Hull etc. The word behaviour is used in a very broad sense. It includes not only motor activities like walking, playing, digging or building but also such activities as gives us knowledge, for example, perceiving, imagining, remembering, thinking or reasoning, and emotional activities like feeling, happy, sad, angry or frightened. They are all activities of the individual; his life depends on them and it is difficult to think what the individual would be without them. They all are included in the term behaviour. "Any manifestation of life is activity" says Woodworth and behaviour is a collective name for all such manifestations. Movements of limbs and acts of hearing, seeing and smelling are as much behaviour as thoughts, emotions and memories. Behaviour expresses the entire life of an individual.

The science of psychology tries to explain how behaviour of one individual differs from that of another. But while it is interested in differences between one individual and another, it seeks to formulate as far as possible, the general laws of behaviour holding good even of very different individual. We define psychology as the science of mental life, the study of interactions of the individual with his environment or the science of the activities of an individual; we are not far from the common objective of understanding, explaining, predicting and controlling behaviour in a systematic and scientific way.

Contributions of Behaviourism to Education

- Behaviourism has given new methods and techniques of understanding the child behaviour.
- It has contributed to the understanding of the emotions of the child.
- It has given new methodology of teaching known as 'programmed learning' which has been successfully employed in several countries.
- It points out that all behaviour is learnt in the process of interaction with environment.
- It emphasizes the importance of environment and its impact on human growth.
- It has led to the development of new approaches, methods and techniques of dealing with maladjustment in children.
- It has brought psychology out from the controversy of mentalistic approach to human behaviour.
- It has greatly contributed to the psychology of learning.
- It has indicated the importance of motivation.

Implication of Behaviourism Learning Theory

- Type of learning environment that is based on Ivan Pavlov's Classical Conditioning. It can be involved in both positive and negative experiences of children in school. This type of learning happens when the children associate their learning experience with something that either make them feel pleasure or uncomfortable at school.
- Type of learning environment that is based on B.F Skinner's Operant Conditioning. Based on giving reinforcement (reward) and punishment. There are two types of reinforcement, i.e. Positive reinforcement and Negative reinforcement.

- Applied behaviour analysis is an application of the principles of operant conditioning to change learner's behaviour. Two usages of Applied Behaviour Analysis are, (a) To increase desirable behaviour and (b) To decrease undesirable behaviour.
- Six operant conditioning strategies to increase child's desirable behaviour: Choose effective reinforcers, make reinforcers contingent and timely, selecting the best schedule for reinforcement, consider contracting, use negative reinforcement, use prompts and shaping.
- Strategies to decrease child's undesirable behaviour: Use differential reinforcement, terminate reinforcement, remove desirable stimuli, and aversive stimuli.

Three Types of Behaviouralism

- **Methodological behaviourism** is a normative theory about the scientific conduct of psychology. It claims that psychology should concern itself with the behaviour of organisms (human and nonhuman animals). Psychology should not concern itself with mental states or events or with constructing internal information processing accounts of behaviour. According to methodological behaviourism, reference to mental states, such as an animal's beliefs or desires, adds nothing to what psychology can and should understand about the sources of behaviour.
- **Psychological behaviourism** is a research programme within psychology. It purports to explain human and animal behaviour in terms of external physical stimuli, responses, learning histories, and (for certain types of behaviour) reinforcements. Psychological behaviourism is present in the work of Ivan Pavlov (1849–1936), Edward Thorndike (1874–1949), as well as Watson. Its fullest and most influential expression is B. F. Skinner's work on schedules of reinforcement.
- **Analytical or logical behaviourism** is a theory within philosophy about the meaning or semantics of mental terms or concepts. It says that the very idea of a mental state or condition is the idea of a behavioural disposition or family of behavioural tendencies, evident in how a person behaves in one situation rather than another.

CONSTRUCTIVISM AS A THEORETICAL BACKING FOR SOCIAL SCIENCE EDUCATION

Constructivism is a theory of knowledge that argues that humans generate knowledge and meaning from an interaction between their experiences and their ideas. It has influenced a number of disciplines, including psychology, sociology, education and the history of science. During its infancy, constructivism examined the interaction between human experiences and their reflexes or behaviour-patterns. Jean Piaget called these systems of knowledge schemata. Constructivism is not a specific pedagogy, although it is often confused with constructionism, an educational theory developed by Seymour Papert, inspired by constructivist and experiential learning ideas of Piaget. Piaget's theory of constructivist learning has had wide ranging impact on learning theories and teaching methods in education and is an underlying theme of many education reform movements. Research support for constructivist teaching techniques has been mixed, with some research supporting these techniques and other research contradicting those results.

Constructivism is basically a theory-based on observation and scientific study - about how people learn. It says that people construct their own understanding and knowledge of the world, through experiencing things and reflecting on those experiences. When we encounter something new, we have to reconcile it with our previous ideas and experience, maybe changing what we believe, or maybe discarding the new information as irrelevant. In any case, we are active creators of our own knowledge. To do this, we must ask questions, explore, and assess what we know. In the classroom, the constructivist view of learning can point towards a number of different teaching practices. In the most general sense, it usually means encouraging students to use active techniques (experiments, real-world problem solving) to create more knowledge and then to reflect on and talk about what they are doing and how their understanding is changing. The teacher makes sure she understands the student's preexisting conceptions, and guides the activity to address them and then build on them.

Definition: Constructivism in psychology is a method of therapy that focuses on both the internal and external systems of meaning-making. Constructivism is an approach that also combines other forms of psychotherapy, including cognitive behavioural therapy, an action- oriented form of therapy that encourages clients to change maladaptive thinking patterns that lead to maladaptive behaviours and negative emotions, and psychoanalysis, a branch of psychotherapy based on theories about the relationship between the conscious and unconscious minds.

Constructivism Theory and Application

Constructivism theory is based on the idea that everyone's sense of knowing is more than a passive expression of the world around us but instead, is a result of our constructions, or our beliefs and emotions about experiences in our lives. In this context, 'construction' simply refers to the ways we build our own understanding of the world around us and how we fit into it. Jean Piaget is considered one of the first constructivism theorists. Constructivism theory is a broad concept that encompasses many disciplines, including sociology and education. It's generally based on Piaget's notion that we are active participants in the construction of our reality.

Clinical psychologist George Kelly was the first to develop a theory of psychotherapy along constructivist lines while working with farmers who were suffering from the effects of the great depression and the dust bowl during the 1920s and 1930s. Kelly designed a procedure where clients were coached to enact fictional identities, they created themselves. Clients acted out the roles with a therapist, allowing the two to discuss the ways the client has built his or her understanding of the world and how that understanding can change. By acting as a different part of themselves, the client sees how they can live differently by acting differently. This procedure of Kelly's came to be known as fixed-role therapy.

In another application, a client might report life experiences and the therapist will pay close attention to how these experiences are being used to create meaning in the present. The therapist then might create an 'action-thought- reaction' scenario, to reveal the impacts of the reactions on the client's life and could continue to have an impact in the future. Narrative therapy, based on the work of Michael white, is a newer application of constructivism, where clients tell stories about their lives and examine those stories for a clearer understanding of how they've assigned meaning to their experiences.

Implication of constructivism for teaching and learning

- Teachers act as facilitators, supports, guides and models of learning.
- Learning concerns adjusting our mental models to accommodate new experiences.
- Learning concerns making connections between information.
- Instruction should be built around more complex problems, not problems with clear, correct answers.
- Context and personal knowledge have high significance.
- Students should help establish the criteria on which their work is assessed.

- Teachers know more and shouldn't let students muddle around.
- Student learning depends on background knowledge – that's why teaching facts is so necessary (reversed).
- Student interest and effort are more important than textbook content.
- It is sometimes better for teachers, not students, to decide what activities are to be done.
- Sense making and thinking are most important, not knowing content.
- Experimentation replaces rote learning.
- Teaching utilizes both skill- based and open-ended approaches.
- Motivation to learn is intrinsic rather than extrinsic (done for its own sake rather than for grades, test scores or rewards).
- Learners often produce unique and personal knowledge.

Constructivist Approach

The nature of the learner: Social constructivism not only acknowledges the uniqueness and complexity of the learner, but actually encourages, utilizes and rewards it as an integral part of the learning process (Wertsch, 1997).

The importance of the background and culture of the learner: Social constructivism or socio-culturalism encourages the learner to arrive at his or her version of the truth, influenced by his or her background, culture or embedded worldview. Historical developments and symbol systems, such as language, logic, and mathematical systems, are inherited by the learner as a member of a particular culture and these are learned throughout the learner's life. This also stresses the importance of the nature of the learner's social interaction with knowledgeable members of the society. Without the social interaction with other more knowledgeable people, it is impossible to acquire social meaning of important symbol systems and learn how to utilize them. Young children develop their thinking abilities by interacting with other children, adults and the physical world. From the social constructivist viewpoint, it is thus important to take into account the background and culture of the learner throughout the learning process, as this background also helps to shape the knowledge and truth that the learner creates, discovers and attains in the learning process (Wertsch, 1997).

Responsibility for learning: Furthermore, it is argued that the responsibility of learning should reside increasingly with the learner (Glasersfeld, 1989). Social constructivism thus emphasizes the importance of the learner being actively involved in the learning process, unlike previous educational viewpoints where the responsibility rested with the instructor to teach and where the learner played a passive, receptive role. Von Glasersfeld (1989) emphasized that learners construct their own understanding and that they do not simply mirror and reflect what they read. Learners look for meaning and will try to find regularity and order in the events of the world even in the absence of full or complete information.

The motivation for learning: Another crucial assumption regarding the nature of the learner concerns the level and source of motivation for learning. According to Von Glasersfeld (1989) sustaining motivation to learn is strongly dependent on the learner's confidence in his or her potential for learning. These feelings of competence and belief in potential to solve new problems, are derived from first-hand experience of mastery of problems in the past and are much more powerful than any external acknowledgment and motivation (Prawat and Floden 1994). This links up with Vygotsky's "Zone of Proximal Development" (Vygotsky 1978) where learners are challenged within close proximity to, yet slightly above, their current level of development. By experiencing the successful completion of challenging tasks, learners gain confidence and motivation to embark on more complex challenges.

The Role of the Instructor

According to the social constructivist approach, instructors have to adapt to **the role of facilitators and not teachers** (Bauersfeld, 1995). Whereas a teacher gives a didactic lecture that covers the subject matter, a facilitator helps the learner to get to his or her own understanding of the content. In the former scenario the learner plays a passive role and in the latter scenario the learner plays an active role in the learning process. The emphasis thus turns away from the instructor and the content, and towards the learner (Gamoran, Secada, & Marrett, 1998). This dramatic change of role implies that a facilitator needs to display a totally different set of skills than that of a teacher (Brownstein 2001). A teacher tells, a facilitator asks; a teacher lectures from the front, a facilitator supports from the back; a teacher gives answers according to a set curriculum, a facilitator provides guidelines and creates the environment for the learner to arrive at his or her own conclusions; a teacher mostly gives a monologue, a facilitator is in continuous dialogue with the learners (Rhodes and Bellamy, 1999). A facilitator should also be able to adapt the learning experience 'in mid-air' by taking the initiative to steer the learning experience to where the learners want to create value. A few strategies for cooperative learning include:

- Reciprocal Questioning: students work together to ask and answer questions
- Jigsaw Classroom: students become "experts" on one part of a group project and teach it to the others in their group
- Structured Controversies: Students work together to research a particular controversy (Woolfolk, 2010)

The Nature of the Learning Process

According to constructivism **learning is an active, social process.** Social constructivism, strongly influenced by Vygotsky's (1978) work, suggests that knowledge is first constructed in a social context and is then appropriated by individuals (Bruning et al., 1999; M. Cole, 1991; Eggan & Kauchak, 2004). According to social constructivists, the process of sharing individual perspectives-called collaborative elaboration (Meter & Stevens, 2000) - results in learners constructing understanding together that wouldn't be possible alone (Greeno et al., 1996). Social constructivist scholar's view learning as an active process where learners should learn to discover principles, concepts and facts for themselves, hence the importance of encouraging guesswork and intuitive thinking in learners (Brown et al.1989; Ackerman 1996). In fact, for the social constructivist, reality is not something that we can discover because it does not pre-exist prior to our social invention of it. Kukla (2000) argues that reality is constructed by our own activities and that people, together as members of a society, invent the properties of the world. Other constructivist scholars agree with this and emphasize that individuals make meanings through the interactions with each other and with the environment they live in. Knowledge is thus a product of humans and is socially and culturally constructed (Ernest 1991; Prawat and Floden 1994). McMahon (1997) agrees that learning is a social process. He further states that learning is not a process that only takes place inside our minds, nor is it a passive development of our behaviours that is shaped by external forces and that meaningful learning occurs when individuals are engaged in social activities.

Collaboration among Learners

Learners with different skills and backgrounds should collaborate in tasks and discussions to arrive at a shared understanding of the truth in a specific field (Duffy and Jonassen 1992). Most social constructivist models, such as that proposed by Duffy and Jonassen (1992), also stress the need for collaboration among learners, in direct contradiction to traditional competitive approaches. One Vygotskian notion that has significant implications for peer collaboration is that of the zone of proximal development. Defined as the distance between the actual developmental level as determined by independent problem-solving and the level of potential development as determined through problem-solving under adult guidance or in collaboration with more capable peers, it differs from the fixed biological nature of Piaget's stages of development. Through a process of 'scaffolding' a learner can be extended beyond the limitations of physical maturation to the extent that the development process lags behind the learning process (Vygotsky, 1978).

Criticism of Educational Constructivism

Several cognitive psychologists and educators have questioned the central claims of constructivism. It is argued that constructivist theories are misleading or contradict known findings. Matthews (1993) attempts to sketch the influence of constructivism in current mathematics and science education, aiming to indicate how pervasive Aristotle's empiricist epistemology is within it and what problems constructivism faces on that account. In the neo-Piagetian theories of cognitive development it is maintained that learning at any age depends upon the processing and representational resources available at this particular age. That is, it is maintained that if the requirements of the concept to be understood exceeds the available processing efficiency and working memory resources then the concept is by definition not learnable. This attitude toward learning impedes the learning from understanding essential theoretical concepts or, in other words, reasoning. Therefore, no matter how active a child is during learning, to learn the child must operate in a learning environment that meets the developmental and individual learning constraints that are characteristic for the child's age and this child's possible deviations from her age's norm. If this condition is not met, construction goes astray.

Kirschner et al. group a number of learning theories together (Discovery, Problem-Based, Experiential, and Inquiry-Based learning) and stated that highly scaffolded constructivist methods like problem-based learning and inquiry learning are ineffective. Kirschner et al. described several research studies that were favourable to problem-based learning given learners were provided some level of guidance and support.

COGNITIVISM IN TEACHING SOCIAL SCIENCE

Cognitivism in teaching social science represents a theoretical framework that places emphasis on the cognitive processes involved in learning and understanding. Rooted in the idea that learning is an active mental process, cognitivism explores how students acquire, organize, and apply knowledge in the realm of social science. This approach recognizes the importance of internal mental structures, such as memory, perception, and problem-solving skills, in shaping the learning experience. In the context of social science instruction, cognitivism encourages educators to design lessons that foster critical thinking, analysis, and the development of higher-order cognitive skills. This approach often involves engaging students in activities that promote deep understanding, such as case studies, discussions, and hands-on projects. By recognizing the cognitive processes at play, cognitivism provides a valuable framework for educators seeking to enhance the intellectual growth and analytical abilities of students within the social science domain. Cognitive learning is a style of learning that focuses on more effective use of the brain. It is an active style of learning that focuses on helping you learn how to maximize your brain's potential. It makes it easier for you to connect new information with existing ideas hence deepening your memory and retention capacity. To understand the process of cognitive learning, it's important to know the meaning of cognition. Cognition is the mental process of gaining knowledge and understanding through the senses, experience and thought.

Cognitive aspects of learning: Cognitive aspects of learning refer to thinking processes and mental procedures involved in the learning process. An important cognitive aspect of learning, that can hinder or facilitate learning, is prior knowledge and prior learning experience of students. Cognition is a term referring to the mental processes involved in gaining knowledge and comprehension. These cognitive processes include thinking, knowing, remembering, judging and problem solving

Functions of Cognitive Learning

- Cognitive learning is an immersive and active process that engages your senses in a constructive and long-lasting way.
- It teaches you to maximize your brain's potential and makes it easier to connect new information with existing ideas, deepening the memory and retention capacity.
- Instead of emphasizing memorization as in the traditional classroom method of teaching.
- Cognitive learning focuses on past knowledge.
- It trains you to reflect on the material and connect it with past knowledge for more robust learning.

- This not only makes cognitive learning a more effective way of gaining knowledge, but it also makes you a better learner for the long-term.

Elements of Cognitive Learning

Cognitive learning is unlike the traditional learning process, where the focus is on memorization rather than achieving mastery of the subject. The following factors are fundamental to the cognitive learning process.

- **Comprehension:** Cognitive learning strategies emphasize comprehension. You need to understand the reason for learning the subject in the first place and the role your knowledge plays in your work.
- **Memory:** Cognitive learning discourages rote learning where you cram materials for memorization. In cognitive learning, the goal is to understand the subject at a deeper level. This creates an immersive effect that helps recall and improves your ability to relate new knowledge to past information.
- **Application:** Cognitive learning strategies encourage you to reflect on the material and how to apply it to current and future situations.

Benefits of Cognitive Learning

The following are the major positive effects of cognitive learning:

- **Enhances learning**: Cognitive learning theory enhances lifelong learning. Workers can build upon previous ideas and apply new concepts to already existing knowledge.
- **Boosts confidence**: Students become more confident in approaching tasks as they get a deeper understanding of new topics and learn new skills.
- **Enhances Comprehension**: Cognitive learning improves learners' comprehension of acquiring new information. They can develop a deeper understanding of new learning materials.
- **Improves problem-solving skills**: Cognitive learning equips students with the skills they need to learn effectively. They are thereby able to develop problem-solving skills they can apply under challenging tasks.
- **Help learn new things faster**: Through the experience of learning, the student will be able to recycle and use the same learning methods that worked previously. This will help them learn new

things a lot faster as they already know what works for them when it comes to obtaining new knowledge.

- **Teaches to form concept formation (think abstract):** Cognitive learning can also teach your students to form a range of different concepts such as easily perceiving and interpreting information that could boost creativity and lead to innovations at the workplace.

Cognitivism in Social Science

Social science instruction plays a crucial role in shaping individuals' understanding of the world around them. It encompasses subjects such as psychology, sociology, anthropology, and political science, among others. One key theoretical framework that guides social science instruction is cognitivism. Cognitivism focuses on the mental processes involved in learning and emphasizes the importance of cognitive structures and strategies. Cognitivism posits that individuals actively construct knowledge through their mental processes, such as perception, attention, memory, and problem-solving. In the context of social science instruction, this means that learners actively engage with the subject matter, seek patterns and connections, and form mental schemas. For example, when learning about the causes of social inequality, learners might identify patterns of discrimination and economic disparities, and develop a mental framework that helps them make sense of these phenomena. Social science instruction that incorporates cognitivist principles can enhance student learning in several ways.

Firstly, it encourages learners to be active participants in their own learning process. Rather than passively receiving information, students are prompted to engage with the material, analyse it critically, and make connections to their prior knowledge. This fosters a deeper and more meaningful understanding of social science concepts.

Secondly, cognitivist-based instruction promotes the development of metacognitive skills. Metacognition refers to the ability to monitor one's own thinking processes and regulate one's learning. By encouraging learners to reflect on their own cognitive strategies, social science instruction can help students become better at planning, monitoring, and evaluating their own learning. For example, students can learn to identify which study techniques work best for them when preparing for a social science exam.

Furthermore, cognitivist principles also support the development of problem-solving and critical thinking skills. In the social sciences, many questions do not have clear-cut answers. Instead, learners are often confronted with complex and ambiguous scenarios where they must draw on their cognitive resources to analyse and evaluate different perspectives. Cognitivist-based instruction helps students develop the skills necessary to approach and solve these kinds of complex problems.

Lastly, cognitivist principles can promote long-term retention of social science knowledge. By actively engaging with the material, forming mental structures, and connecting new information to prior knowledge, learners are more likely to retain what they have learned in the long term. This is especially important in social science instruction, where concepts and theories are interconnected and build upon each other.

In conclusion, cognitivism provides a valuable framework for social science instruction. By emphasizing active participation, metacognitive skills, problem-solving, and critical thinking, cognitivist-based instruction can enhance students' learning experiences in the social sciences. It promotes a deeper understanding of complex social phenomena and provides students with the cognitive tools necessary for analysing and evaluating these phenomena. In this way, cognitivism plays a crucial role in the effective teaching of social sciences.

- Cognitive theories of learning focus on the internal processes of the mind, such as how information is received, organized, stored, and retrieved. These theories have been applied to social science instruction in a number of ways, including:
- *Helping students develop critical thinking skills*. This involves teaching students how to analyse information, identify bias, and draw conclusions. For example, a teacher might have students read a news article and then ask them to identify the author's point of view, the evidence that is presented, and the conclusions that can be drawn from the article.
- *Promoting active learning*: This involves getting students involved in the learning process by having them participate in discussions, solve problems, and create projects. For example, a teacher might have students work in groups to research a historical event and then present their findings to the class.
- *Scaffolding instruction*: This involves providing students with the support they need to learn new concepts and skills. For example, a teacher might provide students with a graphic organizer to help them organize their thoughts about a social science concept.

Cognitive theories can be effective in social science instruction, but it is important to use them in a way that is respectful of students' individual learning styles. For example, some students may prefer to learn by reading, while others may prefer to learn by doing. Here are some additional psychological considerations for social science instruction from a cognitivist perspective:

- *The importance of prior knowledge*: Students are more likely to learn new concepts if they have some prior knowledge about the topic. Teachers can help students build prior knowledge by providing them with background information and by connecting new concepts to students' existing knowledge.
- *The role of schemata*: Schemata are mental models that help us organize and understand information. Teachers can help students develop schemata by providing them with opportunities to practice using new concepts and skills.
- *The importance of feedback*: Feedback is essential for learning. Teachers can provide feedback by giving students specific information about their performance and by helping them identify areas where they need to improve.

By considering these psychological principals, teachers can create social science instruction that is more effective and engaging for students.

HUMANISTIC THEORIES OF LEARNING AND SOCIAL SCIENCE

Humanistic theory is a psychological perspective that emphasizes the study of the whole person and the uniqueness of each individual. It emerged as a reaction to behaviourism and psychoanalysis, which were dominant schools of thought in psychology during the mid-20th century. Humanistic psychology, also known as the third force in psychology, focuses on human experiences, values, and potential for personal growth. Key concepts and ideas within humanistic theory include:

- **Self-Actualization**: One of the central concepts in humanistic psychology is the idea of self-actualization. This refers to the inherent tendency of individuals to fulfill their potential and become the best version of themselves.
- **Maslow's Hierarchy of Needs**: Abraham Maslow, a prominent figure in humanistic psychology, proposed a hierarchy of needs to explain human motivation. According to Maslow, people are motivated to satisfy basic needs (such as food and safety) before progressing to higher-order needs (such as self-esteem and self-actualization).

- **Carl Rogers' Person-Centred Therapy**: Carl Rogers, another influential humanistic psychologist, developed person-centred therapy. This therapeutic approach emphasizes the importance of the therapeutic relationship and the creation of a supportive, non-judgmental environment to facilitate personal growth and self-discovery.
- **Holism**: Humanistic psychology rejects reductionism and focuses on understanding individuals as a whole. This includes considering factors such as emotions, creativity, spirituality, and the pursuit of meaning and purpose in life.
- **Subjective Experience**: Humanistic psychology emphasizes the subjective experience of individuals. This means that researchers and therapists should take into account the unique thoughts, feelings, and perspectives of each person.
- **Free Will**: Humanistic psychology asserts that individuals have free will and the capacity to make choices that shape their lives. This stands in contrast to deterministic views that emphasize the influence of external factors on behaviour.
- **Positive Psychology**: While not originally part of humanistic psychology, the positive psychology movement shares some common themes with humanistic theory. Positive psychology focuses on factors that contribute to a fulfilling and meaningful life, promoting the study of happiness, well-being, and strengths.

Overall, humanistic theory seeks to understand and promote the development of the whole person, acknowledging the importance of subjective experience, personal agency, and the pursuit of meaning and fulfilment in life. Humanistic theories have played a significant role in shaping social science instruction. These theories emphasize the importance of the individual's experience and personal growth, and advocate for a holistic approach to education.

In the context of social science instruction, humanistic theories emphasize the understanding of social phenomena through the lens of human experiences One important aspect of humanistic theories in social science instruction is the recognition and valuing of the individual's unique perspective. Humanistic theories argue that every individual has a subjective experience of the world and that this experience should be taken into account in the learning process. When teaching social science subjects, instructors who adhere to humanistic theories encourage students to share their own experiences, opinions, and perspectives, and use them as a basis for critical inquiry and understanding.

Another key aspect of humanistic theories in social science instruction is the emphasis on personal growth and self-actualization. According to humanistic theories, education should not only be about acquiring knowledge but also about personal development. In the social sciences, this means helping students develop critical thinking skills, empathy, and an understanding of their own values and beliefs. Rather than simply teaching factual information, humanistic approaches to social science instruction encourage students to think critically about societal issues and their own place in the world.

Humanistic theories also emphasize the importance of inclusivity and respect for diversity in social science instruction. These theories argue that all individuals, regardless of their background, experiences, or identities, should be respected and valued within the learning environment. In social science instruction, this means ensuring that students are exposed to a wide range of perspectives and ideas, including those from historically marginalized groups. By doing so, social science instructors can foster a more inclusive, equitable, and diverse learning environment.

An additional benefit of humanistic theories in social science instruction is the promotion of active learning and student engagement. Humanistic theories argue that learning is most effective when it is student-centred and involves active participation. In the social sciences, this means encouraging students to engage in hands-on activities, debates, discussions, and projects that allow them to apply their knowledge and skills in real-world contexts. By actively participating in the learning process, students are more likely to fully understand and internalize social science concepts.

Finally, humanistic theories in social science instruction also emphasize the importance of building positive relationships between students and instructors. These theories argue that when students feel emotionally safe, supported, and connected to their instructors, they are more likely to engage in meaningful learning. In social science classrooms, this means creating a supportive and nurturing environment where students feel comfortable expressing their opinions, asking questions, and challenging existing ideas. By building positive relationships with their students, social science instructors can create a conducive learning environment.

In conclusion, humanistic theories have greatly influenced social science instruction by emphasizing the importance of the individual's experience and personal growth. These theories advocate for a holistic approach to education, taking into account the unique perspectives and backgrounds of students. By valuing inclusivity, promoting active learning, and fostering positive relationships, humanistic theories have shaped social science instruction to be more student-centred, engaging, and meaningful.

Humanistic theories of learning emphasize the importance of the individual learner and their personal growth. These theories have been applied to social science instruction in a number of ways, including:

- *Focusing on the learner's needs and interests*. This involves understanding what motivates students and what they are interested in learning. Teachers can focus on the learner's needs and interests by asking them questions, conducting surveys, and observing their behaviour. Creating a supportive and encouraging learning environment. This involves creating a classroom environment where students feel safe and respected. Teachers can create a supportive and encouraging learning environment by being positive, providing positive reinforcement, and being open to feedback.
- *Promoting student self-direction*. This involves giving students the freedom to choose what they want to learn and how they want to learn it. Teachers can promote student self-direction by providing them with choices, giving them opportunities to make decisions, and supporting their efforts.

Humanistic theories can be effective in social science instruction, but it is important to use them in a way that is respectful of students' individual needs and interests. For example, some students may prefer to learn in a structured environment, while others may prefer to learn in a more flexible environment. Here are some additional psychological considerations for social science instruction from a humanistic perspective:

- *The importance of self-esteem:* Students are more likely to learn if they have high self-esteem. Teachers can promote self-esteem by providing students with positive feedback, helping them set realistic goals, and celebrating their successes.
- *The role of emotions*: Emotions play an important role in learning. Teachers can help students learn by acknowledging their emotions, helping them manage their emotions, and teaching them how to use their emotions to their advantage.
- *The importance of meaning:* Students are more likely to learn if they see the meaning in what they are learning. Teachers can help students find meaning in their learning by connecting new concepts to students' existing knowledge, helping them see how

new concepts apply to their lives, and helping them see how new concepts can be used to solve problems.

By considering these psychological values, teachers can create social science instruction that is more effective and engaging for students. Here are some specific examples of how humanistic theories have been applied to social science instruction:

- The use of role-playing to help students explore different cultures and perspectives.
- The use of creative writing to help students express their thoughts and feelings about social issues.
- The use of journaling to help students reflect on their learning and personal growth.
- The use of service learning to help students apply social science concepts to real-world problems.

These are just a few examples of how humanistic theories can be applied to social science instruction. By understanding these theories, teachers can create lessons that are more effective and engaging for students. In conclusion, when designing and implementing social science instruction, it is crucial to consider the psychological aspects of learning. The behaviourist, cognitivist, constructivist, and humanistic theories provide valuable insights into how students learn and the instructional strategies that can optimize their learning experiences.

By incorporating behaviourist principles, educators can set clear objectives, provide immediate feedback, and reinforce desired behaviours to enhance student learning in social science. Cognitivist considerations focus on activating prior knowledge, organizing information effectively, and promoting metacognitive awareness to facilitate comprehension and deeper understanding. Constructivist principles encourage active learning, social interaction, collaboration, and reflection, enabling students to construct their own knowledge and meaning in the context of social science. Humanistic theory emphasizes the importance of student-centred approaches, autonomy, and creating a positive learning environment that nurtures personal growth and self- actualization.

By understanding and applying these psychological considerations, educators can create engaging, meaningful, and inclusive social science learning environments that cater to the diverse needs, motivations, and abilities of students. It enables students to develop critical thinking skills, foster a deeper understanding of social science concepts, and cultivate a lifelong love for learning in the field of social science.

INCLUSIVE CLASSROOMS: ESSENTIALITIES

An inclusive classroom is a learning environment where all students, regardless of their abilities or disabilities, are welcomed, valued, and provided with equitable opportunities to participate and succeed in education. Inclusion goes beyond just physical placement; it involves creating a supportive and accepting atmosphere that accommodates diverse learning styles, needs, and preferences. Inclusive classrooms have become more important than ever as society recognizes the value of diversity and inclusion in education. Creating an inclusive classroom means that all students, regardless of their abilities, race, ethnicity, or socio-economic status, have equal opportunities to learn and thrive. To achieve this goal, certain essentialities must be present in every inclusive classroom. Inclusive classrooms are learning environments where all students, regardless of their background, disabilities, disorders, impairments, or special needs, are able to participate and succeed. They are characterized by a focus on diversity, equity, and inclusion, and they provide all students with the support they need to learn and grow. Key principles of inclusive classrooms include:

- **Diversity and Individual Differences**: Recognizing and embracing the diversity of students, including those with different abilities, learning styles, cultural backgrounds, and experiences.
- **Equitable Access**: Ensuring that all students have access to the same curriculum, instructional materials, and opportunities for learning. This may involve adapting teaching methods, using assistive technologies, or providing additional support.
- **Collaboration and Teamwork**: Encouraging collaboration among students, teachers, support staff, and parents to create a network of support for each student. This can involve co-teaching, team teaching, or involving special education professionals.
- **Universal Design for Learning (UDL)**: Implementing teaching methods and materials that cater to a broad range of learners. UDL aims to provide multiple means of representation, engagement, and expression to accommodate diverse learning styles and abilities.
- **Positive Behavioural Interventions and Supports (PBIS)**: Establishing a positive and inclusive school culture through proactive strategies to prevent behavioural issues and promote positive behaviour among all students.
- **Flexible Grouping**: Allowing students to work in various groupings based on their strengths, interests, and needs. This may

involve flexible seating arrangements, project-based learning, or other strategies that promote collaboration.

- **Differentiated Instruction**: Tailoring instruction to meet the individual needs of students. This can involve modifying content, process, or product based on students' readiness levels, interests, or learning profiles.
- **Assessment for Learning**: Using a variety of assessment methods to measure student progress and understanding. Assessment should be ongoing, varied, and responsive to individual needs.
- **Cultural Competence**: Developing an understanding and appreciation for the cultural backgrounds of students and incorporating diverse perspectives into the curriculum.
- **Professional Development**: Providing ongoing training and professional development for teachers to enhance their skills in inclusive education and stay informed about best practices.

Inclusive classrooms foster a sense of belonging and contribute to the academic and social development of all students. The goal is to create an environment where every learner can thrive and reach their full potential. Top of Form Creating inclusive classrooms is crucial to ensuring that all students, regardless of their diverse backgrounds, abilities, or learning styles, have equal opportunities to thrive and succeed. Here are some essentialities for establishing inclusive classrooms:

- **Diverse Representation:** Ensure that teaching materials, including textbooks, images, and examples, reflect a variety of cultures, ethnicities, genders, and abilities. Incorporate diverse perspectives into the curriculum to make it more relatable and engaging for all students.
- **Flexible Teaching Strategies**: Use a variety of instructional methods to accommodate different learning styles. Offer multiple ways for students to demonstrate their understanding of the material, such as through projects, presentations, written assignments, or discussions.
- **Universal Design for Learning (UDL):** Implement UDL principles to create flexible and accessible learning environments that cater to the diverse needs of students. Provide options for how information is presented, how students can express their understanding, and how they can engage with the material.
- **Accommodations and Modifications:** Identify and implement reasonable accommodations and modifications for students with

disabilities to ensure equal access to learning opportunities. Collaborate with special education professionals to develop and implement individualized education plans (IEPs) or plans when necessary.

- **Inclusive Language and Communication**: Use inclusive language that respects and acknowledges the diversity of the classroom. Foster open communication and encourage students to share their perspectives and experiences.
- **Culturally Responsive Teaching**: Be aware of and responsive to the cultural backgrounds and experiences of students. Create a classroom environment that values and celebrates diversity.
- **Supportive Classroom Environment:** Foster a positive and welcoming atmosphere where all students feel safe, accepted, and respected. Establish clear expectations for behaviour and address any instances of discrimination or bullying promptly.
- **Professional Development**: Provide ongoing professional development opportunities for teachers to enhance their knowledge and skills related to inclusive education. Encourage collaboration among educators to share best practices and learn from each other.
- **Collaboration with Families**: Involve parents and guardians in the educational process. Maintain open lines of communication with families and seek their input in creating a supportive learning environment for their children.
- **Accessible Physical Environment**: Ensure that the physical space of the classroom is accessible to all students, including those with mobility challenges. Provide assistive technology and tools as needed.
- **Peer Support and Collaboration:** Promote peer support and collaboration among students. Encourage activities that foster teamwork, empathy, and understanding among classmates.

Remember that inclusivity is an ongoing process, and educators should continuously reflect on and refine their practices to meet the evolving needs of their students.

SKILL DEVELOPMENT

Skill development is a continuous process of acquiring and enhancing abilities, knowledge, and expertise to perform tasks effectively. It plays a crucial role in personal and professional growth, allowing individuals to adapt to changing environments and excel in their chosen fields. Here are some key aspects and tips related to skill development:

- *Identify Your Goals*: Clearly define your short-term and long-term goals. Knowing what you want to achieve will help you focus on the specific skills you need to develop.
- *Self-Assessment*: Identify your current skill set. What are your strengths and weaknesses? This self-awareness will guide you in choosing the right areas for improvement.
- *Continuous Learning*: Embrace a mindset of continuous learning. Stay curious and seek opportunities to acquire new knowledge and skills regularly.
- *Stay Updated*: Keep abreast of industry trends and changes. The business landscape evolves, and staying informed ensures that your skills remain relevant.
- *Online Courses and Workshops*: Take advantage of online courses, workshops, and webinars. Many platforms offer a wide range of topics, allowing you to learn at your own pace.
- *Networking*: Connect with professionals in your field. Networking provides opportunities to learn from others, share experiences, and gain insights into industry best practices.
- *Practice Regularly*: Apply what you learn through practical exercises. Whether it's coding, public speaking, or project management, hands-on experience is crucial for skill development.
- *Receive Feedback*: Seek constructive feedback from peers, mentors, or supervisors. Use feedback to identify areas for improvement and refine your skills.
- *Soft Skills Matter*: Don't neglect soft skills such as communication, teamwork, and problem-solving. These skills are often just as important as technical skills in the workplace.
- *Time Management*: Allocate dedicated time for skill development. Consistency is key, and setting aside regular time for learning ensures steady progress.
- *Adaptability*: Be open to change and new challenges. The ability to adapt to different situations and learn on the fly is a valuable skill in today's dynamic world.

Educational Implications of Skill Development

Skill development plays a crucial role in education, and its implications are multifaceted. Here are some educational implications of skill development:

- *Preparation for the Future*: Skill development ensures that students are equipped with the practical abilities needed in the real world. Education becomes a means of preparing individuals for the challenges and opportunities they will face in their personal and professional lives.
- *Relevance and Engagement*: Integrating skill development into the curriculum makes education more relevant and engaging for students. Practical skills enhance the learning experience, making it more meaningful and applicable.
- *Holistic Development*: Beyond academic knowledge, skill development promotes holistic development by addressing various facets of an individual, including cognitive, emotional, social, and physical skills.
- *Adaptability*: Developing a diverse set of skills fosters adaptability. Students become more flexible and better equipped to navigate a rapidly changing world.
- *Critical Thinking and Problem-Solving*: Many skills, such as critical thinking, problem-solving, and decision-making, are crucial for academic success and future professional endeavours. These skills are often transferrable across various disciplines.
- *Collaboration and Communication*: Teamwork, communication, and interpersonal skills are essential for success in most professions. Educational programs focused on skill development often emphasize collaboration, preparing students for effective teamwork in the workplace.
- *Entrepreneurial Mindset*: Skill development can foster an entrepreneurial mindset by encouraging creativity, innovation, and risk-taking. This mindset is valuable in various careers and can also lead to the creation of new opportunities.
- *Technological Literacy*: Given the increasing role of technology in various fields, skill development often includes technological literacy. This prepares students for the digital aspects of many professions and ensures they can navigate technology effectively.
- *Lifelong Learning*: Emphasizing skill development instils a mindset of lifelong learning. Individuals become more proactive in acquiring new skills throughout their lives, adapting to evolving demands in their careers and personal pursuits.
- *Inclusivity and Diversity*: Skill development programs can be designed to be inclusive, addressing the diverse needs and talents

of all students. This promotes equity in education by recognizing and valuing different types of intelligence and skills.

- *Assessment and Evaluation*: Educational systems may need to evolve to incorporate effective methods of assessing and evaluating a broad range of skills. Traditional forms of assessment may need to be complemented with more dynamic and authentic evaluation methods.

MICRO TEACHING

Micro-teaching is a teacher training and faculty development technique whereby the teacher reviews a recording of a teaching session, in order to get constructive feedback from peers and/or students about what has worked and what improvements can be made to their teaching technique. Micro-teaching is a training technique in which a teacher trainee practices with a small group of 5 to 10 pupils for a short duration of 5 to 10 minutes on a selected content/concept in a single skill. Micro-teaching is a stimulated social teaching process to provide feedback to teacher trainees for the modification of the behaviour of teacher trainees. Micro-teaching provides teachers with a practice setting or instruction in which the normal complexities of the classroom are reduced and the teacher gets feedback on their performance. The student teachers are required to teach a single concept using specified teaching skills to a small number of students in a short duration of time.

Characteristic of Microteaching

Microteaching provides adequate feedback. It's a coaching device to organize effective lecturers. Microteaching could be an extremely personalized coaching technique. The use of videotape makes observation terribly objectives. Microteaching could be a coaching technique and not a teaching technique.

Microteaching is scaled down teaching:

- It reduces the category scrutinization to five to ten pupils.
- It reduces the period of amount five to ten minutes.
- It reduces the dimensions of the subject.
- It reduces the teaching talent.

Objectives of Micro-Teaching

Objectives of micro-teaching are given below:

- To find out and assimilate new teaching skills underneath controlled conditions.

- To realize confidence in teaching and mastering a variety of teaching skills on a small size of pupils.
- To utilize the obtainable material and time to the most.
- To modify the teaching method to achieve perfection in teaching.
- To amass mastery during a range of teaching skills.
- To switch the teaching behaviours within the needed manner.
- To scale back the complexities of teaching.
- To amass new teaching skills and refine previous ones.
- To produce needed feedback.

Another objective of micro-teaching is that Micro-teaching aims at providing part skills of the teacher to the teacher trainees at the pre-service level.

Phases of Microteaching

There are three faces of Micro-Teaching. Three phases of the microteaching are as follows:

- **Phase I: Information Acquisition Part (pre-active phase):** In this part, the co-ed teacher tries to amass information regarding the talent, its role in the room, and its part behaviour. S/he reads relevant literature. S/he also observes the demonstration lesson and also the mode of presentation of the talent. It includes 3 vital activities: (a) To produce information and awareness of specific teaching talent, (b) To look at the demonstration of the teaching talent, and (c) To analyses and discuss the demonstration of teaching activities of the talent.
- **Phase II: Talent Acquisition Part (interactive phase):** In this part, the co-ed teacher prepares a small lesson, practices the talent, and carried out the microteaching cycle. Three activities area unit undertook during this phase: (a) To organize a small lesson for teaching talent, (b) To apply the teaching talent in a real room scenario, and (c) To judge the performance. Analysis activity provides the idea to re-plan a similar lesson for reteaching.
- **Phase III: Talent Transfer Part (post-active phase):** After exploiting mastery of the teaching talent, the teacher-trainees area unit was given the opportunity to use the talent within the traditional room scenario rather than a synthetic classroom scenario.

Steps of Microteaching

In microteaching, the trainer should follow the following steps in a systematic manner to achieve the required skills among the trainees.

- **Orientation program with the student-teacher:** The teacher education should provide and enlighten about micro-teaching and its importance in the teaching-learning process to develop teaching efficiency.
- **Discussing teaching skills:** The teacher educator should discuss the definition of the skill and identify different skills, which affect the teacher's behaviour.
- **Selection of a particular skill:** Among the different skills, the teacher educator should select a suitable and particular skill, which is required for the topic in the concerned subject.
- **Presenting a model demonstration lesson on a particular skill:** The teacher educator should demonstrate in a micro lesson in a particular skill, which is selected for demonstration.
- **Observation of the model skill by student teachers and recording their observations on the observation schedule:** The student teachers should observe the model micro lesson performed by the teacher educator.
- **Critical appreciation of the model lesson by student teachers:** The student teachers should discuss the model micro lesson with the teacher educator in detail and achieve the required skill.
- **Creation of a microteaching setting:** The Indian model of micro-teaching developed by NCERT gives the following settings: (a) The number of students is about 5 to 10, (b) The duration of the time is about 5 to 10 minutes, (c) Number of skills only one, (d) Duration of the microteaching cycle: 36 minutes, (e) Observers: peers and teacher educators.
- **Practicing the skill:** The student teachers should practice a particular skill to the satisfaction of the observers.
- **Providing feedback:** The performed micro lesson should be followed by the feedback for knowing not only the mistakes but also modifications in that lesson.
- **Re-planning:** After the feedback on the performed micro lesson, the student-teacher should re-plan the same or different micro lesson by including the suggestions of the observers.
- **Re-teaching:** Re-planed micro lessons should be taught to the same or other groups of students consisting of five to ten students.

- **Providing re-feedback:** Feedback is given again in the re-teaching of a micro lesson as re-feedback. The practice should be continued until the observers are satisfied with the skill achieved.
- **Integration of teaching skills:** Finally, the student teachers should integrate the acquired skills and perform a lesson as link practice.

Advantages of Micro-Teaching

The Advantages of micro-teaching are given below:

- It reduces traditional schoolroom teaching by scaled-down teaching.
- Its objectives square measure well outlined.
- Micro-teaching is helpful for developing teaching potency in pre-service and in-service teacher education programs.
- Micro-teaching is a good feedback device for the modification of teacher behaviour.
- The information and application of teaching skills are given by the utilization of microteaching.
- It provides for self-analysis through the magnetic recorder and videotape.
- Microteaching could be a coaching device for rising teaching apply and prepares effective academics.
- Micro-teaching is coaching for real teaching.
- It minimizes the complexities of traditional schoolroom teaching.
- Micro-teaching facilitates in increase confidence step by step.
- Because it is an associate in personal coaching device, every initiate makes progress at his own rate reckoning on his ability.
- It's simply noticeable, measurable, achievable, modifiable, and practicable.

Disadvantages of Micro-Teaching

The disadvantages of micro-teaching are given below:

- Microteaching is an incredibly time intense technique.
- Microteaching is ability orientated instead of content orientated.
- Scope of microteaching is slim.
- Non-convenience of a microteaching laboratory.
- A sizable number of trainees cannot be given chance for re-teaching and replanning.

- Microteaching is carried with success solely during a controlled environmental state of affairs.
- The fortunate implementation of microteaching needs competent and suitably trained academics.
- Microteaching doesn't take into thought the general setting of teaching.
- It doesn't offer broad, primarily based behaviours in terms of skills.
- It wants sufficient time to impart the teaching skills among all the co-ed teachers.
- It needs video, magnetic recorder, and different devices for creating the small lesson terribly effective. It becomes tough for coaching schools to create such arrangements.

Major Skills of Microteaching practiced in Teacher Training Institutions

- Skill of writing instructional objectives in behavioural terms
- Skill of Introducing a Lesson
- Skill of Black board Writing
- Skill of Fluency in Questioning
- Skill of Probing Questioning
- Skill of Stimulus Variation
- Skill of Explaining
- Skill of demonstration
- Skill of reinforcement
- Skill of achieving closure

MACRO TEACHING

Macro teaching refers to the planning, preparation, and delivery of instruction at the level of the curriculum and the programme. It involves the development of a cohesive and structured learning experience for students, where the teacher focuses on the big picture of the curriculum rather than individual lessons. Macro teaching encompasses a range of tasks, including curriculum design, lesson planning, instructional strategies, and assessment and evaluation.

Strategies for Macro Teaching

The following strategies can help teachers to implement macro teaching effectively:

Curriculum Design

Curriculum design is the foundation of macro teaching. It involves the development of a cohesive and structured plan that outlines the learning objectives, content, and assessment methods. The curriculum design should align with the program's learning objectives and reflect the needs of the students. When designing the curriculum, teachers should consider the following:

- **Learning Objectives:** The learning objectives should be specific, measurable, and achievable. They should reflect the knowledge and skills that students need to acquire to succeed in the program.
- **Content:** The content should be organized, coherent, and aligned with the learning objectives. It should provide students with the knowledge and skills they need to achieve the learning objectives.
- **Assessment Methods:** The assessment methods should align with the learning objectives and the content. They should provide students with feedback on their progress and identify areas where they may need additional support.

Lesson Planning

Lesson planning is a critical component of macro teaching. It involves the development of a structured and organized plan for each lesson, which aligns with the curriculum and the program's learning objectives. Lesson planning should be flexible and adaptable, allowing teachers to adjust their instruction based on the needs of their students. When planning a lesson, teachers should consider the following:

- **Learning Objectives:** The lesson's learning objectives should align with the curriculum and the program's learning objectives. They should reflect the knowledge and skills that students need to acquire to succeed in the program.
- **Content:** The content should be organized, coherent, and aligned with the learning objectives. It should provide students with the knowledge and skills they need to achieve the learning objectives.
- **Instructional Strategies:** The instructional strategies should be chosen based on the learning objectives and the content. Teachers should use a variety of strategies, including lecture, discussion, and hands-on activities, to engage students and promote active learning.
- **Assessment Methods:** The assessment methods should align with the learning objectives and the content. They should provide

students with feedback on their progress and identify areas where they may need additional support.

Instructional Strategies

Instructional strategies are the methods teachers use to deliver instruction to students. Effective instructional strategies engage students, promote active learning, and help students to achieve the learning objectives. Teachers should use a variety of instructional strategies to meet the needs of their students. The following are some effective instructional strategies:

- **Lecture:** Lecture is a traditional instructional strategy that involves the teacher presenting information to students. While lectures can be effective, they can also be passive and disengaging. Teachers should use lectures sparingly and incorporate other instructional strategies to promote active learning.
- **Discussion:** Discussion is an interactive instructional strategy that encourages students to share their ideas and perspectives. Teachers can facilitate discussions by asking open-ended questions, providing feedback, and encouraging students to listen to and respect each other's opinions.
- **Hands-On Activities:** Hands-on activities are instructional strategies that involve students in active learning. These activities can include experiments, simulations, and other activities that allow students to apply what they have learned in a practical context.
- **Technology:** Technology can be an effective instructional strategy that engages students and promotes active learning. Teachers can use a range of technology, including videos, simulations, and online resources, to enhance their instruction.

Assessment and Evaluation

Assessment and evaluation are critical components of macro teaching. They allow teachers to measure student progress and identify areas where students may need additional support. Teachers should use a variety of assessment methods, including formative and summative assessments, to measure student progress. The following are some effective assessment methods:

- **Formative Assessment:** Formative assessment is an ongoing process that provides teachers with feedback on student progress. It can include quizzes, class discussions, and other activities that allow teachers to monitor student learning.

- **Summative Assessment:** Summative assessment is an evaluation of student learning at the end of a unit or course. It can include tests, projects, and other assignments that measure student achievement.
- **Feedback:** Feedback is an essential component of assessment and evaluation. Teachers should provide students with constructive feedback that identifies areas where they have done well and areas where they need to improve.

Best Practices for Macro Teaching

The following best practices can help teachers to implement macro teaching effectively:

- Incorporating Technology: Technology can be an effective tool for macro teaching. Teachers can use a range of technology, including videos, simulations, and online resources, to enhance their instruction. Technology can engage students and promote active learning, and it can help teachers to monitor student progress and provide feedback.
- Differentiated Instruction: Differentiated instruction is an instructional strategy that involves adapting instruction to meet the needs of individual students. Teachers can use differentiated instruction to provide students with the support they need to succeed in the programme. Differentiated instruction can include varying the content, instructional strategies, and assessment methods.
- Collaborative Learning: Collaborative learning is an instructional strategy that involves students working together to achieve a common goal. Teachers can use collaborative learning to promote teamwork, communication, and problem-solving skills. Collaborative learning can include group projects, discussions, and other activities that require students to work together.
- Continuous Professional Development: Continuous professional development is essential for effective macro teaching. Teachers should engage in professional development activities that enhance their knowledge and skills. Professional development activities can include attending conferences, workshops, and training sessions, and collaborating with other teachers.

Educational Implications of Macro Teaching

- *Effective knowledge dissemination*: Macro teaching allows educators to efficiently convey information to a large group of students. However, it is important to supplement macro teaching with interactive and student-centred activities to ensure active engagement and deeper understanding.

- *Classroom management*: Since macro teaching typically involves larger class sizes, effective classroom management strategies are essential. Educators should employ techniques such as clear communication, proactive discipline, and student engagement strategies to maintain an orderly and conducive learning environment.
- *Differentiation and individual support*: Despite the larger group setting, educators should strive to address individual student needs. Differentiation strategies, such as tiered assignments or small-group discussions, can be used to provide personalized support and ensure that diverse learners receive appropriate attention.

PEER TUTORING

Peer tutoring is an instructional strategy in which students with similar or higher academic abilities provide one-on-one or small-group assistance to their peers who may need additional support or guidance. Peer tutoring is an instructional strategy in which students with similar or higher levels of knowledge and skills provide assistance and support to their peers. It involves a collaborative learning approach, where students take on the role of both tutor and learner. Peer tutoring promotes active engagement, mutual understanding, and the reinforcement of learning concepts. It benefits both the tutor and the tutee by fostering deeper comprehension, building interpersonal relationships, and boosting self-confidence. This approach promotes academic growth, builds relationships, and enhances learning outcomes for both the tutor and the tutee.

Here are the key aspects and benefits of peer tutoring:

- **Tutor Selection:** Peer tutors are typically chosen based on their proficiency and mastery of the subject matter. They may be students who have demonstrated strong academic performance or those who have specific expertise in a particular area. Tutoring can take place between students of the same grade level or across different grade levels, depending on the needs and availability of resources.
- **Academic Support:** Peer tutors provide academic assistance to their peers, helping them grasp and master challenging concepts,

review material, or complete assignments. They explain and clarify content, provide examples, offer feedback, and guide the tutees through problem-solving processes. Tutors can adapt their explanations and teaching strategies to meet the individual needs of each tutee.

- **Personalized Learning:** Peer tutoring allows for individualized instruction. Tutors can tailor their approach to match the learning style, pace, and preferences of the tutees. They can provide additional practice opportunities, scaffold learning, and address specific areas of difficulty. This personalized attention and support can accelerate learning and improve academic performance.
- **Confidence and Self-Esteem:** Peer tutoring can boost the confidence and self-esteem of both tutors and tutees. Tutors develop a sense of responsibility, leadership, and competence as they assist their peers. Tutees benefit from the support and encouragement of a peer, which can reduce anxiety, build self-confidence, and improve their attitude towards learning.
- **Improved Academic Performance:** Research has shown that peer tutoring can lead to improved academic performance for both tutors and tutees. Tutors reinforce their own knowledge and understanding of the subject matter through teaching, while tutees receive targeted instruction and support. The active engagement and personalized learning experience contribute to enhanced comprehension, retention, and application of knowledge.
- **Social and Emotional Benefits:** Peer tutoring facilitates social interaction and relationship-building among students. Tutors and tutees develop a supportive and trusting rapport, fostering a positive classroom environment. The tutoring process also promotes empathy, patience, and communication skills as tutors learn to adapt their teaching methods and tutees learn to ask for help and seek clarification.
- **Reinforcement and Mastery:** Peer tutoring provides an opportunity for tutees to reinforce their learning by explaining concepts to their peers. This process of teaching others helps consolidate their own knowledge and deepen their understanding. It also allows tutors to reinforce their mastery of the subject matter by explaining and articulating concepts effectively.
- **Peer Role Models:** Peer tutors serve as role models for their peers. They demonstrate effective study habits, organization skills, and problem-solving strategies. Through their positive example, tutors

can inspire other students to strive for academic success and develop a growth mindset.

- **Inclusive Education:** Peer tutoring promotes inclusive education by providing support and assistance to students with diverse learning needs. It allows students with disabilities or learning differences to receive individualized instruction and encouragement from their peers, fostering a sense of belonging and participation in the learning community.

Peer Tutoring Models

Three widely used peer tutoring models are Class Wide Peer Tutoring (CWPT), Cross-Age Peer Tutoring, and Peer Assisted Learning Strategies (PALS).

- **Class Wide Peer Tutoring (CWPT)**: In CWPT, the entire class participates in the peer tutoring activity simultaneously. The teacher splits the class into groups of two to five students and assigns roles to the students. One student act as the tutor (instructor) and provides a question or stimulus, while the other student(s) acts as the tutee (or learner) and gives an answer or performs a task. These roles are reversed at a designated point during the activity. CWPT requires the teacher to train students in the process and explain the task, but during the CWPT session every student is receiving individualized attention and continuous monitored practice with feedback for correct and incorrect responses.
- **Cross-Age Peer Tutoring**: When an older student is paired with a younger student, it is called cross-age peer tutoring. In this scenario, the older student is the tutor sharing knowledge or providing support to the younger student. Cross-age tutoring can be carefully scripted in nature, or it can be informal. Cross-age tutoring may involve a whole class, or only a few student pairs. Cross-age tutoring is particularly relevant to functional, behavioural, and social skills training and may be used to support students with disabilities or to introduce school routines to younger students at the start of the school year.
- **Peer Assisted Learning Strategies (PALS)**: PALS is based on a specific peer-tutoring model with structured reading and math programs. Students are paired with others of similar ability levels and one student coaches their partner on a specific skill or topic. Partners often switch roles when addressing different skills, so that each student has the chance to both teach and learn.

Advantages of Peer Tutoring

Peer tutoring as a classroom tool has many advantages. When used alongside other educational strategies, peer tutoring can:

- Provide students with extra one-on-one time. Students spend more time having their own responses evaluated and reinforced, rather than observing others.
- Promote active learning. Peer tutoring activities can involve a variety of media and multi-sensory activities.
- Increase student confidence. Peers acting as tutors may understand information better and remember it longer as a result of teaching it.
- Reinforce information and skills as students are taught the same information in a different way.
- Promote the generalization of skills across contexts.
- Create a positive learning environment where each student's input is valued and heard.

Educational Implications of Peer Tutoring:

- *Enhanced learning outcomes*: Peer tutoring promotes active learning and reinforces understanding of concepts. Educators should facilitate structured peer tutoring programs that encourage students to explain, discuss, and teach each other, leading to improved academic achievement.
- *Social and emotional development:* Peer tutoring cultivates positive relationships among students and fosters a supportive learning community. Educators should create a classroom environment that values collaboration, empathy, and respect, allowing students to develop social and emotional skills.
- *Student agency and leadership*: Peer tutoring empowers students to take ownership of their learning and develop leadership skills. Educators should provide opportunities for students to assume tutoring roles, which can boost their confidence, self-esteem, and sense of responsibility.

TEAM TEACHING

Team teaching is an instructional approach that involves two or more teachers collaboratively planning, organizing, and delivering instruction to a group of students. It encourages the sharing of expertise, ideas, and instructional responsibilities among the teachers. Team teaching promotes a dynamic learning environment where teachers can leverage their individual strengths and perspectives. It allows for differentiated instruction, increased student engagement, and the integration of diverse teaching strategies. Team teaching can be particularly effective in addressing the diverse learning needs of students and promoting interdisciplinary learning experiences.

Guiding Principles of Team Teaching

Team teaching for a particular teaching subject is organized under the following basic principles:

- **Principle of pooling the resources:** Team teaching is based on pooling and best utilizing the available resources and expertise in the field of teaching.
- **Principle of joint responsibility and cooperation:** Team teaching is-organized to teach a specific group of students by-a team of personnel headed by a leader. It requires that all the members of the team share joint responsibilities and work together for achieving the ends.
- **Principle of attending the needs of the students:** Team teaching is organized according to the interests, abilities and needs of the learners. Since a team as a whole share the teaching task in it, it provides better opportunities to take care of the difficulties and needs of the individual students.
- **Principle of flexibility in terms of grouping and scheduling:** Team teaching requires adequate flexibility in terms of grouping of the students in the form of large classes, small group or study at the individual level. It also needs flexibility with regard to time factors and scheduling. Here, the time needs to be adjusted according to the requirements of the teaching-learning situation.
- **Principle of appropriate selection of the team members:** Team teaching requires joint responsibility and such responsibility can only be undertaken properly if the members of the team are selected judiciously according to the needs of the instruction.

Objectives of Team Teaching

Team teaching is generally directed to achieve the following objectives:

- To make the best use of expertise of a number of teachers.
- To improve the quality of teaching by utilising and skills of more than one person.

- To develop positive attitudes towards cooperation and group in teaching learning situation.
- To help the students to satisfy the needs and solve the difficulties relating special content areas.
- To develop the sense of shared responsibility in teaching and evaluation.
- To minimise the scope of teaching wrong things to the students by any individual teacher.

Characteristics of Team Teaching

Team teaching has following characteristics:

- It utilises the service of two or more teacher in the process of teaching the same class.
- It is an instructional strategy rather than training strategy.
- In team teaching a group of teachers are responsible for realisation of the educational objectives, rather than an individual teacher.
- A team of the teachers of the same subjects work together to deal relevant content area to the same group of students.
- It can term as co-operative teaching, in which teachers plan together to pool resources, interests and expertise for teaching the same content for the same group of students.
- Every individual teacher of the team gets an appropriate role in the instructional process in accordance with one's special competencies or area of specialisation.
- The group of teachers involves have shared responsibilities in planning, organising, leading, controlling and evaluating.
- In team teaching, the group of teachers has to jointly consider the needs of their pupils.

Merits of Team Teaching

- It stimulates thought and discussion among teachers who are jointly responsible for a group of students.
- A strong sense of involvement and responsibility develops among the students.
- It gives adequate opportunities to students for free expression.
- It affords opportunities to the students to develop human relations essential for social adjustment.
- Teachers are motivated to work hard for the development of their professional proficiency.

- Students get the opportunity to be benefitted by the special knowledge of the teachers constituting the team.
- It makes proper use of the staff, equipment and the school building.
- It helps in the maintenance of discipline as it makes the best use of the time and energy of the students.
- It helps teachers to evaluate the work of one another and provides opportunities for improving one's own teaching.
- It provides a flexible class size.
- Teachers work in the totality of a situation.
- It helps in the improvement of instruction.

Demerits of Team Teaching

- In team teaching, numbers of teachers are not available according to requirement. It however, they are arranged, they have no enough efficiently and abilities.
- For this method, a large hall is required which is hardly there in school.
- There is a lack of coordination among there the teachers required.
- A teacher cannot teach his permanent experience as it affects his freedom.
- This method requires new researches which may make up its shortcomings.
- Traditional methods cannot be used in this method.

Educational Implications of Team Teaching:

- *Interdisciplinary learning*: Team teaching enables educators from different disciplines to collaborate and integrate their expertise. This promotes interdisciplinary learning experiences, allowing students to make connections between subjects and develop a holistic understanding.
- *Diverse instructional strategies*: Team teaching encourages the use of a variety of instructional approaches, catering to different learning styles and preferences. Educators can incorporate cooperative learning, project-based learning, and other innovative methods to engage students and enhance learning outcomes.
- *Shared expertise and professional growth*: Team teaching creates opportunities for educators to learn from one another and develop professionally. Collaborative planning sessions, regular feedback,

and reflection can enhance teaching skills and promote a culture of continuous improvement among educators.

In conclusion, the various teaching methodologies related to skill development, such as micro teaching, peer tutoring, macro teaching, and team teaching, offer valuable educational implications. These approaches highlight the significance of practical application, individualized instruction, reflective practice, peer feedback, collaboration, enhanced learning outcomes, social and emotional development, student agency, effective knowledge dissemination, classroom management, differentiation, interdisciplinary learning, diverse instructional strategies, shared expertise, and professional growth. By incorporating these educational implications into teaching practices, educators can create dynamic and inclusive learning environments that cater to the diverse needs of students. It fosters active engagement, critical thinking, and skill development, enabling students to acquire not only knowledge but also the necessary competencies to succeed in various aspects of life. Furthermore, these teaching methodologies empower educators to continuously improve their instructional strategies and create meaningful learning experiences.

ICT INTEGRATION

Information and Communication Technology (ICT) integration in education refers to the use of technology tools and resources to enhance teaching and learning experiences. ICT encompasses a wide range of technologies, including computers, tablets, interactive whiteboards, the internet, and various software applications. Here are some key aspects of ICT integration in education:

- **Enhanced Teaching and Learning**: (a) **Interactive Learning**: ICT tools can facilitate interactive and engaging learning experiences through multimedia content, simulations, and educational games. (b) **Access to Information**: The internet provides students and teachers with access to a vast amount of information, enabling research and exploration beyond traditional textbooks.
- **Collaborative Learning**: (a) **Online Collaboration**: ICT allows students and educators to collaborate on projects, share resources, and communicate seamlessly, breaking down geographical barriers. (b) **Digital Platforms**: Learning Management Systems (LMS) and other online platforms enable teachers to share assignments, resources, and assessments.

- **Personalized Learning**: (a) **Adaptive Learning Software**: ICT can be used to tailor learning experiences to individual students' needs, providing personalized feedback and adapting content to their pace and learning style. (b) **Digital Assessments**: Online assessments and quizzes can help teachers gauge students' understanding and provide timely feedback.
- **Teacher Professional Development**: (a) **Online Courses and Resources:** Teachers can use ICT for their professional development through online courses, webinars, and digital resources. (b) **Collaborative Networks:** Online communities and social media platforms allow educators to connect, share best practices, and stay updated on the latest educational trends.
- **Digital Literacy Skills**: (a) **Digital Citizenship:** ICT integration promotes the development of digital literacy skills, teaching students to use technology responsibly and ethically. (b) **Problem Solving:** ICT tools encourage critical thinking and problem-solving skills as students navigate digital environments and solve real-world problems.
- **Cost and Resource Efficiency**: (a) **Electronic Textbooks:** Digital textbooks and resources can be more cost-effective and environmentally friendly than traditional print materials. (b) **Remote Learning:** ICT facilitates remote and online learning, making education more accessible, especially during times of crisis.
- **Challenges and Considerations**: (a) **Infrastructure:** Adequate technology infrastructure, including reliable internet access and devices, is essential for successful ICT integration. (b) **Teacher Training:** Educators need training to effectively integrate ICT into their teaching practices. (c) **Equity:** Ensuring equal access to technology and addressing the digital divide is crucial for equitable education.
- **Emerging Technologies**: (a) **Artificial Intelligence (AI):** AI can be used for personalized learning, intelligent tutoring systems, and data analytics to enhance educational outcomes. (b) **Virtual Reality (VR) and Augmented Reality (AR):** These technologies offer immersive and experiential learning opportunities.

ICT integration in education requires a thoughtful and strategic approach, considering the unique needs and contexts of learners and educators. Continuous support, professional development, and evaluation are essential for the successful implementation of ICT in educational settings.

E LEARNING

E-learning - also called *electronic learning* or *web-based training* - is anywhere, anytime instruction delivered over the internet or a corporate intranet to students and other learners via a browser. Contrary to traditional learning methods, e-learning lets students, employees in training and casual learners participate in an organized learning experience regardless of their physical location. In its formative years, e-learning tools primarily enabled the delivery of learning material directly from a teacher to a learner. Now, the e-learning experience has evolved to enable more multidirectional communication using increasingly interactive tools. Learners have greater freedom in choosing how they receive and respond to e-learning content, and any number of peers can be involved. Online education is delivered using a combination of static and interactive methods. Static approaches include learning portals, hyperlinked pages, screen cam tutorials, streamed audio and video and live web broadcasts. Interactive methods are approaches such as discussion forums, chats and desktop video conferencing. There are three main criteria an enterprise should follow to ensure an effective e-learning programme, viz.

- **Mobile-friendly:** People live on their devices, and e-learning must take advantage of that. Training prompts, other reminders and congratulations on training achievements should be sent to smartphones and other mobile devices through mobile apps.
- **Social features:** Social media, or a platform that emulates social media's basic features, can give learners a way to receive updates, respond to training requirements and communicate with peers and managers.
- **Instructional design:** E-learning experiences should use a wide range of offerings to suit diverse learning styles, including quizzes, infographics, podcasts, demonstrations and narrative-based training materials. E-learning course development apps use authoring tools that allow even those without coding experience to create these different offerings.

Types of e-learning

There are two primary models of web-based learning systems: **synchronous**, also known as instructor-led, and **asynchronous** or self-directed and self-paced. Basically, synchronous e-learning requires participants to be present, albeit virtually, at the same time, whereas asynchronous e-learning does not. Examples of synchronous e-learning methods include the use of scheduled and timed online tests, virtual classrooms, web conferencing technology and interactive shared whiteboards that learners can use to collaborate. Examples of asynchronous e-learning methods include the use of discussion boards, discussion groups and self-paced learning courses.

Advantages of e-learning

There are many benefits of e-learning, which proponents believe outweigh the disadvantages. They include the following:

- **On-demand availability:** E-learning tools and services meet the needs of those with busy schedules because they're commonly always available on demand. Learners can access material delivered online as long as they have access to the e-learning application.
- **Not requiring travel:** E-learning is especially conducive to cohort learning where groups of people who live in different locations work on obtaining a new skill or knowledge set
- **Cost efficiency:** In a traditional, in-person classroom setting, the cost of the space, infrastructure, maintenance and materials adds up. Most of these costs go away when learners online.
- **Flexibility:** Web-based training and e-learning enable flexibility, letting learners consume information at their own pace.

Disadvantages of e-learning

Critics point out the following disadvantages related to e-learning:

- **Need for human contact:** Web-based training is a good alternative for independent, self-motivated students, but the need for human contact limits its usefulness for students with other learning styles. For example, a learner using an asynchronous e-learning method might not be able to successfully complete an e-learning course without the structure of a deadline. They might also need instant responses to questions that an asynchronous system doesn't provide.
- **Technical issues:** Students connecting virtually often must use their own devices to attend online classes and complete assignments. Connecting and staying connected requires the right devices and network access that all students might not have.
- **Lack of transparency:** Sometimes the quality and credibility of the content or the teacher isn't always clear and transparent on every e-learning platform. This is especially an issue on free and easily accessible resources.

ONLINE LEARNING

Online learning refers to the use of the internet and digital technologies to deliver educational content and facilitate communication between students and instructors. This mode of learning has become increasingly popular in recent years, offering flexibility and accessibility to a wide range of learners. Online learning, also known as distance education or eLearning, refers to the delivery of educational content and instruction through the internet. It allows students to take courses and earn degrees remotely, without the need to be physically present on campus. Online learning can take many different forms, such as web-based courses, video conferencing, and self-paced learning programs. It is becoming an increasingly popular way for students to access education, as it offers flexibility and convenience.

Advantages and Disadvantages of Online Learning

There are both advantages and disadvantages to online learning. Some of the main advantages include:

- **Flexibility:** Online courses allow students to learn at their own pace and schedule, as they can access course materials and complete assignments whenever it is convenient for them. One of the primary advantages of online learning is flexibility. Learners can access course materials and participate in discussions at any time and from anywhere with an internet connection. This flexibility is particularly beneficial for individuals with busy schedules, such as working professionals or students with other commitments.
- **Cost:** Online courses are often less expensive than traditional in-person courses, as there are no transportation or relocation costs.
- **Access to a wider range of courses:** Students who live in rural areas or who have busy schedules may have limited access to certain courses or programs. Online learning allows students to take courses from anywhere in the world. Online learning provides access to a wide range of courses and educational resources that may not be available locally. This is especially important for individuals in remote areas or those who have limited access to traditional educational institutions.
- **Self-paced learning:** Online courses allow students to work at their own pace and spend as much time as they need on each lesson. Many online courses allow learners to progress at their own

pace. This is beneficial for individuals who may need more time to grasp certain concepts or want to accelerate their learning. It also accommodates different learning speeds among participants.

- **Cost-Effectiveness:** Online courses often cost less than traditional, in-person courses. There are no commuting costs, and materials are typically available digitally, reducing the need for physical textbooks. Additionally, some online resources and courses are available for free.
- **Diverse Learning Materials**: Online courses can incorporate various multimedia elements such as videos, interactive quizzes, simulations, and discussion forums. This diversity in learning materials can cater to different learning styles, making the educational experience more engaging.
- **Global Collaboration**: Online learning platforms enable collaboration among individuals from different geographic locations. This fosters a diverse and global learning community, providing opportunities for networking and exposure to different perspectives.
- **Skill Development**: Online courses often focus on practical skills relevant to specific industries. Learners can acquire and enhance skills that are directly applicable to their professional development, making online learning a practical choice for career advancement.
- **Continuous Learning Opportunities**: Online learning encourages a culture of continuous learning. Learners can update their skills or acquire new ones throughout their careers, contributing to ongoing professional development.
- **Personalized Learning**: Some online platforms use adaptive learning technologies to personalize the learning experience. These systems can assess individual progress and tailor content to address specific learning needs, enhancing the effectiveness of the educational process.
- **Environmental Impact**: Online learning can have a lower environmental impact compared to traditional in-person education. Reduced commuting means less energy consumption and a smaller carbon footprint.

Some of the main disadvantages of online learning include:

- **Lack of face-to-face interaction:** Online courses do not offer the same level of interaction and support as in-person courses.

- **Technical difficulties:** There is a risk of technical issues such as internet outages or computer problems that can disrupt learning.
- **Limited access to resources:** In-person courses often have access to resources such as laboratories or studios that may not be available to online students.
- **Self-motivation:** Online courses require a high level of self-motivation, as there is no instructor present to provide structure and support.
- **Limited Social Interaction**: Online learning can be isolating, as students may miss out on the face-to-face interaction with peers and instructors. The lack of a physical classroom environment can lead to feelings of loneliness and reduced opportunities for networking.
- **Technical Issues:** Technical problems, such as internet connectivity issues, software glitches, or hardware malfunctions, can disrupt the learning experience. Not everyone has access to a reliable internet connection or the necessary devices, which can create barriers to participation.
- **Self-Motivation and Discipline:** Online learners need to be highly self-motivated and disciplined to manage their time effectively and stay on track with coursework. Without the structure of a traditional classroom, some students may struggle to stay organized and focused.
- **Limited Hands-On Learning**: Certain subjects, particularly those requiring hands-on or practical experience, may be challenging to teach and learn online. Science labs, art studios, or other hands-on activities may be difficult to replicate in a virtual environment.
- **Dependence on Technology:** Online learning is heavily dependent on technology. If there are technical issues, or if a student is not comfortable using digital tools, it can hinder the learning process. Additionally, not everyone has access to the latest technology or devices.
- **Lack of Immediate Feedback:** In a traditional classroom setting, students can receive immediate feedback from instructors. In online learning, the feedback may be delayed, and the communication may be less personal, potentially affecting the quality of the learning experience.
- **Cheating Concerns:** The remote nature of online learning can make it more challenging to monitor and prevent cheating during

assessments. Maintaining academic integrity can be a concern, and some students may be tempted to engage in dishonest practices.

- **Isolation and Motivational Challenges:** Some students may feel isolated and disconnected from the learning community. The absence of face-to-face interactions with instructors and peers can contribute to a lack of motivation and engagement.
- **Not Suitable for All Learning Styles:** Online learning may not cater to every learning style. Some students thrive in hands-on or interactive environments, which may be lacking in certain online courses.
- **Limited Networking Opportunities**: Building professional networks and relationships with peers and instructors can be more challenging in an online setting. Traditional education often provides more opportunities for networking and socializing.

How is Online Learning helpful for kids?

Online learning can be helpful for kids in a number of ways:

- **Flexibility:** Online learning allows kids to learn at their own pace and schedule, which can be especially helpful for those with busy schedules or who need to accommodate other commitments.
- **Access to a Range of Courses:** Online learning allows kids to take courses that may not be offered at their school or in their local area.
- **Self-Paced Learning:** Online courses can be tailored to the individual needs and learning style of each child, allowing them to work at their own pace and spend as much time as they need on each lesson.
- **Improved Critical Thinking and Problem-Solving Skills:** Online learning can encourage kids to be more independent and self-directed learners, as they are responsible for managing their own learning and seeking out additional resources as needed.
- **Technology Skills:** Online learning can help kids develop important technology skills such as navigating online platforms, using communication tools, and completing assignments electronically.

How is Online Learning not helpful?

There are a few ways in which online learning may not be helpful for some students:

- **Lack of face-to-face interaction:** Online courses do not offer the same level of interaction and support as in-person courses, which can be challenging for some students who prefer a more traditional classroom setting.
- **Technical Difficulties:** There is a risk of technical issues such as internet outages or computer problems that can disrupt learning and make it difficult for students to complete assignments.
- **Limited access to resources:** In-person courses often have access to resources, such as laboratories or studios, that may not be available to online students.
- **Self-Motivation:** Online courses require a high level of self-motivation, as there is no instructor present to provide structure and support. This can be challenging for students who need more support and guidance.
- **Limited access to certain programmes:** Some programs, such as those in the arts or hands-on fields, may not be fully available online. This can limit access for students who are interested in these areas of study.

M-LEARNING

Mobile learning, or m-Learning, is an online learning facility that learners can benefit from anywhere and anytime by using their mobile devices. It does not require additional components or changes to a regular smartphone or tablet. Students can enrol in course programs, study assigned lessons, watch video lectures, attend live classes, and take tests/exams from their devices with location and schedule conditions. It is similar to e-learning, but a major difference is the use of a mobile device for content access.

Key Characteristics of M-Learning

The major characteristics of mobile learning that make it effective for training/educating purposes are as follows:

- **Microlearning content**: Mobile learning often delivers microlearning content that lasts about 2-5 minutes. The crisp and relevant information maintains learners' attention and bolsters retention.
- **Social learning**: Mobile learning employs social learning to boost engagement. It can include a newsfeed, forums, chat function, or comments section for learners to interact with one another, ask questions, and share their insights.

- **Seamless access**: Several mobile-based training solutions have done away with the login process or embedding content directly into the native app to remove friction and increase engagement.
- **Privacy**: Users get optimal privacy. Nobody can intrude on and check their scores, performance or any details they would not like to share.

Pros of Mobile Learning

- **Availability**: Learners get easy access to helpful materials whenever they need them.
- **Usability**: M-learning is task-oriented and practical. It provides valuable information in the form of how-tos, concise guides, step-by-step tutorials, and mini exercises that help put new skills into practice.
- **Convenient size**: The courses and exercises fit seamlessly into daily schedules.
- **Social touch**: Learners can connect with their peers or instructors for assistance and discussions. They can leave comments and stay connected as a community.
- **Engagement**: It creates no burden on the learner. The training and learning process becomes interactive.
- **Cost-effective**: It is more cost-effective than traditional classroom training. It cuts down the brick-and-mortar expenses, physical tools, travel expenses to and from the venue, and the in-person trainer salaries. Learners use their personal devices for training, eliminating the cost of tech labs.

Cons of Mobile Learning

- **Tech discrepancies**: Mobile devices can have varying storage and processing capacities that hinder the mobile learning experience.
- **Poor wireless connection**: Remote places often have insufficient cell coverage and thus poor internet access.
- **Distractions**: Mobile notifications and an urge to scroll social media can reduce training effectiveness.

Difference between Mobile Learning and E-learning

The use of mobile devices for content learning is not the only point of difference between mobile learning from eLearning. Mobile learning is not just a smaller portable version of eLearning. Rather it has some strikingly different characteristics. The major differences between the two are as follows:

- **Different purposes**: While e-learning is more suitable for in-depth fundamental knowledge, mobile learning is ideal for refresher training or systematically acquiring knowledge. Mobile learning increases learning support and diversification. The learners have instant access to small and independent information pieces that they can study on the go.
- **Different lesson lengths**: Traditional online courses via computers or laptops can vary from 15 to 90 minutes. They are lengthier when compared to mobile learning content. The content developed for mobile devices is broken into smaller chunks, usually 3 to 5 minutes. They are easier for the learners and allow them to learn without disturbing their regular schedule.
- **Different output**: eLearning doesn't need special software as it works right in a browser. Contrastingly, m-Learning needs an application of at least two versions: iOS and Android. eLearning courses can be accessed on mobile devices via browsers. Mobile apps are specially curated for mobile devices and cannot be accessed on the web. These apps make the user experience smoother with cameras, audio, barcode scanning, and built-in sensors.

OPEN AND DISTANCE LEARNING (ODL)

Open learning refers to an educational approach that allows learners to have greater control over their learning experience. It emphasizes flexibility, self-paced learning, and learner autonomy. In open learning, students have the freedom to choose their courses, study materials, and learning methods according to their individual needs and interests. It often involves a mix of online resources, textbooks, multimedia materials, and interactive platforms. Open and Distance Learning (ODL) is an educational approach that allows students to pursue their studies remotely, without being physically present in a traditional classroom setting. ODL utilizes various forms of technology, such as the internet, online platforms, and multimedia resources, to deliver educational content to learners wherever they are. ODL has gained popularity due to its flexibility, accessibility, and the ability to reach a wide range of learners, including those who may not have access to traditional educational institutions. It provides opportunities for individuals who cannot attend regular classes due to work commitments, geographical constraints, personal responsibilities, or other reasons. Here are some key features and components of Open and Distance Learning in education:

- **Flexibility**: ODL allows learners to study at their own pace and convenience. They can choose when and where to study, providing them with the flexibility to balance their education with other commitments.
- **Open access**: ODL aims to provide equal access to education for everyone. It eliminates barriers such as location, time, and eligibility criteria, allowing individuals from diverse backgrounds to pursue education.
- **Learning materials**: ODL utilizes a variety of learning materials, including online textbooks, multimedia resources, recorded lectures, interactive simulations, and virtual labs. These materials are often accessible through online platforms or learning management systems.
- **Communication and interaction**: ODL incorporate communication tools such as email, discussion forums, video conferencing, and social media platforms to facilitate interaction between learners and instructors. This helps create a sense of community and allows for discussions, collaboration, and feedback.
- **Assessment and feedback**: ODL employ various methods for assessing student learning, such as online quizzes, assignments, projects, and exams. Feedback is typically provided electronically, allowing students to track their progress and make improvements.
- **Student support services**: ODL institutions typically offer support services to assist learners throughout their educational journey. These may include academic advisors, online tutoring, counselling services, and technical support to address any issues or challenges faced by students.
- **Accreditation and recognition**: ODL programs and institutions may be accredited and recognized by educational authorities to ensure quality and credibility. Accreditation ensures that the educational standards are met and that the qualifications obtained through ODL are recognized by employers and other educational institutions.
- **Self-Paced Learning**: Open learning enables students to progress through the course material at their own pace. They can review and revisit topics as needed, focusing on areas that require more

attention and moving quickly through areas where they are already proficient.

- **Personalized Learning**: Open learning recognizes that learners have different needs, learning styles, and interests. It offers a range of learning materials and resources, allowing students to tailor their learning experience according to their preferences and goals.
- **Accessible Education**: Open learning aims to make education accessible to a wider audience, including individuals who may face barriers to traditional forms of education, such as geographical constraints, financial limitations, or disabilities. It provides opportunities for lifelong learning and skill development.

ODL has proven to be an effective approach in expanding educational opportunities, especially in remote areas, developing countries, and for individuals who face barriers to traditional education. However, it also requires self-discipline, motivation, and effective time management skills on the part of the learners to succeed in a self-directed learning environment

Distance Education

Distance education refers to a method of delivering education to learners who are physically separated from the educational institution or instructor. It utilizes various technologies and communication tools to bridge the gap between learners and educators. Distance education can take different forms, including online courses, correspondence courses, teleconferencing, and video lectures.

Key Features of Distance Education:

- **Independent Learning**: Distance education places a strong emphasis on independent learning. Students are provided with study materials and resources, and they are responsible for managing their own learning process, completing assignments, and preparing for assessments.
- **Communication and Interaction**: Despite the physical separation, distance education promotes communication and interaction between learners and instructors. It may involve virtual classrooms, discussion forums, email, chat rooms, or video conferencing, enabling students to ask questions, seek clarification, and engage in collaborative learning activities.

- **Assessment and Feedback**: Distance education incorporates various assessment methods, such as online quizzes, assignments, projects, and examinations, to evaluate student progress and learning outcomes. Feedback and support from instructors are provided through digital means to guide students' learning and improvement.
- **Support Services**: Distance education institutions often provide support services to assist students throughout their learning journey. These services may include online tutoring, academic advising, technical support, library resources, and access to online learning platforms.

Advantages of Open Learning and Distance Education:

- **Flexibility and Accessibility**: Open learning and distance education offer opportunities for individuals who cannot attend traditional on-campus classes due to various constraints, such as work, family commitments, or geographical distance.
- **Lifelong Learning**: Open learning and distance education promote lifelong learning by enabling individuals to update their knowledge and acquire new skills at any stage of their lives.
- **Personalized Learning**: These approaches allow students to customize their learning experience according to their needs, interests, and learning styles.
- **Technology Integration**: Open learning and distance education harness the power of technology to deliver educational content and facilitate communication and collaboration between students and instructors.
- **Cost-Effective**: Distance education can be a cost-effective alternative to traditional education, as it eliminates expenses related to commuting, accommodation, and campus facilities.

Challenges and Considerations:

- **Self-Motivation and Discipline**: Open learning and distance education require self-motivation and discipline, as learners must take responsibility for managing their time and keeping up with coursework.
- **Digital Literacy and Technical Requirements**: Distance education relies heavily on technology, so students need to possess basic digital literacy skills and have access to reliable internet connectivity and appropriate devices.

- **Social Interaction**: The lack of face-to-face interaction and social engagement in open learning and distance education can be a challenge for some students. Efforts should be made to foster virtual communities and facilitate peer-to-peer interaction.
- **Quality Assurance**: Ensuring the quality and effectiveness of open learning and distance education programs is crucial. Institutions must design and deliver courses that meet established educational standards and provide adequate support for student success.

VIRTUAL LEARNING

Virtual learning refers to an environment where students study a digital-based curriculum taught by instructors that lecture online via video or audio. This instruction can take place either in a self-paced (asynchronous) environment or in a real-time (synchronous) environment.

Benefits of Virtual Learning

The virtual learning environment is a good choice for people who enjoy learning on their own, without restrictions on space and time. Some virtual learning options have classes to attend at scheduled times, while others allow you to learn at your own pace. With this self-paced option, you have a lot of autonomy with the intensity and cadence of your learning while still enjoying the benefits of guided lessons. Virtual learning can be convenient, flexible, and affordable.

Types of Virtual Learning

Not all virtual learning is the same. There are three different ways you may learn in a virtual environment: synchronous, asynchronous, and hybrid.

- **Synchronous virtual learning** typically asks students to attend online live-streamed lectures. The instructor streams their presentation or lecture, allowing students to ask questions in real-time via webcam, microphone, or live chat, for a more hands-on learning experience. If you benefit from the constant structure and pacing of the material, synchronous virtual learning could be a good choice for you.
- **Asynchronous virtual learning** features pre-recorded lectures that students can watch on their own time. The instructor will post either a video or audio file along with lecture notes. Often there will be a quiz on the material to ensure students are watching lectures and up to date with the class schedule. Typically, the

instructor or an assistant is available via email or text chat. Current students, and sometimes past students, usually have some form of communication with each other, such as a forum, where they can discuss the material and flesh out details they may not have gathered from the lecture.

- **Hybrid learning** will make use of both virtual and in-person learning. This is the most common for classes that also require a lab component. If you want the freedom to learn at the best times for you, but also want some structured lessons and communication with the instructor, consider enrolling in a hybrid course.

Advantages of Virtual Learning

Virtual learning gives students access to coursework from anywhere, at any time, making learning super convenient. Asynchronous classes also give an immense amount of flexibility for lectures and studying. Even with the flexibility of the course, online courses are associated with higher retention rates and graduation rates. A study conducted by Arizona State University found that students taking virtual classes benefit from increased access and cost savings of as much as 50 percent. Completing courses virtually can also increase students' digital aptitude, preparing them for life in the workforce. In addition to these advantages, the nature of virtual learning allows teachers to conduct more frequent assessments to help ensure students are staying on track. Since tests can be turned in digitally, you can also get near-immediate feedback and scoring.

Disadvantages of virtual learning

Technology offers us wonderful opportunities like the ability to learn from home, but it also may lead to momentary malfunctions, like interruptions or downtime. Since virtual learning takes place on a screen, you might feel that the course isn't as fully immersive compared to in-person instruction. You may feel a lack of collaboration or networking since you're not sitting next to others as in a classroom setting. For some, that's a con, but it may not be an issue for people who prefer a more individualistic learning approach. For some students, the ability to study and learn comfortably from home could be a huge benefit. For others, learning at home can be distracting. Interruptions from family members and access to a phone and entertainment can make focusing more difficult, and some people may even feel isolated. There is also somewhat of a lack of accountability with virtual learning, so students will need to have a good sense of self-motivation or know where to go for help. Virtual learning can require learning new programs for both students and teachers. For the school or course provider, this will likely require additional funds to ensure the instructors are fully fluent in the necessary technologies.

TELE-CONFERENCING

Teleconferencing means meeting through a telecommunications medium. It is a generic term for linking people between two or more locations by electronics. There are at least six types of teleconferencing: audio, audio graphic, computer, video, Business Television (BTV), and distance education. The methods used differ in the technology, but common factors contribute to the shared definition of teleconferencing:

Interactive Technologies

The new systems have varying degrees of interactivity – the capability to talk back to the user. They are enabling and satellites, computers, teletext, view data, cassettes, cable, and videodiscs all fit the same emerging pattern. They provide ways for individuals to step out of the mass audiences and take an active role in the process by which information is transmitted. The new technologies are de-massifier so that a special message can be exchanged with each individual in a large audience. They are the opposite mass media and shift control to the user. Many are asynchronous and can send or receive a message at a time convenient for individuals without being in communication at the same time. This overcomes time as a variable affecting communication. A video, data and voice delivery system reduce travel costs. When the material is retrieved and saved to a video tape or disc, the material can be used at any time or anyplace. As more interactive technologies emerge, the value of being an independent learner will increase. Research shows that learning from new technologies is as effective as traditional methods. Large groups are cost-effective and everyone gets the same information.

Types of Teleconferences

- **Audio Teleconference:** Voice-only; sometimes called **conference calling**. Interactively links people in remote locations via telephone lines. Audio bridges tie all lines together. Meetings can be conducted via audio conference. Preplanning is necessary which includes naming a chair, setting an agenda, and providing printed materials to participants ahead of time so that they can be reviewed. Distance learning can be conducted by audio conference. In fact, it is one of the most underutilized, yet cost effective methods available to education. Instructors should receive training on how to best utilize audio conferences to augment other forms of distance learning.

- **Audio graphics Teleconference:** Uses narrow-band telecommunications channels to transmit visual information such as graphics, alpha-numeric, documents, and video pictures as an adjunct to voice communication. Other terms are desk-top computer conferencing and enhanced audio. Devices include electronic tablets/boards, freeze-frame video terminals, integrated graphics systems (as part of personal computers), Fax, remote-access microfiche and slide projectors, optical graphic scanners, and voice/data terminals. Audio graphics can be used for meetings and distance learning.
- **Computer Teleconference:** Uses telephone lines to connect two or more computers and modems. Anything that can be done on a computer can be sent over the lines. It can be synchronous or asynchronous. An example of an asynchronous mode is electronic mail. Using electronic mail (E-Mail), memos, reports, updates, and newsletters can be sent to anyone on the local area network (LAN) or wide area network (WAN). Items generated on computer which are normally printed and then sent by facsimile can be sent by E-Mail. Computer conferencing is an emerging area for distance education. Some institutions offer credit programs completely by computer. Students receive texts and workbooks via mail. Through common files assigned to a class which each student can assess, teachers upload syllabi, lectures, grades and remarks. Students download these files, compose their assignment and remarks off-line, and then upload them to the common files. Students and instructors are usually required to log on for a prescribed number of days during the week. Interaction is a large component of the students' grades. Through computers, faculty, students and administrators have easy access to one another as well as access to database resources provided through libraries. The academic resources of libraries and special resources can be accessed such as OCLC, ERIC, and Internet. Administrators can access student files, retrieve institutional information from central repositories such as district or system offices, government agencies, or communicate with one another. Other resources can be created such as updates on state or federal legislation.
- **Video Teleconference:** Combines audio and video to provide voice communications and video images. Can be one-way video/

two-way audio, or two-way video/two-way audio. It can display anything that can be captured by a TV camera. The advantage is the capability to display moving images. In two-way audio/video systems, a common application is to show people which creates a social presence that resembles face-to-face meetings and classes and enables participants to see the facial expressions and physical demeanour of participants at remote sites. Graphics are used to enhance understanding. There are three basic systems: freeze frame, compressed, and full-motion video. Video conferencing is an effective way to use one teacher who teaches to a number of sites. It is very cost effective for classes which may have a small number of students enrolled at each site. In many cases, video conferencing enables the institution or a group of institutions to provide courses which would be cancelled due to low enrolment or which could not be supported otherwise because of the cost of providing an instructor in an unusual subject area. Rural areas benefit particularly from classes provided through video conferencing when they work with a larger metropolitan institution that has full-time faculty.

Through teleconferencing, institutions are able to serve all students equitably, via (a) Use a telecommunications channel, (b) Link people at multiple locations, (c) Interactive to provide two-way communications, and (d) Dynamic to require users' active participation.

Benefits of Using Teleconferencing

- **Move Information – Not People:** Electronic delivery is more efficient than physically moving people to a site, whether it is a faculty member or administrator.
- **Save Time:** Content presented by one or many sources is received in many places simultaneously and instantly. Travel is reduced resulting in more productive time. Communication is improved and meetings are more efficient. It adds a competitive edge that face-to-face meeting do not.
- **Lower Costs:** Costs (travel, meals, lodging) are reduced by keeping employees in the office, speeding up product development cycles, improving performance through frequent meetings with timely information.
- **Accessible:** Through any origination site in the world.
- **Larger Audiences**: More people can attend. The larger the audience, the lower the cost per person.

- **Adaptable:** Useful for business, associations, hospitals, and institutions to discuss, inform, train, educate or present.
- **Flexible:** With a remote receive or transmit truck, a transmit or receive site can be located anywhere.
- **Security:** Signals can be encrypted (scrambled) when it is necessary. Encryption prevents outside viewers.
- **Unity:** Provides a shared sense of identity. People feel more a part of the group…more often. Individuals or groups at multiple locations can be linked frequently.
- **Timely:** For time-critical information, sites can be linked quickly. An audio or point-to-point teleconference can be convened in three minutes.
- **Interactive:** Dynamic; requires the user's active participation. It enhances personal communication. When used well for learning, the interactivity will enhance the learning and the teaching experience.

Disadvantages of using teleconferencing

As you work your way up the corporate ladder, you might increasingly be asked to participate in meetings, and many of these may be conducted via the telephone. If you start your own business, travel expenses might make in-person meetings cost-prohibitive and teleconferencing a more viable option. Body language, facial expressions and work samples you use to shine when communicating face to face won't help you during teleconferences, so weigh the pros and cons of in-person meetings vs. teleconferencing, especially if you are selling a product, service or yourself.

- **Lack of Body Language:** Teleconferencing doesn't let you read other participants' body language, which can give you clues as to whether you need to change your direction during a meeting. For example, if the person you're meeting with crosses his arms, it might be a sign of defensiveness and that you are not connecting. Seeing this, you would be able to soften your message. Someone slouching or tapping their fingers can signal they are losing interest, letting you know to change the subject or finish your point. In a teleconferencing situation, you do not get these cues to make changes in your presentation.
- **Lack of Eye Contact:** Eye contact is another key benefit you lose when teleconferencing. Someone who looks down at the floor might be lying, giving you a clue not to take him at his word if you are interviewing him for a job or involved in a sales call. If

someone's eyes dart around the room, they might be bored. If you or your meeting partners absolutely can't make an in-person meeting, ask about videoconferencing capabilities. Using the video cameras on our computers and the availability of low-cost and free video services such as Skype, it might be just as easy to organize a video meeting.

- **Interruptions:** People who teleconference do so using landlines, cell phones and voiceover Internet protocol, or VOIP, phones. Plan on interruptions during telephone meetings when calls are dropped and Internet connections go dead. Many people attend teleconferences while driving, talking on cell phones that can create static or other noise as the user moves in and out of dead zones. Some people take advantage of teleconferences to stay at home that day, leading to crying babies, barking dogs or people at the door disrupting your call.
- **No Visual Presentation:** The ability to share graphs, charts, photos, reports, drawings, videos, product samples and other visual messages is important to make a sale, whether you're trying to get a customer to buy, co-workers to understand a new procedure or your boss to agree with a pitch you're making. When organizing or attending a teleconference that would benefit from visuals, upload documents or videos to a company or personal website or email information to attendees before the meeting starts.

SCAFFOLDING STRATEGIES

Scaffolding is a classroom teaching technique in which instructors deliver lessons in distinct segments, providing less and less support as students master new concepts or material. Much like scaffolding on a building, this technique is meant to provide students with a framework for learning as they build and strengthen their understanding. When students reach the intended level of comprehension or mastery, the teacher can step back and gradually remove their support. For example, a middle school biology teacher may show students a video on mitosis, then have them take a short, open-book quiz aided by a glossary. After a class wide discussion on the topic, during which the teacher shows examples of mitosis and answers students' questions, students may retake the quiz without textbooks to measure their comprehension.

The scaffolding approach differs from traditional "independent learning" model, in which a teacher asks students to read an article as homework, write a five-page essay and hand it in by the end of the week without providing any additional structured support. (Students are typically able to ask questions, but many are hesitant.) In this scenario, students would be responsible for navigating their own way through new course content, which would likely prove challenging for students who do not learn well via independent study.

The term "scaffolding" was first used in an educational context in the mid-1970s, coined by American psychologist Jerome S Bruner. In *The Child's Conception of Language* (ed. A. Sinclair, et al, 1978) Bruner describes scaffolding as: "…the steps taken to reduce the degrees of freedom in carrying out some tasks so that the child can concentrate on the difficult skill she is in the process of acquiring." Scaffolding can also be explained by the phrase "I do, we do, you do," wherein the teacher demonstrates, guides, then hands the reins to the students.

Scaffolding vs. Differentiation

Unlike scaffolding, which involves all students following discrete steps to master a concept, differentiation presents students with different types of lessons based on their abilities and preferences. For example, a teacher may assign most of the class to read a chapter of a book, then write a short paragraph discussing the chapter. However, there may be one or more students in the class for whom this type of assignment poses a challenge. For these students, the teacher may ask them to read a shortened or altered version of the text, then show they understand by answering some multiple-choice questions about the text. The teacher is differentiating the type of assessments these students need in order to be successful.

Scaffolding and differentiation are used to achieve similar goals, in that they provide a way for educators to help students succeed while still being challenged and building upon existing knowledge. Both approaches may also be combined in a single lesson. Teachers may identify students who need differentiated lessons by first scaffolding their lessons, then determining whether students need alternative assignments to keep pace with their peers.

It may take some time for teachers to identify which students respond best to scaffolding or differentiation, if they don't receive insight from students' previous teachers and guidance counsellors. However, knowing how to effectively engage all of their students can be extremely beneficial for overall classroom management. The concepts of scaffolding and the "zone of proximal development" are sometimes used interchangeably, as both were developed around the same time. Psychologist Lev Semyonovich Vygotsky explained his zone of proximal development, or ZPD, as the difference between what a learner can do without help and what they can achieve with guidance from a teacher. Therefore, the ZPD refers to the skills a learner is on the cusp of mastering, while scaffolding provides the support needed for the student to reach successive points of comprehension.

Benefits of Scaffolding in Education

Even before it was given a name, the concept of scaffolding has proven itself an essential approach to education. Teachers find that scaffolding:

- Improves the likelihood that students will retain new information
- Helps connect foundational knowledge to new concepts
- Engages students with their learning and tracking their own progress
- Gives students more autonomy and independence in the classroom
- Bridges student learning gaps in traditionally difficult course content
- Reduces students' feelings of frustration, confusion and negative self-perceptions in the classroom
- Improves communication between students and teachers
- Allows students to "fail productively" and encourages asking for help
- Keeps classes organized and on schedule

When both teachers and students can follow an instructional roadmap and actively participate in the transfer of knowledge, fewer students are likely to become lost and give up on difficult concepts. If a teacher chooses to scaffold differentiated lessons for certain students, overall student performance is likely to soar. If teachers are new to scaffolding, implementing the strategy into practice can be challenging or time consuming. However, the benefits of improved learning retention and better overall performance far outweigh the effort expended. Soon, scaffolding will become a natural part of the lesson planning process.

Strategies for Scaffolding in the Classroom

No matter the instructional approach, teachers should always introduce new concepts to students in a way that meets their current level of comprehension. A tenth-grade geometry teacher wouldn't begin a unit on the Pythagorean theorem without first ensuring that students knew what a hypotenuse was. Once teachers establish their students' starting point, they can scaffold new course content by following this process:

- Break the new lesson into discrete units

- Create assignments for each unit
- Talk students through each assignment before they begin work
- Explain the purpose of the lesson or assignment - answer the age-old question, "Why do we need to know this?"
- Divide students into groups to discuss the assignment, plan their approach and support each other
- Provide students with tips or examples of the completed assignment so they can compare their progress
- Have students present their work for feedback and/or take an assessment to gauge understanding

Examples of some of these steps can be illustrated with specific scaffolding strategies, including:

- **Show and tell:** The teacher models a process or final product so students can see what they are meant to be creating. Show and tell can be used to demonstrate algebra equations, scientific models, artistic techniques and much more. Teachers can even extend show and tell to doing the first assignment along with the students following their initial demonstration.
- **Making real-life connections:** Sometimes, it can be challenging for students to understand why they need to know something or how it connects to the world outside of school. As the teacher, share an example of how an academic concept applies to your own life, then ask students if they have any similar examples.
- **Start with vocabulary:** If a student encounters a word they don't recognize in a text about a new concept, they may start to feel out of their depth, and their engagement may falter. Before embarking on a new lesson or assigning independent reading, make sure students understand key vocabulary words so they don't become lost. Again, connect new words to concepts students are already familiar with, and have students create their own vocabulary flash cards or "cheat sheets" (with examples) to refer back to.
- **Use visual aids:** There are countless studies demonstrating the increase in retention of visual over auditory information. Specifically, it's been found that seeing images or visual demonstrations helps students understand and remember key concepts better than simply listening to the teacher explain them. Charts, models, slideshows, videos and other visual tools can all support student learning.

Not every student will feel they need the same amount of scaffolding as others; some students may be able to demonstrate certain algebraic equations after one lesson, while others may need a week's worth of teacher demonstrations and in-class exercises before they grasp the concept. It's best to structure lessons to serve the greatest number of learners possible at once, and build in a chance to address both high achievers and those who need extra support.

Scaffolding Learning Activities

As they scaffold a lesson on new material, teachers must first confirm that students have adequate context. This can even be basic, foundational information — for example, as a teacher embarks on a lesson about the Boston Tea Party, they need to confirm that their students know where Boston is, what taxes are, why tea was so important at the time and why Britain might care if a shipload of it ended up in Boston Harbor. "No taxation without representation!" means nothing if students don't understand what each of those words means. Once the teacher establishes a baseline for student understanding, whether through an in-class discussion or short exploratory quiz, they can identify the goals of the lesson and begin to create a lesson plan. Here are some activities students can follow as they begin to explore new concepts:

- **Fish bowl:** Give students a topic to discuss, perhaps guided by a set of questions. Select about one quarter of the class to sit in a circle or group in the middle of the classroom. Have all other students sit around the edges of the central group and listen while this group discusses the topic. Observers are not allowed to speak while the smaller group is talking amongst themselves. After about 15–20 minutes of discussion, divide the smaller group up among the rest of the class and divide into new groups of equal size. The observers can now discuss what they heard with members of the smaller group, offer different perspectives, ask questions and come to new conclusions together.
- **Think-aloud:** This technique works well for reading comprehension exercises, but can also work for mathematical exercises. The teacher reads a passage aloud as the students follow along. Whenever the teacher reaches a potential point of confusion for students — such as an unfamiliar vocabulary word or place name — they stop and think through the issue aloud, perhaps with the aid of some predetermined questions. As they continue to read the passage aloud, the teacher will stop and pose some of

their questions for the students to answer. Eventually, students are asked to take over reading aloud (if they are able), pausing to think through or pose questions to their classmates.

- **Mind maps and concept maps:** To demonstrate their grasp of a new topic, teachers can direct students to create a mind map as a visual representation of that topic. For example, if students have just learned about penguins in the Arctic, they should begin to draw a diagram with "penguin" at the centre, then make "branches" off of that central topic that led to the penguin's characteristics, including what it eats, where it lives and what its predators are.

In a concept map, students are asked to take everything they know about a larger topic — for instance, the Arctic — and connect all the disparate concepts they know about that topic. An Arctic concept map might connect penguins to elements of the landscape and climate, other animals and the effect of humans on their habitat. Often, a lack of engagement results from students not understanding the purpose of school work, or the intended end result of a certain lesson or assignment. Showing and explaining to students what they are meant to create or achieve is not giving them the answers. Rather, providing students with a blueprint can help them take ownership of the learning process and, by extension, the finished product — their new knowledge.

MODULAR EXPLORATIONS AND DEVELOPING LEARNING PACKAGES

Modular explorations and the development of learning packages in education are strategies that aim to enhance the learning experience and provide flexibility for students. This approach involves breaking down the curriculum into smaller, self-contained modules or units of study that can be combined or rearranged to create customized learning paths. Here are some key aspects to consider when developing learning packages using a modular exploration approach:

- **Curriculum Design**: Start by analysing the curriculum or learning objectives and identifying the core concepts, skills, and knowledge areas. Divide the curriculum into smaller modules based on these elements.
- **Learning Outcomes**: Clearly define the learning outcomes for each module. What specific skills or knowledge should students acquire by completing the module? Design assessments or activities that align with these outcomes.

- **Flexibility and Adaptability**: Ensure that the modules are designed to be flexible and adaptable. Students should be able to progress through the modules in a non-linear fashion, allowing them to customize their learning journey based on their interests, prior knowledge, and learning pace.
- **Sequencing and Prerequisites**: Determine the logical sequence of modules, considering any prerequisites or dependencies between them. Some modules may need to be completed before others to ensure progressive learning.
- **Engaging Resources**: Develop high-quality learning resources for each module, such as readings, videos, interactive activities, or simulations. These resources should be engaging, relevant, and aligned with the learning outcomes.
- **Assessments and Feedback**: Design assessments that align with the learning outcomes of each module. Provide timely feedback to students to guide them learning progress and address any misconceptions.
- **Learning Pathways**: Consider different learning pathways that students can follow based on their interests or career goals. Allow students to choose from a variety of modules and create personalized learning paths.
- **Integration and Interconnections**: Identify opportunities to integrate concepts or skills from different modules. Highlight the interconnections between modules to help students see the bigger picture and understand how different topics relate to each other.
- **Collaboration and Reflection**: Encourage collaborative activities and reflection within the modules. Foster opportunities for students to interact with their peers, discuss ideas, and engage in critical thinking.
- **Continuous Improvement**: Regularly gather feedback from students, educators, and stakeholders to improve the learning packages. Evaluate the effectiveness of the modules, assess student outcomes, and make necessary adjustments to enhance the learning experience.

Overall, modular explorations and learning packages offer flexibility, customization, and increased student engagement. By breaking down the curriculum into smaller, interconnected modules, educators can provide students with a more personalized and meaningful learning experience.

MODELS OF TEACHING

Development of Models of Teaching is one of the innovations in teaching. The core of teaching process is the arrangement of environments with in which the students can interact and study how to learn. A model of teaching is a description of learning environments. An important purpose of models of teaching is to assist the teacher to have a wide range of approaches for creating a proper interaction environment for learning. A model of teaching is a plan or pattern that can be used to shape curricula, to design instructional materials and to guide instruction in the classroom and other settings. Basically, models of teaching are prescriptive teaching strategies designed to accomplish particular instructional goals. They are prescriptive in the sense that the teacher's responsibility during the planning, implementing and evaluating stages are clearly defined.

Teaching models have long histories behind them; they have been refined through experiences so that they can be used comfortably and effectively in classroom. Furthermore, they are adaptable they can be adjusted to the learning styles of students and to the requirements of the subject matter. Again, there is evidence that they work. Besides being validated by experiences, all are backed by some amount of formal research that tests their theories and abilities to gain effects. Weil and Joyce (1978) say that, "A model of teaching consists of guidelines for designing educational activities and environments. It specifies ways of teaching and learning that are intended to achieve certain kinds of goals."

Main Characteristics of a Teaching Model: Some common identifiable characteristics of good models are;

- Specification of Learning Outcome: All models of teaching specify what students should perform after completing an instructional sequence.
- Specification of Environment: A teaching model specifies in definite terms the environmental conditions under which a student's response should be observed.
- Specification of Criterion of Performance: A model of teaching specifies the criterion of performance which is expected from the students.
- Specification of Operations: A model of teaching specifies the mechanism that provides for the reaction of students and interaction with the environment.
- Specification of Procedure: A model of teaching is based on a

systematic procedure to modify the behaviour of the learner. It is not a haphazard combination of facts.

Fundamental Elements of Models of Teaching

For using a model, the teacher must know the theoretical orientation and practical implementation of the model. Thus, the fundamental elements of a model of teaching are; Focus of the model, Syntax, The social system, Principles of reaction, The support system, Applications of the model, and Instructional and nurturant effect.

- **Focus of the Model**: Focus describes the goals and objectives of the model, theoretical assumptions, the principles and major concepts underlying the model. It gives the description of the environment also. So, the focus constitutes the objectives of teaching and environmental description.
- **Syntax:** Syntax includes the sequence of steps involved in the organization of the complex program of teaching.
- **The social system:** The social system describes students and teacher roles and relationships and the kind of norms that are encouraged. The leadership roles of teacher vary greatly from model to model. The teacher may be a reflector or a facilitator of group activity in some models. In some other models the teacher may be the centre of activity.
- **Principles of Reaction:** This aspect tells the teacher how to regard the learner and how to respond to what the learner does. Principles of reaction provide the teacher with rules of thumb by which to tune into the students and select model.
- **Support system:** The support system relates to the additional requirements other than the usual human skills or capacities of the teacher and facilities usually available in the ordinary class room. These requirements refer to special skills, special knowledge of the teacher and special audio-visual materials like films, self-instructional material, visit to special places etc.
- **Application of the model:** Several types of teaching models are available. Some models are developed for some specific purpose, whereas others have very wide general applications. For e.g. some are designed to develop social relationships; some are designed to develop social development along with academic and personal development.
- **Instructional and Nurturant Effects**: The description of the effects of model can validly be categorized as the direct

or instructional effect and indirect or nurturant effects. The instructional effects are those directly achieved by leading the learner in certain directions. The nurturant effects come from experiencing the environment created by the model.

GROUP INVESTIGATION MODEL

The Group Investigation Model of teaching is an instructional strategy that emphasizes student-centred and collaborative learning. This approach encourages students to work together in small groups to investigate, explore, and solve problems.

Key Components and Features of the Group Investigation Model:

- *Formation of Groups*: Students are organized into small groups. Group size can vary depending on the task and the teacher's preferences, but typically, groups consist of 3-5 students.
- *Selection of Topics or Problems*: Students are given the freedom to choose or are assigned a specific topic or problem to investigate. This could be related to the curriculum, real-world issues, or specific areas of interest.
- *Research and Investigation*: Groups engage in research and investigation to explore their chosen topic or problem. This may involve library research, internet research, interviews, experiments, or other methods depending on the nature of the investigation.
- *Collaborative Learning*: The emphasis is on collaborative learning, where group members work together to share ideas, information, and resources. This fosters teamwork, communication skills, and the ability to work effectively in a group setting.
- *Teacher as Facilitator*: The teacher takes on the role of a facilitator rather than a traditional instructor. The teacher provides guidance, support, and resources, but the students take an active role in their own learning.
- *Presentation of Findings*: After conducting their research, groups present their findings to the class. This could be in the form of presentations, reports, posters, or other creative formats.
- *Reflection and Evaluation*: Students and the teacher engage in reflection and evaluation of the group investigation process. This may involve discussing what worked well, challenges faced, and how the group could improve in future projects.

- *Assessment*: Assessment can be based on various criteria, including the quality of the investigation, the effectiveness of the group's presentation, individual contributions to the group, and the ability to apply critical thinking skills.

Benefits of the Group Investigation Model:

- *Promotion of Critical Thinking*: Students are encouraged to think critically and problem-solve as they explore and investigate their chosen topics.
- *Enhanced Communication Skills*: Working in groups helps students develop effective communication and interpersonal skills.
- *Increased Engagement*: Students often find group investigations more engaging and relevant compared to traditional lecture-based learning.
- *Ownership of Learning*: Students take ownership of their learning process, fostering a sense of responsibility and independence.
- *Real-world Application*: The model encourages students to apply their learning to real-world situations, making the knowledge more practical and meaningful.

SOCIAL INQUIRY MODEL

The Social Inquiry Model of teaching is an instructional approach that emphasizes active student engagement in the learning process through social interaction, collaboration, and inquiry-based methods. This model is rooted in the constructivist philosophy of education, which posits that learners actively construct their own understanding of the world through meaningful experiences and interactions.

Key components of the Social Inquiry Model:

- *Inquiry-Based Learning*: The model promotes inquiry as a fundamental aspect of the learning process. Students are encouraged to ask questions, explore topics of interest, and actively seek answers through research and investigation.
- *Collaboration*: Social interaction and collaboration are central to the Social Inquiry Model. Students often work together in groups to share ideas, discuss findings, and solve problems. Collaborative learning fosters the development of communication skills, teamwork, and a sense of shared responsibility for learning outcomes.

- *Real-World Connections*: The model emphasizes the application of learning to real-world situations. Students are encouraged to connect their knowledge and skills to practical, everyday contexts, making the learning experience more meaningful and relevant.
- *Critical Thinking*: The Social Inquiry Model aims to develop students' critical thinking skills. This involves the ability to analyse information, evaluate evidence, and make informed decisions. Critical thinking is often cultivated through the exploration of open-ended questions and complex problem-solving tasks.
- *Teacher as Facilitator*: In this model, the role of the teacher shifts from being a traditional "sage on the stage" to a facilitator or guide on the side. Teachers support and guide students in their learning journey, providing resources, posing thought-provoking questions, and offering guidance when needed.
- *Reflection*: Reflection is an integral part of the Social Inquiry Model. Students are encouraged to reflect on their learning experiences, consider the process they went through, and evaluate their understanding. Reflection helps learners become more metacognitive, understanding how they learn and how to improve their learning strategies.
- *Student Autonomy*: The model promotes student autonomy and self-directed learning. Students are given more control over their learning process, allowing them to take ownership of their education and become more independent learners.

Benefits of Social Inquiry Model

- *Active Learning*: Social inquiry encourages students to actively engage in the learning process. Through inquiry-based activities, students are involved in hands-on experiences, investigations, and discussions, which can lead to a deeper understanding of the subject matter.
- *Critical Thinking Skills*: The social inquiry model promotes critical thinking by encouraging students to analyse information, ask questions, and evaluate evidence. This helps them develop the ability to think critically and make informed decisions, skills that are valuable in various aspects of life.
- *Problem-Solving Skills*: By engaging in inquiry-based learning, students are often confronted with real-world problems and challenges. This approach helps them develop problem-solving skills as they work collaboratively to find solutions and make decisions.

- *Collaboration and Communication*: Social inquiry often involves collaborative learning experiences where students work together in groups. This fosters communication and teamwork skills, helping students learn how to effectively express their ideas, listen to others, and work collaboratively toward common goals.
- *Relevance to Real Life*: The social inquiry model connects classroom learning to real-world situations. This relevance can enhance students' motivation and engagement, as they see the practical applications of the knowledge and skills they are acquiring.
- *Intrinsic Motivation*: Inquiry-based learning allows students to pursue their interests and curiosity, fostering intrinsic motivation. When students have the opportunity to explore topics that genuinely interest them, they are more likely to be motivated to learn and take ownership of their education.
- *Lifelong Learning*: The skills developed through the social inquiry model, such as critical thinking, problem-solving, and effective communication, are essential for lifelong learning. Students are better equipped to adapt to new information and challenges throughout their lives.
- *Social Awareness and Empathy*: Social inquiry often involves exploring issues and topics that have societal implications. This can contribute to the development of social awareness and empathy as students gain a deeper understanding of diverse perspectives and societal challenges.
- *Preparation for the Future*: In today's rapidly changing world, the ability to think critically, solve problems, and collaborate with others is highly valuable. The social inquiry model helps prepare students for the challenges they may face in their future academic, professional, and personal lives.
- *Personalized Learning*: Inquiry-based learning allows for a degree of personalization, as students can explore topics that align with their interests and learning styles. This can contribute to a more individualized and engaging educational experience.

CONCLUSION

In conclusion, Unit four has provided a comprehensive exploration of key strategies for effective social science instruction. Delving into the psychological underpinnings, we examined behaviourist, cognitivist, constructivist, and humanistic theories, gaining insights into the diverse ways learners engage with and internalize social science concepts. The unit emphasized the importance of inclusive classrooms, highlighting essentialities to create an environment that caters to diverse learning needs. Additionally, we delved into skill development through micro teaching, peer tutoring, macro teaching, and team teaching, acknowledging the significance of collaborative and varied instructional approaches. The integration of information and communication technology (ICT) was thoroughly examined, encompassing online learning, e-learning, m-learning, open and distance learning (ODL), virtual learning, and teleconferencing. Scaffolding strategies were explored as crucial tools to support learners at various levels. Furthermore, modular explorations guided us in the development of learning packages, fostering a structured and adaptable learning experience. Finally, models of teaching, including the group investigation model and social inquiry model, were presented as effective frameworks for engaging students in critical thinking and inquiry. This unit equips educators with a diverse toolkit to enhance the delivery of social science instruction, fostering an enriched and inclusive learning environment for students.

UNIT - 5

SOCIAL SCIENCE TEACHER EDUCATOR

INTRODUCTION

Welcome to Unit five: "Social Science Teacher Educator." This unit delves into the multifaceted role of a Social Science Teacher Educator, addressing various aspects crucial for effective teacher education. Throughout the unit, we will explore pedagogic priorities, emphasizing innovative practices and the cultivation of creativity in the teaching-learning process. The unit also delves into the concept of reflective teaching, offering insights into strategies that enable Social Science Teachers to become reflective practitioners. With a focus on roles and responsibilities, we examine the diverse functions that Teacher Educators undertake. Professional development is a key theme, encompassing the understanding of the learner (Teacher Educand), continuing education for Teacher Educators, and the ethical dimensions of their practice. Furthermore, we explore the Teacher Educator's role as a Techno-Pedagogue, Curriculum Designer, and Researcher, shedding light on the development of research potential within this critical educational role. Join us on this educational journey as we navigate the intricacies of preparing Social Science educators for the challenges and opportunities in the contemporary teaching landscape.

PEDAGOGIC PRIORITIES, INNOVATIVE PRACTICES, EXPLORING CREATIVITY

In the realm of education, pedagogic priorities play a crucial role in shaping the learning experiences of students. Two priorities that have gained increasing recognition in recent years are innovative practices and exploring creativity. Innovative practices refer to the incorporation of new and unconventional approaches to teaching and learning, which seek to enhance student engagement and foster critical thinking skills. On the other hand, exploring creativity emphasizes the importance of nurturing students' creative potential by providing opportunities for self-expression and problem-solving through various artistic and imaginative activities. These pedagogic priorities not only contribute to a more dynamic and vibrant learning environment but also equip students with the necessary skills to thrive in an ever-evolving world. The pursuit of innovative practices in education acknowledges the need to adapt teaching methods to meet the changing demands of the 21st century. With advancements in technology and the globalized nature of today's society, traditional teaching approaches may no longer be sufficient. Innovative practices aim to break away from the traditional lecture-based model and instead promote active learning, collaboration, and real-world problem-solving. This can be achieved through project-based learning, flipped classrooms, and the use of educational technologies, among others. By encouraging students to take an active role in their learning process, innovative practices foster critical thinking, creativity, and adaptability – essential skills for the future workforce.

In addition to innovative practices, exploring creativity is another crucial pedagogic priority that recognizes the immense value in nurturing students' creative abilities. Creativity serves as a catalyst for innovation and enables individuals to think outside the box, find novel solutions, and adapt to changing circumstances. By integrating the arts, such as music, visual arts, and drama, within the curriculum, students are able to unleash their imaginative potential and develop a holistic set of skills. Furthermore, exploring creativity fosters self-expression, empathy, and cultural understanding, as it allows students to explore different perspectives and communicate their thoughts and emotions in unique ways. This pedagogic priority encourages students to embrace their individuality and curiosity, ultimately promoting a love for learning and a lifelong passion for creativity. Exploring creativity and incorporating innovative practices in pedagogy can greatly enhance the learning experience for students. Here are some pedagogic priorities and innovative practices that can help foster creativity in education:

- **Project-Based Learning (PBL):** Encourage students to work on projects that require critical thinking, problem-solving, and creativity. PBL allows students to apply theoretical knowledge to real-world situations, fostering creativity in finding solutions.

- **Flipped Classroom:** Flip the traditional classroom model by having students engage with course content outside of class through videos or readings. In-class time can then be used for discussions, collaborative activities, and hands-on projects, promoting active learning and creativity.
- **Inquiry-Based Learning:** Pose open-ended questions and problems to stimulate curiosity and encourage students to explore topics independently. This approach cultivates a sense of discovery and creativity as students actively seek answers and solutions.
- **Technology Integration:** Incorporate technology tools and platforms that allow students to express themselves creatively, such as multimedia presentations, digital storytelling, or coding projects. Virtual reality, augmented reality, and simulations can also provide immersive learning experiences.
- **Cross-Disciplinary Collaboration:** Foster collaboration between different subject areas to promote a holistic understanding of concepts. Integrating diverse perspectives and knowledge from various disciplines can spark innovative thinking and creative problem-solving.
- **Flexible Learning Spaces:** Create environments that support different learning styles and encourage collaboration. Flexible seating arrangements, collaborative workspaces, and interactive technology can contribute to a more dynamic and creative learning atmosphere.
- **Student-Centred Approaches:** Tailor instruction to students' interests and abilities, allowing them to take ownership of their learning. Providing choices and autonomy can fuel intrinsic motivation and creativity.
- **Cultivate a Growth Mindset:** Encourage students to view challenges as opportunities for growth rather than obstacles. Emphasize the importance of effort, perseverance, and learning from mistakes in the creative process.
- **Arts Integration:** Incorporate arts (visual arts, music, drama, etc.) into different subjects to stimulate creativity and enhance understanding. Creative expression through the arts can provide a unique outlet for students to convey their thoughts and ideas.
- **Global and Cultural Perspectives:** Explore diverse perspectives and cultures to broaden students' understanding of the world. Exposure to different ways of thinking can inspire creative thinking and innovative solutions.

In conclusion, pedagogic priorities encompassing innovative practices and exploring creativity have become increasingly essential in contemporary education. By adopting innovative teaching methods, such as active learning and incorporating technology, students are engaged in their learning process and equipped with the necessary skills to thrive in a rapidly evolving world. Simultaneously, exploring creativity through the integration of arts nurtures students' imagination and unleashes their potential for innovation, self-expression, and lifelong learning. As education continues to adapt to the changing needs of society, it is imperative to embrace these pedagogic priorities to ensure that students are prepared for the challenges and opportunities of the future.

REFLECTIVE TEACHING: CONCEPTS AND STRATEGIES FOR MAKING SOCIAL SCIENCE TEACHERS REFLECTIVE PRACTITIONERS

Reflective level of teaching is that teaching which is problem-centred in nature in which the learner is engaged. In an original imaginative and critical approach to the subject and does deep or serious kind of thinking. The learner examines facts and generalizations and seeks out a new one. Memory and understanding levels of the teaching of the content are the pre-requisite for this level of teaching. Reflective teaching is a process in which educators engage in thoughtful and intentional consideration of their teaching practices. It involves looking back on experiences, critically analysing them, and using the insights gained to inform future actions and decisions in the classroom. This reflective process is continuous and helps teachers grow personally and professionally. Here are some key aspects of reflective teaching:

- **Self-awareness:** Reflective teaching starts with self-awareness. Teachers need to be conscious of their beliefs, values, teaching methods, and the impact these factors have on their students.
- **Critical analysis:** Reflection involves critically analysing teaching methods, instructional strategies, and classroom management techniques. Teachers may consider what worked well, what didn't, and why.
- **Goal setting:** Reflection is not just about looking back; it's also about setting goals for improvement. Teachers can identify specific areas for growth and develop strategies to enhance their teaching.
- **Feedback:** Seeking and incorporating feedback from peers, students, and administrators is an essential part of reflective teaching. Constructive feedback provides different perspectives

that can contribute to a more comprehensive understanding of teaching practices.

- **Action research:** Some teachers engage in action research, a systematic inquiry into one's own teaching practice. This involves identifying a specific issue or question, collecting data, and using the findings to make informed decisions about instructional practices.
- **Professional development:** Reflection often leads to a commitment to ongoing professional development. Teachers may seek out workshops, conferences, or additional education to stay informed about new teaching strategies, technologies, and educational research.
- **Adaptability:** Reflective teachers are adaptable. They are open to change and willing to adjust their methods based on the needs of their students and the evolving educational landscape.
- **Collaboration:** Collaborating with colleagues can provide valuable insights. Discussing teaching practices, sharing experiences, and learning from others can contribute to the reflective process.

Developing reflection among prospective teachers call for developing a disposition, whereby, they are motivated for a change within. Pollard et al. (2005) have described that 'reflective teaching implies an active concern with aims and consequences as well as means and technical competence. The central objective of reflective teacher education is to develop reasoning among student teachers on why a particular teaching method should be employed and how they can improve their teaching to have positive impact on learners. This process of change can be encouraged and facilitated by teacher educators through various means. In order to promote reflection, the teacher educator should:

- Help student teacher to become aware of his/her learning needs.
- Offer student teachers multiple perspectives of issue under consideration;
- Facilitate student teachers in finding useful experiences;
- Help student teachers to reflect on these experiences in detail.

By reflecting on their past experiences, the trainee teachers may become conscious of their learning needs, and by formulating learning needs they often become aware of necessary learning situations. In our school experience programmes we have the provision of supervisor's feedback and post teaching discussion which is usually utilized as a routine affair providing little opportunity to trainee teachers for reflection and further improvement or either not utilized at all. Discussions with mentor or supervisor after practice teaching may be crucial source to enable trainee teachers reflect on their own experiences. Here technology could play important role and audio or video recording of at least few lessons of trainee teachers may serve as mirror of reflection for them. Such recording offers an opportunity to replay certain important events of classroom practice and facilitate trainee teacher to analyse problems and achievements of his/her classroom practice.

Promoting reflective practice among social science teachers is essential for their professional development and the improvement of teaching and learning in the classroom. Reflective practitioners are educators who actively engage in self-reflection, critically analyse their teaching practices, and seek ways to enhance their effectiveness. Here are some key concepts and strategies to foster reflective practice among social science teachers:

Concepts:

- **Critical Reflection:** Encourage teachers to engage in critical reflection, which involves questioning assumptions, examining beliefs, and considering alternative perspectives. Help teachers analyse their teaching practices in-depth, focusing on the why and how, rather than just the what.
- **Continuous Learning:** Emphasize that reflective practice is an ongoing, lifelong process. Learning and adapting should be continuous throughout a teacher's career. Encourage teachers to stay informed about current research, educational trends, and advancements in social science education.
- **Action Research:** Promote the use of action research, where teachers systematically investigate and reflect on their own teaching practices to improve student outcomes. Provide support and resources for teachers to conduct small-scale research projects within their classrooms.
- **Collaboration and Peer Observation:** Facilitate a culture of collaboration where teachers can share experiences, insights, and challenges with their peers. Encourage peer observation and feedback to promote a supportive and constructive professional community.
- **Student-Centred Approaches:** Advocate for student-centred teaching approaches that empower students to take an active role in their learning. Encourage teachers to reflect on how

their instructional methods align with the diverse needs of their students.

Strategies:

- **Journaling and Blogs:** One strategy for making teaching more reflective is keeping a reflective journal. This journal serves as a personal record of teaching experiences, reflections, and insights. It allows teachers to document their thoughts and feelings about various aspects of their teaching practice, such as lesson planning, classroom management, and student interactions. By reflecting on these experiences, teachers can identify patterns, strengths, and areas for growth. The journal also serves as a tool to track the effectiveness of teaching strategies and interventions, allowing for informed decision-making and future improvements.
- Have teachers maintain reflective journals or blogs to document their thoughts, experiences, and insights. Provide prompts or questions to guide their reflections, such as "What worked well in today's lesson? What could be improved?"
- **Professional Learning Communities (PLCs):** Establish PLCs where teachers can collaboratively discuss teaching strategies, share resources, and reflect on their classroom practices. Create a structured format for meetings that includes time for reflection and goal setting.
- **Workshops and Training:** Conduct workshops on reflective teaching practices, focusing on specific strategies and tools for self-reflection. Provide training on the use of technology tools that support reflection, such as video analysis of teaching.
- **Mentorship Programs:** Implement mentorship programs pairing experienced teachers with those new to the profession. Encourage mentor-mentee discussions focused on reflective practices and professional growth.
- **Feedback Mechanisms:** Establish formal feedback mechanisms, including peer evaluations, administrator observations, and student feedback. Emphasize constructive feedback that helps teachers identify strengths and areas for improvement.
- **Incorporate Professional Development Opportunities:** Support attendance at conferences, workshops, and seminars focused on social science education and reflective teaching practices. Encourage participation in online courses or webinars that promote continuous professional development.

- **Regular Self-Assessment:** Another strategy for reflective teaching is engaging in regular self-assessment. Teachers can utilize various assessment tools, such as surveys, questionnaires, or self-reflection worksheets, to assess their teaching practices. These assessments can focus on various aspects of teaching, including instructional strategies, classroom management techniques, and student engagement. The gathered data allows teachers to identify their strengths and weaknesses and make informed decisions regarding professional development and instructional modifications.
- **Discussions:** Discussion is the basic teaching tool where the teacher tries to create understanding by providing opportunity to student teachers for exchanging information, opinions, or experiences while working towards a common goal. The facilitator (teacher educator) observes and encourages group discussion without being directly involved. One of the approaches in discussion that is useful in developing reflective thinking among learners is Brainstorming which helps the trainee teachers to freely share their views and encourage uninhabited participation of learners.
- **Cooperative Learning:** Cooperative learning can improve individual's achievement more than the traditional approaches of instruction, if implemented effectively, which also ensures high learner motivation, active involvement and more time on various tasks. However, in order to be effective, it has to be well planned and systematically executed by the teacher. We cannot ensure learning just by dividing learners in various groups and assigning them some tasks to accomplish. There are very specific methods to ensure the success of group work. In cooperative group every learner has a specific task and everyone is involved in learning. The essential components of cooperation are positive interdependence, face-to-face interaction, individual and group accountability, interpersonal and small group skills and group processing.
- **Role Play:** The use of Role play as an educational or training technique is part of reflective teaching. The idea of role play in its simplest form is that of asking someone to imagine that they are either themselves or another person in a particular situation. They are then asked to behave exactly as they feel that persons would. As a result of doing this they, and rest of the participants learn something about the person or situation. Situations for role play may be simple or elaborate, familiar or strange. They may

be described in detail or left to the imagination of the role player. Participants in role play can be made to relive a particular work situation, so that they can get the real feel of the roles they are called upon to play. The experience enhances their knowledge and helps them understand the behaviour of others as well as their own emotions and feelings.

- **Peer observations**: Peer observations provide an excellent opportunity for teachers to reflect on their teaching practices. By inviting colleagues to observe their lessons and provide constructive feedback, educators can gain invaluable insights into their teaching methods. Peer observations encourage collaborative learning and foster a culture of continuous improvement. Teachers can reflect on the feedback received, identify areas for growth, and make adjustments accordingly. Furthermore, observing other teachers' practices can inspire new ideas and approaches that can be incorporated into one's own teaching.
- **Dialogue and Feedback:** Engaging with students through dialogue and feedback is another essential strategy for making teaching more reflective. By soliciting students' perspectives and valuing their opinions, teachers can understand the impact of their practices on student learning. Additionally, providing timely and constructive feedback to students promotes growth and reflection in their own learning processes. This reciprocal feedback loop between teachers and students cultivates a supportive and inclusive learning environment.

TEACHER EDUCATORS: ROLES AND RESPONSIBILITIES

Teacher educators play a crucial role in shaping the future of education by cultivating the knowledge, skills, and attitudes of future teachers. As professionals who guide aspiring educators through their training, teacher educators possess distinct roles and responsibilities in ensuring the development of competent and committed teachers. Their expertise not only encompasses subject matter knowledge but also pedagogical strategies, as well as a deep understanding of the complexities of the educational landscape. This essay explores the roles and responsibilities of teacher educators, shedding light on their essential contributions to the field of education. Teachers are a very important contributor and part of society. They have the responsibility of moulding the future generation. Apart from educating students and helping them achieve their goals, there are important **roles teachers** play in the lives of every student. Such as:

- **Counsellor:** Being able to counsel your students properly is one of the most important roles and responsibilities of a teacher. The role of teachers as counsellors comes naturally to most teachers. Most schools employ counsellors to deal with problems and non-academic issues that affect a student's academic development. However, a lot of teachers themselves volunteer as student counsellors. Typically, this is because students feel more at ease confiding in a teacher, they already like than the school counsellor. A class teacher spends a lot of time with kids in the classroom. Thus, they might be the first to notice an issue the student might be dealing with and need some help.
- **Facilitator:** In the entire teaching-learning process, there are many **roles and responsibilities of a teacher** that plays a crucial role. After all is said and done, the teacher is still the one who can make education the most valuable human endeavour. Being a facilitator to your students will help them give encouragement to those students who lack self-assurance, reassure those who are shy, not reject but divert an answer, aid in the search for solutions, and allow the opportunity to build on ideas and share personal experiences.
- **Collaborator:** In a collaborative learning strategy, two or more people work together to comprehend a shared learning topic and finish a shared assignment. To complete the goal, they rely on one other's resources, knowledge, and abilities. Joint accountability exists for obligations and mistakes if any. They work individually on various parameters while assessing one another's work to raise the calibre of the final product.
- **Delegator:** A teacher is a person who distributes the responsibilities among the students and overviews the functioning of the class. Teachers, as delegators, don't get too involved in the class. Rather they let the students have ownership of the tasks. Delegation is one of the major roles of a teacher. These types of roles and responsibilities of a teacher are best suitable for group activities and subjects that require teamwork.
- **Role as a Club Patron:** Beyond classroom teaching, some teachers volunteer to work as club sponsors. This is logical in certain cases as the course assignments of their teaching profession are a logical extension of the club. For instance, the fine arts teacher might be the best guide for an art exhibition, and the business teacher might be the right person to support students with their startup ideas. A

math class teacher will best guide the math team, and a science teacher will play an important role in the innovation club. Besides, students are already comfortable with their teachers. Hence, club activities will be fun for them.

- **A Resource:** Teachers are the biggest resources for students. Teachers are like a library to students. They are the resource for every information. The information passed by the teacher is very trusting for the students. For the students, the teacher is like a help to get them past the hurdles they face while studying, and this builds the trust of students in the teacher.

Responsibilities of a Teacher

The role of teachers in the classroom is extremely varied. She has to serve as a teacher, mentor, critic, counsellor, motivator, and sometimes a friend in the class room. The roles and responsibilities of a teacher can, however, go beyond the classroom. To foster the growth of a strong relationship with students or for other reasons, many teachers take responsibility outside the classroom.

- **Planning:** One of the biggest roles and responsibilities of a teacher is to plan and prepare lesson plans and prepare for their lectures, the study material, the activities, and everything that is important to be planned before the actual lecture is delivered in the classroom.
- **Assessing student progress and participation:** Not every student is so open to participating in every new thing or trying a new activity. This becomes one of the most important roles and responsibilities of teachers to encourage students to participate and try to explore every activity, learn new things, and understand what they like and dislike. Keeping track of your student's progress will help you provide them with proper guidance whenever needed.
- **Providing feedback:** The most effective teaching and learning technique is feedback. Feedback helps in providing proper instructions to students, thereby helping them to better their learning process. It helps in assisting them in understanding the subject they are studying. Giving and taking feedback on a regular basis helps both students and teachers to improve their performance every day.
- **Maintaining classroom discipline:** Having a disciplined classroom environment leads to positive outcomes. To make

your teaching more effective, it is important to have a disciplined classroom.

- **Responsibility for improving their teaching:** Each student has a particular personality and requirements of his own. Teachers have to constantly change their teaching methods to address their needs. Precisely adapting their teaching styles to meet each student's skills and shortcomings takes a lot of time and work. Effective teaching requires the use of instructional tactics.

PROFESSIONAL DEVELOPMENT OF SOCIAL SCIENCE TEACHER EDUCATORS

Professional development is the enrichment training provided to teachers over a period of time to promote their development in all aspects of content and pedagogy. Becoming an effective teacher is a continuous process that stretches from pre-service experiences to the end of the professional career. Professional development for teachers is more than training or classes as it functions as an agent for change in their classroom practices. The growth of a teacher's skill and understanding is developed through personal reflections, interaction with colleagues and mentoring which gives confidence by engaging them with their practices and reaffirming their experiences. It could have a positive impact on teachers' pedagogical content knowledge as many teachers feel challenged with teaching of curricular subjects due to lack of previous experience with hands-on activities, lack of content knowledge, lack of confidence and lack of interest to acquire there. Professional development plays a crucial role in enhancing the knowledge, skills, and expertise of social science teacher educators. As educators in the field of social sciences, it is essential for teacher educators to continuously learn and grow in order to effectively prepare future social science teachers. Let's explore the importance of professional development for social science teacher educators and discuss various strategies that can be adopted to promote their professional growth.

Firstly, professional development empowers social science teacher educators with the latest knowledge and research in the field. The realm of social sciences is constantly evolving, with new theories, methodologies, and resources being developed. By participating in professional development activities such as attending conferences, workshops, and seminars, teacher educators can stay updated with the latest trends and approaches in social science education. This allows them to provide their students with accurate and relevant information, ensuring effective teaching and learning experiences in the classroom.

Furthermore, professional development equips social science teacher educators with the necessary pedagogical skills to effectively teach and mentor future social science teachers. Teaching methods and strategies are constantly evolving, and it is essential for teacher educators to continuously refine their instructional techniques. By engaging in professional development activities, teacher educators can enhance their understanding of instructional methodologies, assessment techniques, and classroom management strategies. This enables them to adopt innovative and effective teaching practices in their own classrooms, as well as effectively guide and mentor aspiring social science teachers. Additionally, professional development provides social science teacher educators with opportunities for collaboration and networking. By attending professional development events, teacher educators can connect and interact with their peers from different institutions and regions. This exchange of ideas, experiences, and best practices provides valuable insights and perspectives, fostering a sense of community among teacher educators. Collaborative initiatives such as research projects, curriculum development, and lesson planning can be undertaken, strengthening the collective expertise and knowledge base of social science education.

Professional development is essential for social science teacher educators to ensure that they are providing their students with the best possible training. There are three key areas of professional development for social science teacher educators: understanding the learners, continuing education for teacher educators, and professional ethics.

- **Understanding the Learners (Teacher Educand):** Social science teacher educators need to have a deep understanding of the learners they are teaching. This includes understanding their prior knowledge, their learning styles, and their cultural backgrounds. Teacher educators need to be able to create learning experiences that are relevant and engaging for their students.
- **Continuing education for teacher educators**: Social science teacher educators need to continue their education throughout their careers. This includes keeping up-to-date with the latest research in social science education, as well as learning about new teaching methods and technologies. Teacher educators also need to be involved in professional organizations and networks, where they can share ideas and learn from others.
- **Professional ethics**: Social science teacher educators have a responsibility to act in an ethical manner. This includes being honest and fair in their dealings with students, colleagues, and

the public. Teacher educators also need to be aware of the ethical implications of their teaching, such as the potential for bias or discrimination.

The main objectives of initial professional preparation of teachers are as follows:

- To acquire knowledge and understanding of the instructional planning, preparation, transaction and evaluation.
- To apply the knowledge and understanding to the new and unfamiliar teaching situations.
- To develop proper interests, attitudes and values relating to teaching profession and procedures.
- To develop the abilities for effective classroom management.
- To acquaint with different approaches of teaching and communication techniques.

Major issues related to Initial Professional Preparation of Teachers are as follows:

- The curriculum taught at pre-service teacher education level is not appropriate for development of right attitude and skills among student - teachers required for teaching profession. Certain topics in some subjects are obsolete and have no relevance to present educational and social scenario. The curriculum should be activity-centred and integration of ICT should be introduced in it. The pre-service teacher education curriculum does not commensurate with the emerging needs of school curriculum and contemporary educational and social scenario.
- The school-based teaching activities are mostly dominated by traditional methods of teaching. The student-teachers mostly employ teacher dominant method for their classroom teaching during practice teaching.
- Lack of coordination between student-teachers/pre-service teacher training institutions and schools is also a major issue that needs to be addressed. This is mainly on the part of secondary teacher training institutions which do not make any contact with schools and school teachers during whole academic session to infuse the component of reality in teacher education course. It is therefore of much importance that coordination and linkage between schools and teacher training institutions be developed so that a component of reality can be induced into teacher training imparted by secondary teacher education institutions.

Professional development is crucial for social science teachers to enhance their effectiveness in the classroom and stay abreast of the latest educational trends. Here are some key aspects of professional development for social science teachers:

Understanding the Learner (Teacher Educand)

- **Pedagogical Strategies**: Stay updated on effective teaching methods and pedagogical strategies that cater to diverse learning styles within the social science classroom.
- **Cultural Competence**: Develop cultural competence to understand and connect with students from various backgrounds. This includes recognizing and valuing diverse perspectives in the teaching of social sciences.

Continuing Education for Teacher Educators:

- **Workshops and Seminars**: Attend workshops and seminars that focus on new developments in social science education, technology integration, and innovative teaching methods.
- **Advanced Degrees**: Pursue advanced degrees or certifications in social science education to deepen subject knowledge and pedagogical skills.
- **Online Learning**: Explore online courses and webinars to stay informed about the latest research, teaching methodologies, and technological advancements.

Professional Ethics:

- **Code of Conduct**: Familiarize oneself with the professional code of conduct and ethical guidelines for teachers. Understand the responsibilities and obligations associated with being a social science educator.
- **Reflective Practices**: Engage in reflective practices to assess one's teaching methods, ethical decisions, and overall professional conduct. Seek feedback from peers and supervisors.

Collaborative Learning Communities:

- **Professional Learning Communities (PLCs)**: Join or establish PLCs with fellow social science teachers to share experiences, resources, and best practices. Collaborative learning fosters a supportive professional environment.

- **Peer Observation**: Participate in peer observation programs to receive constructive feedback and observe effective teaching practices from colleagues.

Technology Integration:

- **Digital Literacy**: Enhance digital literacy skills to integrate technology into social science lessons effectively. Stay informed about educational apps, online resources, and interactive tools that can enhance the learning experience.
- **Blended Learning**: Explore blended learning approaches that combine traditional teaching methods with online resources, providing students with a more dynamic and engaging educational experience.

Research and Scholarship:

- **Stay Informed**: Keep up with current research in social science education and related fields. Subscribe to academic journals, attend conferences, and engage in scholarly discussions to stay informed about the latest theories and practices.
- **Action Research**: Engage in action research within the classroom, identifying areas for improvement, implementing changes, and assessing the impact on student learning.

In-Service Teacher Education Programmes

In-service teacher education refers to a recurrent, organized and need-based continuing education of teachers already on the job to update and enrich their professional competencies, strengthen their commitment and enhance their professional performance in the classroom as well as in the school and community. In-service teacher training programmes can be described as a process of learning whereby teachers who have completed a certain level of teacher training are provided with means of meeting their needs for further personal development in teaching. This implies that in their career, teachers need to go through some periodic study aimed at retaining them and enhancing their pedagogical and academic competencies. The objectives of in-service teacher education programmes are as follows:

- To make teachers aware of the new developments in the disciplines and the subject they teach.
- To help teachers know their problems and solve them by using the resources and wisdom.

- To enable the teachers, meet the requirements of changing educational and social contexts and concerns.
- To increase the level of motivation of teachers, develop self-confidence, promote the spirit of inquiry and help them to be committed and reflective teachers.
- To provide a support system to teachers in the areas of their deficiency.
- To provide a support system to teachers in the development of new skills in the areas of emerging trends.
- To upgrade the qualification of teachers who are either under-qualified or unqualified.
- To foster the desire for life-long learning and to empower teachers 'learning to learn' and 'learning to be'.
- To train teachers for contemporary thematic issues like MLL, joyful learning, meeting educational needs of the deprived, disadvantaged and disabled children, use of mass media in education, community participation in educational etc.
- Eliminating deficiencies in teachers' preparation, fulfil the gaps of pre- service education, remove its inadequacies and make it more realistic.
- To sensitize teachers with the educational problems of the neglected sectors.

Strategies for addressing the issues of Professional Development of Teachers

- Development of a network among institutions and individuals of SCERTs/SIEs, IASEs and CTEs and University Education Departments.
- Organization of workshops for content and pedagogy enrichment.
- Developing training capacity for action research projects and ICT applications.
- Development of a set of indicators and benchmarks to track in-service professional development of teachers and the institutions which organize them.
- Development of short-term courses for continuous professional development and upload them on their websites.
- Devise open and distance learning (ODL) strategies for professional development of the teacher.

TEACHER EDUCATOR AS A TECHNO PEDAGOGUE

A Techno- Pedagogue is a person who focuses on the user of technology and whose expertise is in electronic pedagogy methods and theory. A techno pedagogue is not a systems administrator. Education system is now witnessing a paradigm shift from traditional chalk-board teaching methodology to digitalizing pedagogical approach through technical devices. So, teachers have to change their pedagogy. Teachers should give up mechanical approach and make teaching interesting by integrating technology to pedagogy. This transformation not only increase the capability of teachers but also widen the knowledge base of students so as to make them competitive in the international arena.

The techno pedagogue is a person who can see the practical uses and appropriate uses of technology to attain their educational goals. This person's expertise is grounded in educational theory curriculum development and course design. This person stays abreast of new developments in technology and helps to flitter new information to other teachers in a manner that can be understood by the less techno savvy. The techno pedagogue also designs, model courses that use technology. Techno pedagogy is a type of bilingualism one foot in pedagogy and the other in technology and all its potential. A techno pedagogue can oversee the design, production and even implementation of online environments, interfaces and tools that supports learning on diverse processes. Needs, assessment and technical specifications are both part of the techno pedagogue daily work. This bridge is part of the new reality of digital society, the capacity to maximise the potential of technological tools to meet needs that are lest we forget always human. Techno pedagogy refers to the united potential of technology to transform individual and organisational practices. It is rich and nuanced conversation between the technological possibilities.

The TPACK Framework

TPACK is a framework to understand and describe the kinds of knowledge needed by a teacher for effective pedagogical practice in a technology enhanced learning environment. The idea of pedagogical content knowledge (PCK) was first described by Lee Shulman (Shulman 1986) and TPACK builds on those core ideas through the inclusion of technology.

The TPACK framework argues that effective technology integration for teaching specific content or subject matter requires understanding and negotiating the relationships between these three components: Technology, Pedagogy, and Content. A teacher capable of negotiating these relationships represents a form of expertise different from, and (perhaps) broader than, the knowledge of a disciplinary expert (say a scientist or a musician or sociologist), a technology expert (a computer engineer) or an expert at teaching/pedagogy (an experienced educator). The TPACK framework highlights complex relationships that exist between content, pedagogy and technology knowledge areas and may be a useful organizational structure for defining what it is that teachers need to know to integrate technology effectively (Archambault & Crippen, 2009).

TPACK consists of 7 different knowledge areas:

- Content Knowledge (CK),
- Pedagogical Knowledge (PK),
- Technology Knowledge (TK),
- Pedagogical Content Knowledge (PCK),
- Technological Content Knowledge (TCK),
- Technological Pedagogical Knowledge (TPK), and
- Technological Pedagogical Content Knowledge (TPCK).

Teaching with technology is complicated further considering the challenges. In our work, the word technology applies equally to Analogue and digital, as well as new and old, technologies. As a matter of practical significance, however, most of the technologies under consideration in current literature are newer and digital and have some inherent properties that make applying them in straightforward ways difficult. At the heart of good teaching with technology are three core components: content, pedagogy, and technology, plus the relationships among and between them. The interactions between and among the three components, playing out differently across diverse contexts, account for the wide variations seen in the extent and quality of educational technology integration. These three knowledge bases (content, pedagogy, and technology) form the core of the technology, pedagogy, and content knowledge (TPACK) framework.

Techno Pedagogic Domains

- Lifelong learning – techno pedagogue should be a lifelong learner updating with all new technologies
- Collaborative working methods - online tools facilitate sharing between techno pedagogues.
- Participatory sharing - encourages and facilitate sharing of content while respecting the creators.
- Social networking - connect people on common base.

In the era of rapid technological advancements, educators need to adapt to the changing landscape of education and embrace technology as a powerful pedagogical tool. Teacher educators, who play a pivotal role in preparing future teachers, must themselves become techno - pedagogues – instructors who effectively integrate technology into their teaching practices. This essay explores the importance of teacher educators embracing technology, highlighting their role in fostering student engagement, implementing innovative teaching approaches, and facilitating lifelong learning.

Engaging 21st Century Learners

To effectively engage 21st-century learners, teacher educators must leverage technology to create dynamic and interactive learning environments. Utilizing multimedia tools, such as videos, simulations, and interactive presentation software, not only captures students' attention but also facilitates content retention and understanding. By employing technology, teacher educators can bridge the digital divide and reach diverse learners, enhancing inclusivity and accessibility of their instruction.

Implementing innovative teaching approaches

Techno-pedagogues employ innovative instructional strategies that leverage technology to enhance student learning. By embracing digital platforms, such as learning management systems, virtual classrooms, and online collaborative tools, teacher educators can foster active learning and enable personalized instruction. The integration of online discussions, forums, and social media platforms further fosters engagement and knowledge sharing among students, promoting critical thinking and collaborative problem-solving.

Facilitating lifelong learning

In an ever-evolving world, teacher educators must equip their students with the necessary skills to become lifelong learners. Technology can facilitate this process by providing access to vast repositories of information, enabling students to conduct independent research, and encouraging self-directed learning. Teacher educators themselves must model effective use of technology as a means to staying abreast of current research and professional development opportunities, inspiring their students to follow suit.

Addressing challenges and ethical considerations

While integrating technology offers numerous benefits, teacher educators also face challenges and ethical considerations. It is crucial for them to address issues such as privacy, digital citizenship, and the responsible use of technology to ensure a safe and inclusive learning environment. Additionally, technological advancements may require teacher educators to continuously update their own skills and knowledge to effectively navigate the ever-changing technological landscape.

Fostering teacher candidates' technological proficiency

To equip future teachers with the necessary skills, teacher educators must provide training and mentorship in educational technology tools and strategies. By doing so, teacher educators empower their candidates to effectively integrate technology into their own teaching practices, preparing them for the demands of modern classrooms. This proficiency ensures that teacher candidates are capable of designing and implementing technology-enhanced lessons that cater to diverse learners' needs.

Promoting creativity and innovation

Technology opens new avenues for creativity and innovation in teaching and learning. Teacher educators often serve as role models, demonstrating how technology can be leveraged to design engaging and innovative instructional materials and assessments. Encouraging teacher candidates to embrace emerging technologies, such as virtual reality and augmented reality, fosters creative problem-solving and enhances student engagement by enabling immersive and interactive learning experiences.

Collaboration and global connections

Techno-pedagogues recognize the importance of fostering collaboration among teacher candidates, enabling them to establish global connections and engage in cross-cultural exchanges. Through online platforms, teacher educators can facilitate collaborations with educators from different geographic regions, offering valuable opportunities for sharing experiences, best practices, and diverse perspectives. Such interactions cultivate a global mindset and empower future teachers to prepare their students to thrive in a globalized world.

Evaluation and assessment

Technology allows for innovative assessment practices that provide timely and meaningful feedback to both teacher candidates and teacher educators. Through learning analytics, digital portfolios, and online quizzes, teacher educators can monitor student progress and identify areas for improvement more efficiently. Additionally, teacher educators can leverage technology to conduct formative and summative assessments that align with current educational standards, ensuring the accountability of teacher education programs.

In short, teacher educators must embrace the role of a techno-pedagogue to effectively prepare future teachers for the demands of the 21st century classroom. By harnessing technology, teacher educators can engage learners, foster innovation, and facilitate lifelong learning. The integration of technology into teacher education promotes creativity, collaboration, and global connections, while also addressing the challenges and ethical considerations that arise. Ultimately, the techno-pedagogical approach empowers teacher candidates to become effective educators equipped with the skills and knowledge necessary to navigate the evolving landscape of education.

TEACHER EDUCATOR AS A CURRICULUM DESIGNER

In the rapidly evolving world of education, teachers are no longer just transmitters of knowledge but rather serve as vital architects of curriculum design. With learners becoming more diverse and educational needs expanding beyond traditional boundaries, educators must possess the skills to design and deliver high-quality instruction. This section explores the role of teachers as curriculum designers, focusing on their intelligence and comprehension in meeting the demands of a graduate school-level student. A teacher educator who also serves as a curriculum designer plays a crucial role in shaping the education and professional development of future teachers. The responsibilities and tasks involved in this role can be diverse, but generally, it involves designing, implementing, and revising educational programs and materials to ensure that they effectively prepare teachers for their roles. The role of a teacher in curriculum design is crucial, as teachers are at the forefront of implementing and delivering educational content. While curriculum design is often a collaborative effort involving education experts, administrators, and policymakers, teachers play a central role in shaping and refining the curriculum to meet the needs of their students.

Key Aspects of a Teacher's Role in Curriculum Design

- **Understanding Student Needs:** Teachers have a deep understanding of their students' abilities, learning styles, and interests. They can provide valuable insights into what works best for their particular group of students.

- **Alignment with Educational Goals:** Teachers ensure that the curriculum aligns with broader educational goals and standards. They bridge the gap between theoretical curriculum design and the practical needs of the classroom.
- **Adaptation for Diverse Learners:** Teachers consider the diverse needs of their students, including different learning styles, abilities, and backgrounds. They may suggest modifications or accommodations to make the curriculum accessible to all learners.
- **Feedback and Evaluation:** Teachers provide feedback on the effectiveness of the curriculum based on their classroom experiences. They can identify areas that need improvement, suggest changes, and share success stories that can inform future revisions.
- **Integration of Real-World Context:** Teachers bring real-world context into the curriculum, making it more relevant and engaging for students. They can connect academic content to practical applications, fostering a deeper understanding of the subject matter.
- **Incorporating Technology:** Teachers, being on the frontline of educational technology use, can provide insights into how technology can be integrated into the curriculum to enhance learning experiences.
- **Flexibility and Adaptability:** Teachers understand the dynamic nature of the classroom environment. They contribute to designing a curriculum that is flexible and adaptable to changing needs, allowing for adjustments based on student progress and feedback.
- **Professional Development:** Teachers may be involved in their own professional development to stay updated on educational trends, methodologies, and best practices. This knowledge can inform curriculum design decisions.
- **Assessment Strategies:** Teachers play a role in designing assessment methods that align with the curriculum. They can provide input on the types of assessments that accurately measure student understanding and progress.
- **Continuous Improvement:** Teachers contribute to the ongoing improvement of the curriculum by participating in reflection sessions, collaborating with colleagues, and staying informed about educational research and innovations.
- **Planning:** Teachers know their students' needs better than others involved in the curriculum process. While state or federal standards

often dictate the skills covered by the curriculum, a teacher can provide insight into the types of materials, activities and specific skills that need to be included. Teachers from multiple grade-levels may collaborate to identify skills students need at each level and ensure that the curriculum adequately prepares students to advance to the next grade-level and to meet the standards.

- **Creation:** Because teachers must use the curriculum, they should have input in its creation. A teacher can gauge whether an activity will fit into a specified time frame and whether it will engage students. If multiple teachers will use the curriculum, allow as many of them as possible to provide input during the creation stage. As teachers provide input, they will gain ownership in the final product and feel more confident that the curriculum was created with their concerns and the needs of their particular students in mind.
- **Implementation:** Teachers must implement the curriculum in their own classrooms, sticking to the plan that has taken so much time, careful planning and effort to create. When a teacher fails to properly implement a strong curriculum, she risks not covering standards or failing to implement effective practices in the classroom. That does not mean a teacher cannot make minor changes. In fact, a strong curriculum is designed to allow a teacher to be flexible and to insert a few personalized components or choose from among a selection of activities.
- **Reflection:** Reflecting on a curriculum allows teachers and others involved in the process to find any weaknesses in the curriculum and attempt to make it better. Teachers reflect on curriculum in multiple ways, such as keeping a journal as they implement the curriculum, giving students surveys and reviewing the results or analysing assessment data and individual student performance. Not only can reflection serve to improve a specific curriculum, it may guide the creation of new curriculum.
- **Understanding the Complexities of Curriculum Design:** Teachers as curriculum designers must possess a deep understanding of the complexities associated with developing a comprehensive curriculum. They must intricately comprehend the relationship between key content areas, educational objectives, and pedagogical strategies. Mastery of subject matter enables them to identify essential knowledge, skills, and competencies, shaping learning experiences to foster intellectual growth.

- **Creating Engaging and Relevant Learning Experiences**: Intelligence in curriculum design involves designing lessons that engage students in a meaningful and relevant manner. By incorporating real-world scenarios, hands-on activities, and technological advancements, teachers can cater to the diverse learning styles and abilities of graduate school students. This comprehension ensures that the curriculum remains current and applicable in a rapidly changing society.
- **Personalized Learning Approaches**: Understanding the unique needs and abilities of learners is a crucial aspect of curriculum design. Higher education students often possess varying levels of prior knowledge and skills, requiring teachers to tailor their instruction to accommodate individual differences. By offering differentiated activities, assessments, and resources, teachers promote personalized learning experiences that optimize student growth.
- **Cultivating Critical Thinking and Problem-Solving Skills**: Curriculum designers with advanced comprehension methods employ teaching strategies that foster critical thinking and problem-solving skills among graduate school students. By integrating inquiry-based learning, project-based assessments, and collaborative activities, educators encourage students to think critically, analyse information, and make informed decisions. This intelligence facilitates the development of well-rounded individuals equipped to tackle complex challenges.
- **Nurturing Creativity and Innovation**: Teachers as curriculum designers must also possess the comprehension to foster creativity and innovation among students. By incorporating open-ended tasks, interdisciplinary projects, and autonomy in the learning process, educators can inspire and stimulate graduate school-level learners to think outside the box. Harnessing their intelligence to create an innovative learning environment nurtures inventiveness and imagination.
- **Incorporating Technology-Enhanced Learning**: An intelligent curriculum designer efficiently comprehends the power of technology as an educational tool. By integrating innovative digital resources, virtual learning platforms, and blended learning approaches, teachers can harness technology's potential to provide rich, interactive learning experiences. Such implementation facilitates engagement, collaboration, and information processing among graduate school students.

- **Emphasizing Authentic and Lifelong Learning:** An advanced comprehension of curriculum design empowers teachers to emphasize authentic and lifelong learning experiences. By integrating real-world applications, problem-based scenarios, and experiential learning opportunities, educators nurture graduate school students' ability to transfer knowledge to practical settings. This approach cultivates a passion for continuous learning beyond the classroom walls.
- **Collaboration with Stakeholders:** Intelligence in curriculum design extends beyond the teacher's professional expertise. Effective curriculum designers understand the importance of collaborating with stakeholders such as administrators, fellow educators, parents, and industry professionals. In involving all stakeholders, teachers can gather insights, perspectives, and expertise necessary to create a holistic and relevant curriculum for graduate school students.

In short, the role of teachers as curriculum designers plays an integral part in shaping the education landscape. Through intelligence and comprehension, educators can design curricula that foster critical thinking, creativity, personalized learning, and lifelong learning. By embracing the evolving educational landscape and adequately responding to the needs of graduate school students, teachers can truly prepare them for success in the 21st century society.

TEACHER EDUCATOR AS A RESEARCHER: DEVELOPMENT OF RESEARCH POTENTIAL

In recent years, the role of teacher educators has evolved significantly, giving rise to increased attention towards the development of educational research. As primary agents of change within the education system, teacher educators are increasingly encouraged to engage in research to enhance their own professional growth and positively impact the field of education. This essay explores the notion of teacher educator as a researcher, highlighting the importance of developing research skills and knowledge within the graduate school student population.

Traditionally, teacher educators have been seen primarily as facilitators of learning, preparing aspiring teachers to effectively manage classrooms and deliver quality instruction. However, there has been a paradigm shift that emphasizes the importance of teacher educators as researchers. These individuals are expected to engage in scholarly inquiry in order to contribute to the knowledge base of the teaching profession. The involvement of teacher educators in research offers numerous benefits. Firstly, it enables them to stay up-to-date with current educational trends and advancements. By continually engaging in research, teacher educators can ensure that their knowledge and expertise remain relevant and applicable to the evolving needs of students and the education system. Moreover, research allows teacher educators to critically evaluate their own teaching practices and implement evidence-based strategies that enhance student learning outcomes.

While the development of research skills is crucial, teacher educators often face various challenges when transitioning into the role of a researcher. These challenges can include inadequate support systems, limited time for research, and a lack of familiarity with research processes. Addressing these challenges requires a collaborative effort between graduate school programs, educational institutions, and policymakers to provide the necessary resources and support structures for teacher educators to thrive as researchers. In order to cultivate a strong research culture among teacher educators, it is crucial to provide ongoing professional development opportunities. These opportunities allow teacher educators to continually refine their research practices and expand their research interests. Research-based professional development programs can also foster collaborations and networking among teacher educators, enhancing the exchange of ideas and promoting a culture of research within the education community.

Research-informed teaching is the cornerstone of effective instruction. Teacher educators who engage in research are better equipped to translate their findings into actionable classroom strategies. By leveraging evidence-based practices, teacher educators can effectively address the diverse needs of their students and promote inclusive and equitable education. Research-informed teaching also encourages an iterative and reflective approach to pedagogy, leading to continuous growth and innovation within the field of education. Being a teacher educator as a researcher involves engaging in systematic inquiry to enhance educational practices, contribute to the scholarship of teaching and learning, and foster professional development. Developing research potential in this context entails a combination of knowledge, skills, and dispositions. Here are some key aspects to consider:

- **Stay Informed:** Keep abreast of current educational research, trends, and innovations. Subscribe to journals, attend conferences, and participate in professional development opportunities.
- **Continuous Learning:** Develop a habit of continuous learning. Stay curious and open-minded about new theories, methodologies, and technologies relevant to education.

- **Network and Collaboration:** Collaborate with other teacher educators and researchers. Establishing professional networks can provide support, mentorship, and opportunities for collaborative research projects.
- **Identify Research Questions:** Identify pressing questions or challenges in teacher education. Develop research questions that align with your interests and have the potential to contribute to the field.
- **Research Design and Methodology:** Acquire skills in research design and methodology. Understand different research paradigms, data collection methods, and statistical analyses to choose the most appropriate for your research questions.
- **Ethical Considerations:** Familiarize yourself with ethical guidelines in educational research. Ensure that your research respects the rights and well-being of participants, and adhere to ethical standards.
- **Grant Writing:** Develop skills in writing research proposals and applying for grants. Funding opportunities can support your research initiatives and provide resources for data collection, analysis, and dissemination.
- **Dissemination:** Share your research findings through publications, presentations, and workshops. Disseminating your work contributes to the broader knowledge base and enhances your visibility in the academic community.
- **Reflective Practice:** Engage in reflective practice. Regularly assess and reflect on your teaching and research practices, identifying areas for improvement and growth.
- **Mentorship:** Seek mentorship from experienced researchers in the field of education. Learning from their experiences and guidance can be invaluable in developing your own research potential.
- **Utilize Technology:** Stay updated on technological tools that can enhance your research, such as data analysis software, online survey platforms, and collaborative writing tools.
- **Contribute to Policy and Practice:** Consider how your research can inform educational policies and practices. Engage with policymakers and practitioners to bridge the gap between research and application.
- **Contributing to Educational Knowledge:** Conducting research allows teacher educators to contribute to the body of knowledge

in education. By investigating various aspects of teaching and learning, they can generate new insights, theories, and practical applications.

- **Staying Informed about Current Trends:** Engaging in research helps teacher educators stay informed about the latest trends, methodologies, and innovations in education. This knowledge can be directly applied to teacher training programs, ensuring that educators are well-prepared to meet the evolving needs of students.
- **Promoting Evidence-Based Practices:** Teacher educators, as researchers, have the opportunity to promote evidence-based practices in education. By conducting rigorous research studies, they can identify effective teaching strategies and methods, helping to bridge the gap between educational theory and practice.
- **Modelling Research Skills for Future Educators:** Teacher educators serve as role models for aspiring teachers. By actively engaging in research, they demonstrate the importance of being lifelong learners and the value of integrating research skills into teaching practices. This modelling can inspire future educators to adopt a reflective and evidence-based approach to their own teaching.
- **Informing Policy and Practice:** Research conducted by teacher educators can have a direct impact on educational policies and practices. By disseminating their findings, they contribute valuable information that can influence decision-makers at the school, district, and even national levels.
- **Enhancing Pedagogical Content Knowledge:** Through research, teacher educators deepen their own understanding of pedagogical content knowledge. This enhanced knowledge can inform the development of teacher training programs, ensuring that pre-service and in-service teachers receive the most relevant and effective instructional strategies.
- **Fostering a Culture of Inquiry:** Teacher educators can foster a culture of inquiry within their institutions. By promoting research as a key component of professional development, they encourage both faculty and students to engage in critical thinking, question assumptions, and seek evidence to inform their teaching practices.
- **Addressing Educational Challenges:** Researchers in education have the opportunity to address and provide solutions to pressing educational challenges. Teacher educators can focus their research

on areas such as student achievement gaps, inclusive education, technology integration, and other issues that impact the quality of education.

In short, the role of teacher educators as researchers holds immense potential for transforming the education landscape. By developing research skills and knowledge, graduate school students can become effective agents of change, contributing to the knowledge base of education and improving student outcomes. The challenges faced by teacher educators as researchers can be overcome through collaborative efforts, emphasizing the importance of ongoing professional development and robust support systems. Ultimately, research-informed teaching allows teacher educators to maintain relevance, promote evidence-based practices, and drive positive change in the field of education.

CONCLUSION

In conclusion, Unit five has delved into the multifaceted role of a Social Science Teacher Educator, addressing various dimensions that contribute to the effective preparation and professional development of future educators. The exploration of pedagogic priorities, such as innovative practices and the cultivation of creativity, sets the stage for engaging and dynamic teaching methods. The emphasis on reflective teaching introduces essential concepts and strategies, fostering a culture of continuous improvement among Social Science teachers. By elucidating the roles and responsibilities of Teacher Educators, the unit underscores the significance of their impact on shaping the next generation of educators. The focus on professional development, including understanding the teacher educand, continuing education, and professional ethics, emphasizes the holistic growth of Teacher Educators. Furthermore, the unit highlights the evolving roles of Teacher Educators as techno-pedagogues, curriculum designers, and researchers, reflecting the dynamic nature of the field. Overall, Unit five serves as a comprehensive guide for Social Science Teacher Educators, equipping them with the knowledge and skills needed to navigate the complex and evolving landscape of teacher education.

UNIT - 6

ASSESSMENT IN SOCIAL SCIENCE EDUCATION

INTRODUCTION

In the realm of social science education, assessment serves as a pivotal component in gauging student learning, understanding, and application of knowledge. As we delve into the final chapter of our book, "Advanced Methodology and Pedagogical Practices of Social Science Education," we embark on a comprehensive exploration of assessment strategies, methodologies, and principles that play a fundamental role in shaping effective teaching and learning experiences. Assessment in social science education encompasses a diverse array of techniques, ranging from traditional examinations to innovative classroom assessment techniques (CATs), portfolios, rubrics, self-reflection, and peer evaluation. Each of these methods offers unique insights into students' comprehension, critical thinking abilities, and application of social science concepts in real-world contexts. Moreover, this chapter delves into the principles of grading, shedding light on the complexities surrounding grade inflation and the importance of maintaining fairness, consistency, and rigor in evaluating student performance. We examine how grading practices align with educational objectives, ensuring that assessment measures accurately reflect students' mastery of social science content and skills. Furthermore, the assessment of student performance extends beyond mere academic achievement to encompass internal evaluation, student progression, quality, innovation, leadership, internship experiences, and community involvement. We explore how these multifaceted dimensions contribute to a holistic understanding of students' growth and development within the social science discipline. Additionally, this chapter delves into the role of examinations as a feedback mechanism, considering the efficacy of open-book examinations and online tests in providing meaningful insights into students' comprehension and analytical abilities. By embracing innovative assessment methodologies, educators can leverage technology and pedagogical advancements to enhance the assessment process and promote deeper learning outcomes. In essence, this final chapter serves as a comprehensive guide to designing, implementing, and evaluating assessment practices in social science education. Through a nuanced exploration of assessment strategies and principles, educators can cultivate a dynamic learning environment that empowers students to thrive as critical thinkers, problem solvers, and engaged citizens in an ever-evolving global society.

DESIGNING LEARNER EVALUATION

Evaluation is the process of determining whether the designed instruction meets it's intended goals. Evaluation helps us to determine whether learners can transfer the skills and knowledge learned back into long-term changes in behaviour and skills required for the target context Evaluation sits at the centre of the instructional design model. It provides feedback to all other stages of the design process to continually inform and improve our instructional designs. Evaluation ensures that the instruction being designed both meets the identified need for instruction and is effective in achieving the intended learning outcomes for participants. Evaluation ensures that the instruction being designed both meets the identified need for instruction and is effective in achieving the intended learning outcomes for participants.

CLASSROOM ASSESSMENT TECHNIQUES

"Classroom Assessment" is a formative rather than a summative approach to assessment. Its purpose is to improve the quality of student learning, not to provide evidence for evaluating or grading students. It provides faculty with feedback about their effectiveness as teachers, and it gives students a measure of their progress as learners. The aim of classroom assessments is to provide faculty with information on what, how much, and how well students are learning. Classroom Assessment Techniques (CATs) are flexible and can be both speedy and anonymous for students (although they need not be).

Benefits to Faculty: Classroom Assessment helps faculty to focus on student learning. By determining what students have learned and what is unclear, instructors can focus the class more effectively to meet the learning needs of that group. This may mean reviewing some areas, or spending less time in other areas. Unlike student evaluation surveys [summative evaluation] which are typically given at the end of the semester, Classroom Assessment provides an on-going formative evaluation. The instructor can find out what can be changed immediately to help students to learn.

Benefits to Students: Students may be hesitant to ask questions during class. Classroom Assessments give students opportunities to provide anonymous feedback to their instructor about their learning. Students often discover, as the instructor reviews the feedback, that others in the class had similar questions. Classroom assessment activities can themselves be positive learning activities for students; they can be developed both to promote (and not just measure) writing skills or critical thinking skills, and to increase student motivation and their learning more seriously. In addition, students may become more involved in their learning when they find that others in the class learned some interesting things that they had not picked up from the class session. Through greater involvement, students are likely to become more self-directed learners, and may be more motivated to successfully complete the class.

Objectives in classroom assessment techniques: The purpose of classroom assessment is both formative during instruction, to improve student learning, and summative, documenting student proficiency at the end of an instructional unit. Recent research on student learning and motivation has clear implications for implementing effective classroom assessment.

PORTFOLIO

Portfolio is a purposeful collection of student's work that exhibits the student's efforts, progress and achievement in one or more areas. The collection must include student participation in selecting contents, the criteria for selection, the criteria for judging merit and evidence of student self-reflection. It is a collection of student work compiled over time to showcase a learner's progress, skills, and achievements. This can include project work samples, finished assignments, case studies, and self-reflections. Student portfolios can be digital or physical and tailored to specific subjects or projects. portfolio can also mean a collection of drawings or photographs, typically bound in book form, or in a folder.

Why use portfolio?

- It produces an accurate holistic of the student
- It involves student in decision about the choice of the inclusion and quality of work completed

- It allows students to exhibit differences
- It keeps recodes that accompany children from one year level to the next
- It provides means for evaluating programme effectiveness

Scope of Portfolio Assessment in Student's Performance

- It helps the teacher to assess the progress of a student over a period of time.
- It enables the teacher to determine the efficiency of the teaching method.
- It enables the teacher to develop a connection with the parents of the learners.
- It also helps teachers to identify the weak points in the teaching learning process.
- It also helps the teacher to evaluate the education program.

Uses of Portfolio Assessment in Student's Performance

- It can present the learners with a wide perspective and enables them to receive continuous feedback
- Students can also gain self-assessment for their academic learning and review their progress.
- Students can gain visual proofs about their interests, skills, and strengths.
- It also helps learners to develop strong qualities such as critical thinking and self- assessment.
- Teachers can also become reflective practitioners and more self-directed.

Types of Portfolios

- **Assessment Portfolios:** If you're trying to wow someone, then an assessment portfolio is perfect for you. This type of portfolio displays products or works that need to be judged. Professionals can use these portfolios to win over clients, and students can use them to present materials that will eventually be graded.
- **Showcase (Presentation) Portfolios:** Think about a showcase at a museum. The best items are on display and may be even put under a spotlight. A showcase portfolio works the same way, showing off your finest work in one place. This portfolio should contain samples, products, and assignments that make you look amazing.

- **Process (Learning) Portfolios:** It's not like your work is magically put together by elves. There's a process to get from start to finish. The mistakes that occurred along the way, prototypes, and initial drafts can all be seen in a process portfolio.
- **Development Portfolios:** A development portfolio can be thought of as a timeline that shows where you started to where you've come. It's meant to demonstrate growth, whether it's in terms of your business, your art, or any other body of work.
- **Working Portfolios:** Let's say you're not quite done with your project. In that case, a working portfolio is right for you. This is a display of a "work in progress," which means there should be space left at the end for the finished product.
- **Product Portfolios:** A product portfolio has physical samples of a product. This type of portfolio is typically used by businesses so they can show off their best goods at trade shows, expos, and conventions.
- **Hybrid Portfolios:** As the name suggests, a hybrid portfolio is a combination of a few different types of portfolios. This type of portfolio will take up a lot of space, so make sure to carry it in a bigger carrying case, or if it's digital, on a large USB flash drive.

RUBRICS

A rubric is a scoring tool that teachers use to assess student learning after a lesson, using a set of criteria and standard. Rubric is a document that articulates the expectations for an assignment by listing the criteria and describing level of quality from excellent to poor.

Types of Rubrics

The main purpose of a rubric is its ability to assess student's performance or work. Rubrics can be tailored to each assignment or to the course to better assess the learning objectives. Two types of rubrics discussed as under:

Analytic Rubrics

An analytic rubric is a tool for grading that has a variety of subsections and levels of quality. Analytic rubrics usually use a grid format to communicate grading requirements. Analytic rubrics can communicate expectations and feedback clearly to students. Instead of wondering why they were placed on a single level, students can see where they scored in various areas. The multi-topic scoring process also allows for more specific and fair grades since students are scored based on their performance in each area instead of finding themselves placed in one overall section based on fewer criteria. Analytic rubrics can also shorten grading time for complex assignments, including essays and longer projects. Analytic rubrics do take a significant time to develop, however, and rubrics that use confusing or obscure descriptions will be of little help to both instructors and students in determining a reasonable grade or recognizing what might have been done differently for a better score.

Advantages of Analytic Rubrics: It help students understand the expectations and standards of the writing task, and guide them through the writing process. Second, they can help teachers provide specific and constructive feedback to students, and pinpoint areas for improvement.

Drawbacks of Analytic Rubrics: Takes more time to create and use than a holistic rubric. And unless each point for each criterion is well-defined ratters may not arrive at the same score

Holistic Rubrics

A holistic rubric is a simple guide for giving feedback, usually with a scale of 1 to 4 or 1 to 5 and only one description per level. Holistic rubrics can assess skills and behaviours. Holistic rubrics are useful when teachers are scoring simple skills or behaviours that do not have many components. Feedback is a simple process wherein an instructor only has to select one description that best fits the student's work, and students generally have an easy time understanding the category in which they were placed. However, holistic rubrics should be avoided in instances where teachers would like to determine a student's scores based on various requirements. Holistic rubrics also limit the depth of a teacher's feedback since students might be left wondering which specific elements they fulfilled and which were lacking. Holistic rubrics work best for skills and behaviours; major projects, essays, or assignments with many components should use an alternative rubric type.

Advantages of holistic rubrics: Emphasis on what the learner is able to demonstrate, rather than what s/he cannot do. Saves time by minimizing the number of decisions raters make. Can be applied consistently by trained raters increasing reliability.

Disadvantages of holistic rubrics

Does not provide specific feedback for improvement. When student work is at varying levels spanning the criteria points it can be difficult to select the single best description. Criteria cannot be weighted.

Advantages and Disadvantages in Rubrics

Advantages	Disadvantages
Rubrics encourages learners to develop critical thinking about their own scores and work.	Rubric scale has various different options due to which it may be a little difficult to use it.
Rubrics can also help in producing more insightful learners by developing the meta-cognition.	The language of rubrics is not as clear as it is supposed to be.
It helps teachers to make better decisions due to its focus on "criterion- referenced rather than norm-referenced" scoring.	The lower scale may use negative terms to describe student performance which may discourage the learners.
Rubrics makes the learning goal clearer to learners enabling increased fair treatment for learners.	Each level should also be more measurable and observable.
It decreases the chances of student preference by teachers.	There is a need for more detailed specification.

SELF REFLECTION

Self-reflection is an essential skill for personal growth. Without it, we walk around unconscious and often reactive to others and even our own selves. Self-assessment and self-reflection involve students reviewing their work and reflecting on their learning progress. This helps students participate in and take ownership of their own learning.

Types of self-reflection

Two main types of reflection are often referred to – reflection-in-action and reflection-on-action. The most obvious difference is in terms of *when* they happen.

Reflection-in-action: This is the reflection that takes place whilst you are involved in the situation, often a patient interaction. Reflection-in-action involves using analysis of observation, listening and/or touch or 'feel' to problem solve. It therefore sounds a lot like clinical reasoning – where reflection differs is that the problem-solving leads to a change in the practitioner's view of self, values and beliefs. It is like 'thinking on your feet' but the focus is on gaining a new perspective, rather than just solving the problem. Because it is happening on the spot, this type of reflection often appears very intuitive. It can take some time to develop the skills of reflection-in-action – it often is a skill associated with the development of expert practice.

Reflection-on-action: This type of reflection involves a stepping back from the situation, meaning that it happens at some time after the situation has occurred. Therefore, it demands a time commitment – something that is often a challenge. Despite this, it has an important place in professional development.

Importance of self-reflection: Self-reflection influences learning in a significant way. This was recognized by the International Baccalaureate (IB) in 2018 as they took the step of removing reflection as a key concept and fully integrated the practice through all learning and teaching to strengthen ongoing inquiry. This proves the importance of self-reflection because it's recognized as a more dynamic, continuous process. Self-reflection is also ideal for metacognition – how can you be a better learner if you don't consider your own thought process? When we learn passively, we don't have enough time to reflect on our learning or the lessons, which means we are unlikely to draw upon the information again. Additionally, self-reflection also means students have a chance to evaluate their own strengths and weaknesses and establish a path of positive self-evaluation that, importantly, includes speaking about any negatives. This helps students to track their own achievements and progress, promotes ownership over their work for growth and allows students to analyse their own learning.

PEER EVALUATION

Peer assessment or peer review provides a structured learning process for students to critique and provide feedback to each other on their work. It helps students develop lifelong skills in assessing and providing feedback to others, and also equips them with skills to self-assess and improve their own work.

Purpose of Peer Evaluation

- Peer evaluation helps empower children because the process of peer evaluation involves taking responsibility for their own learning, as well as helping classmates.
- Children can learn effectively through peer evaluation because they are refreshing on course content by marking their peer's work. This can be a helpful way to motivate children with their work.
- Peer assessment in education often involves a discussion aspect. Children will identify examples of what their peers did well on and areas that they may be able to improve on next time, and then will discuss this with the person whose work they have marked. This is a great way to help young children become more confident in their social and communication skills and will help prepare them

for later years of education when group work and peer assessment begins to feature more frequently.

- As children will be taking on the role of the assessor during peer assessment, they will develop new, valuable skills, such as evaluation and critical thinking through analysing and commenting on their peer's work. Allowing them to see their work and the work of others through a different lens is one of the main purposes of peer assessment.

Objectives of Peer Evaluation: Peer Evaluation of Teaching consists of the review of teaching performance by colleagues, usually in the same or a similar discipline, with the purpose of assessing and improving the quality of teaching. Peer review puts faculty in charge of the quality of their teaching.

Advantages of Peer Evaluation: Empower students to take responsibility for and manage their own learning. Enable students to learn to assess and give others constructive feedback to develop lifelong assessment skills. Enhance students' learning through knowledge diffusion and exchange of ideas.

Disadvantages of peer evaluation: Peer pressure and friendship can influence the reliability of grades given by students. Students may have a tendency to give everyone the same mark (for example, there may be collusion in return for good grades). Students are not experienced in assessing each other.

GRADING

Grading in education is the process of applying standardized measurements for varying levels of achievements in a course. Grades can be assigned as letters, as a range, as a percentage, or as a number out of a possible total. In some countries, grades are averaged to create a grade point average.

Principles of grading: Grading should inform students about their progress toward course goals. Grading should use a weight system that communicates to students that learning is the result of skill building. Grading practices should acknowledge the limitations of our assessments in productive ways.

Features of Grading

- It is a score
- It identifies students' performance level with a wide range

- When students level of performance is classified in to a few classificatory units using letter grade system of assessment is called grading system
- In grading classification is made on 5,7,9 point scale
- It involves the use of set of specialized symbols whose meaning ought to be objectively defined in terms of specific criteria

Grade Inflation

Grade inflation (also known as grading leniency) is the awarding of higher grades than students deserve, which yields a higher average grade given to students. The term is also used to describe the tendency to award progressively higher academic grades for work that would have received lower grades in the past. However, higher average grades in themselves do not prove grade inflation. For this to be grade inflation, it is necessary to demonstrate that the quality of work does not deserve the high grade. Grade inflation is frequently discussed in relation to education in the United States, and to GCSEs and A levels in England and Wales. It is also an issue in many other nations, such as Canada, Australia, New Zealand, France, Germany, South Korea, Japan, China and India.

Types of Grade Inflation

- *Static Grade Inflation*: occurs when grades overstate the students' content knowledge or academic performance. It grades the student performance overtly at a fixed point in time. Although exams are imperfect and some students might have faced extenuating circumstances that can cause them to underperform, static grades suggest a disconnect between grades and content mastery at a given point in time.
- *Dynamic Grade Inflation*: occurs when the level of content knowledge associated with a given grade decreases over time. Here, the link between the student's grades and their performance changes with time. This is troubling because those who rely on the information provided by student grades cannot know how to interpret it at a given point in time.
- *Differential Grade Inflation*: occurs when the association between knowledge and grades is different because of the students' background or school type. The relationship between the students' grades and performance differs according to the school/student type. Differential grade inflation can occur in either a static or dynamic environment.

Causes of Grade Inflation

Many factors contribute to grade inflation. Some of these factors are a decrease in the academic standards of the students or an increase in the student performance, and it could also be both. There are also pressure factors that cause grade inflation. For example, a teacher may try to reduce the pressure mounted on him/her by the students' parents, from the school and the student. Also, when a teacher cannot determine whether the student understands the content of the lesson or not. Another reason an instructor or teacher might be involved in grade inflation is if the supervisors and the colleagues of this instructor are questioning the work ethics of this instructor. In a move to appear as performing excellently, the instructor might indulge in grade inflation. The responsibility of the faculty member is to ensure there are no incidents of grade inflation by examining the grades of the students through progress tracking and personalized feedback. If a faculty member fails to perform this responsibility, teachers and students will get away with grade inflation. When students who put in the work in their courses do not receive support or get any feedback, they may be inclined to receive grade inflation.

Effects and Implications of Grade Inflation on Students

There are many implications of grade inflation on students and we are going to look at some of them:

- When students are aware, they are getting better grades than they are supposed to, they may develop lesser interest and become disillusioned. They may even decide to stop studying or putting in more effort, as that would be considered a waste of time to them.
- The level of students' creativity will drop. This is because they've realized they can do substandard work and still get above-average grades.
- With top grades, students should wonder if grade inflation is benefiting them or their university's reputation.
- In reality, grade inflation does not help students or the universities that use it. There is no one clear path to end grade inflation, but deflating grades is necessary to protect the integrity of college as a learning environment and not just a credential factory.

How to Avoid Grade Inflation?

- The teachers or instructors should not forget that the grading experience is for the improvement of their students. The educational process should be a learning experience for the students. Students will readily accept lower grades if they're helped to understand the reason why they have the grade and they can see, or you can show them ways to improve the grades.

- Completely avoid general expressions or statements that could cover the entire work of the students without specification. Expressions such as "great work" should be avoided. As a teacher, be specific while praising your students. Praise them in their areas of strength or where they excel, and communicate with them clearly, the areas where they need to improve.
- Show them examples of previous works. Let them see why one work has an "A" grade while the other has a "C". This has proven helpful.
- Personalize the feedback. That way the student will feel supported. And that will also allow the management to justify the grades of the students in terms of its fairness.
- You can use quizzes and assignments to track the progress of students in a particular course. The result over time can help the faculty member to support the students that may be struggling by providing them with an intervention.
- Rubrics that focus on the strengths of the students and acknowledge them to grade them. Be specific to use rubrics that grade their area of strength and their weak areas accordingly.
- Use Rubrics to grade your students fairly. Rubrics are recommended because it has been proven to demonstrate an accurate and fair grading system. So, if your grading is ever questioned, you are assured that you have substantial evidence to back you up.

ASSESSING STUDENT PERFORMANCE

Assessment of student performance and the evaluation of courses and teaching are critical elements in the teaching-learning environment and are central to each higher education institution's mission of preparing students for the future. There are increasing internal and external pressures for institutions to review and improve their practice in this area. While a vast knowledge-base exists to inform good practice in assessment of student performance, change in practice seems to be slow. A framework for improving assessment practice, based on a simple quality management model, is provided as are some examples which illustrate application of the model/framework. Some suggestions are also made about support mechanisms and resources required for effecting significant improvement to practice.

INTERNAL EVALUATION

Internal evaluation is a process of quality review undertaken within an institution for its own ends (with or without the involvement of external peers). Internal review is something an institution does for its own purposes. Internal evaluation supports formative and diagnostic evaluation. This is conducted to know the learning progress of the students and the difficulties that they face during the process of teaching and learning. Internal evaluation is also providing a base for remedial teaching to the identified students.

- Internal Evaluation Process: Internal evaluation involves asking good questions, gathering fit-for-purpose data and information, and then making sense of that information. Much more than a technical process, evaluation is deeply influenced by your values and those of your community.
- Role of Internal evaluation: Internal evaluation involves asking good questions, gathering fit-for-purpose data and information, and then making sense of that information. Much more than a technical process, evaluation is deeply influenced by your values and those of your community.

Advantages of internal evaluation

- Examination based on more memory of the student can be avoided
- Minimize the over anxiety and nervousness
- Motivation to active participatory in both curricular and co-curricular activities
- Help in identifying the strength and weakness of the student and to impart instructions

Disadvantages of internal evaluation

- Cannot replace external examination
- Requires a lot of time to undertake the activities
- Increased work load of evaluators
- May be biased

STUDENT PROGRESSION

Student progression is a process which ensures all students are passing required units to progress through to graduation. At the end of each semester student grades are reviewed to determine whether progress in your studies is satisfactory.

Aim of Student Progression: Learning progressions are essential tools for understanding students' progress in their learning. In the classroom, learning progressions enable teachers to identify where students are at in their learning and convert student assessment results into meaningful descriptions of their learning progress.

Purpose of Student Progression: The main purpose of education is to provide the opportunity for acquiring knowledge and skills that will enable people to develop their full potential, and become successful members of society.

ROLE OF THE TEACHERS IN ENHANCING QUALITY EDUCATION

Quality education specifically entails issues such as appropriate skills development, gender parity, provision of relevant school infrastructure, equipment, educational materials and resources, scholarships or teaching force. The success of any education system depends on the quality of teachers, which, in turn, depends on the effective teaching / learning process. Teachers' role is of vital significance for the development of society and appropriate changes in the society. Thus, the quality of higher education depends upon quality of those who impart it. Teachers are the most important components of any educational system. Teachers play most crucial role in the development of the education system as a whole and also in imparting and maintaining the standards of higher education. The role of the teachers in enhancing quality education given as under:

- **Dedication and Commitment**: Dedication and commitment of teachers plays a crucial role in improving the quality of education and shaping the future of nation.
- **Motivation**: A teacher should act as a motivational force and should be able to create a learning environment in which students are encouraged to think carefully, rationally and express their thoughts and decide on the situations and difficulties. It is the responsibility of teacher to create a context in which the students' desire and ability to learn can work most effectively. A teacher should act as the role model for the students
- **Skill Development**: Skill development is crucial to the success of students in the job market. Skill development of students, on

par with their counterparts elsewhere is an important aspect of enhancement of quality of higher education. With liberalization and globalization of economic activities, the need to develop skilled human resources of a high calibre is imperative. Consequently, the demand for internationally acceptable standards in higher education is evident. Therefore, preparing the students to achieve core competencies, to face the global requirements successfully is very important. This requires that the teachers should be innovative, creative and entrepreneurial in their approach, to ensure skill development amongst the students. By various means such as establishment of collaborations with industries, social organizations, networking with the neighbourhood agencies/ bodies and fostering a closer relationship between the "world of skilled work" and the "world of competent learning", it is possible to develop required skills.

- **Imparting Value Based Education**: It is said that skills are of less importance in the absence of appropriate value systems. Hence, teachers should shoulder the responsibility of inculcating the desirable value systems amongst the students. In a country like India, with cultural pluralities and diversities, it is essential that students imbibe the appropriate values commensurate with social, cultural, economic and environmental realities, at the local, national and universal levels. Whatever be the pluralities and diversities that exist in the country, there is ample scope for inculcating the core universal values like truth and righteousness. The seeds of values sown in the early stages of education, mostly aimed at cooperation and mutual understanding, have to be reiterated and re-emphasized at the higher educational institutions, through appropriate learning experiences and opportunities. Values are the guiding principles of life, which are conducive to all round development. They give direction to life and bring joy, satisfaction and peace to life. In ancient India, more importance was given to morality, honesty, duty, truth, friendship, brotherhood, etc and these were considered to be the themes of Indian culture and society. Imparting value-based education was the only aim of the teachers of ancient age. But in the present scenario, due to large number of changes, there is a considerable decrease in the quality of value-based education.
- **Impact of calibre**: It has been revealed by many research studies that the calibre of teachers has tremendous impact on the calibre of the students. Hence, a teacher, who is a permanent learner has to

update the subject knowledge continuously and should be aware of latest development in their subject.

- **Lateral Thinking**: Lateral thinking, sometimes called horizontal thinking or divergent thinking, is defined as an approach to problem-solving that strives for creative solutions rather than the most straightforward answer. Through spontaneous, free-flowing brainstorming, lateral thinking disrupts traditional step-by-step thinking patterns to develop as many varied creative ideas as possible. Psychologist Edward de Bono developed this concept in his 1967 book, The Use of Lateral Thinking. De Bono argued that the human brain has been trained to think "inside the box" and seek typical, predictable solutions, even if those aren't the best options. He proposed lateral thinking as a new way to move past our cognitive biases and be more inventive. Lateral thinking instead combines imagination and intuition. You consciously try to generate ideas and scenarios that imagine uncertainties outside the information you already have. It places more importance on the ideas themselves and doesn't dwell on the outcome until later. Despite their differences, vertical and lateral thinking can work together to make ideas the best they can be. Lateral thinking can stimulate more creative logic in vertical thinking, and vertical thinking fine-tunes lateral thinking's big ideas.
- **Use of Resources**: Efficient use of resources helps to produce uniquely educated, highly satisfied and employable graduates. Motivated teachers can enrich their teaching with resources and co-curricular activities. Use of ICTs in teaching-learning process makes the lecture effective and improves the quality of teaching. Continuous updating of teaching methods and use of innovative teaching methods help to improve the quality of teaching.
- **Curriculum Design**: The quality of higher education can be enhanced by designing need-based curriculum, keeping in view the demands in the employment sector at national and international level.
- **Special Attention to Research**: Promotion of research is crucial for improving the quality of higher education system. It is one of the factors, which influences the quality of teaching. Educational research must be strengthened as an instrument for improving educational quality and results of such research must be communicated to teachers in a better way. The link between classroom teaching and research is extremely important. It must

be a link operating in two directions: Lateral thinking is solving problems through approach, using reasoning that is not immediately obvious and involving ideas that may not be obtainable by using only traditional step-by-step: (a) Information to the teachers about latest findings, (b) Information to the researchers about the problems.

- **Academic Development:** To teach is the life-long process of learning – Teachers are the most important components of the higher education system. Academic development of teachers is crucial and necessary for the success of the higher education system because teachers are the prime movers and catalysts for all round development of students. Teachers play a significant role not only in improving the quality of higher education but also maintaining it; the professional competency of teachers has to be of such a high level so as to impart quality knowledge to the students. This would call the continuous upgrading of the professional development of the teachers, which is key guarantee of quality education.

INNOVATION

Innovation is production or adoption, assimilation, and exploitation of a value-added novelty in economic and social spheres; renewal and enlargement of products, services, and markets; development of new methods of production; and the establishment of new management systems. It is both a process and an outcome.

- **Use of Innovation Education:** Innovation in education can lead to better overall outcomes in the school environment. Innovative classrooms are filled with students who are developing stronger communication skills and building engagement capacity amongst their peers.
- **Characteristics of Innovation:** There are certain product and service characteristics that affect the diffusion process and can influence consumer acceptance of new products and services; the five factors that can impact the diffusion process and the rate of adoption are relative advantage, compatibility, complexity, trial-ability, and observability.
- **Relative Advantage:** The relative advantage of the innovative product/service offering over already existing products/services, accelerates its rate of adoption by the target market. The degree to which customers perceive a new product/service as superior

to similar existing products determines the relative advantage. A product/service that provides advantage over other existing products is indicative of being superior to existing alternatives, and thus higher in terms of "value". The more radical a change, and the higher the relative advantage, the faster would be the diffusion. The relative advantage may lie in terms of it being a modified product (with better features, attributes, benefits, form etc), or at a lower price (better deals, discounts, terms of payment, warranty and exchange), or more accessible in terms of availability (physical store format, or virtual electronic format), or better communication. Thus, while product-based advantages are more attractive in nature, the other components of the marketing mix like price, place and promotion can also provide a basis for relative advantage. Examples of innovations that provide relative advantage are, flash drives versus compact discs, laptops versus computers, or digital libraries versus traditional libraries, ATMs versus bank teller counters.

- **Compatibility:** The compatibility of the innovative product and service offering with the existing backgrounds, behaviour and lifestyle patterns of consumers also affects its adoption by the consuming public. The compatibility of a product/service measures how closely it relates to needs, value systems and norms, lifestyles, culture etc. The higher the level of compatibility, the quicker the diffusion; and the lower the compatibility, the slower the diffusion. A product will diffuse more quickly if it does not require consumers to change their values, norms, lifestyles, cultures and day to day behaviours. Continuous and dynamically continuous innovations are higher on compatibility than discontinuous innovations. Fast food in the form of pizzas, burgers, noodles etc. took considerable amount of time to get diffused into the Indian society, as it contrasted heavily with the dal roti meal concept. The pace of adoption quickened in the 1990s and more so in the 2000s with the new generation, and their preference towards packaged foods and fast food. Another example that can be mentioned here is, coconut oil as a medium of cooking would be incompatible to people staying in North India. Even if positioned as "healthy and natural cooking medium", it would be slow to penetrate and may even fail if launched in North India. The same would penetrate easily in South India, as it is culturally more compatible.
- **Complexity:** The level of complexity in a product purchase and usage also affects the diffusion process. An innovative offering

would be easily diffused when there is ease of understanding, purchase and use. The easier it is to understand and use a product, the more likely it is to be accepted quickly, and vice versa. While speaking of complexity, technological complexity acts as a barrier to diffusion. People resist adoption of new products because of fear of complexity in purchase and usage. This is well understood by high tech industries. Let us take the example of the electronic goods industry, e.g. microwave cookers or vacuum cleaners. While designing their communication, the marketer illustrates ease of use, so as to encourage quicker acceptance; prospects are provided with demos and trials; once purchased, arrangements are made for providing installation at home. Another example is the mobile phone industry; realizing the problem of complexity, simpler models are introduced for those who desire the mobile set just for making and receiving calls and messages. It would be noteworthy to mention here that the youth are more techno savvy and have accepted electronic goods like MP3s and 4s, laptops, I-pods, ATMs etc much faster than the older generation. This is because the former have been able to deal with the complexity with a higher level of comfort than the older generation.

- **Trialability:** The ease with which the product or service can be tested and tried also determines the rate of acceptance. The higher the degree of trialability, the greater would be the rate of diffusion. This is because the prospects get an opportunity to try the product/service, assess it and decide to accept/reject it. Trialability can be encouraged by providing free samples, or providing smaller packs and smaller-than-average sizes, (for FMCG and household goods) or even through demos and test- runs (for consumer durables). Consumers could try out the innovative offering, evaluate it and then decide on a purchase commitment by accepting/rejecting it. Trials leading to purchase can be encouraged through guaranty and warranty schemes. Such trials encourage a product/service to be diffused easily.
- **Observability:** Observability refers to the ease with which the product can be observed. Observability in an innovative product refers to the degree to which a product/service's benefits can be observed, imagined and perceived by a potential consumer. The higher the degree of observability, the greater the chances of the innovative offering being accepted by the prospects. Those new product offerings that are (a) tangible, (b) have social visibility, and (c) whose benefits are readily observed (without much time

gap), are more readily diffused than those that are intangible, or have no social visibility or whose benefits accumulate over long periods of time. Thus, relative advantage, compatibility, complexity, triability, and observability have an impact on the rate of diffusion. While all these factors relate to the product, they are dependent on consumer perception. A product/service offering that is relatively superior to existing ones, is more compatible to existing consumption behaviours and usage, is less complex, easy to use and observable, is more likely to be purchased quickly by the public, than when it is not.

- **Leadership:** Leadership is the process of encouraging and helping others to work enthusiastically towards objectives. It is the behaviours of an individual when he is directing the activities of a group towards a shared goal. It is the relationship in which one person influences others to work together willingly on related task to attain goals desired.

Features of Leadership

- *Influence the behaviour of others*: Leadership is an ability of an individual to influence the behaviour of other employees in the organization to achieve a common purpose or goal so that they are willingly co-operating with each other for the fulfilment of the same.
- *Inter-personal process*: It is an interpersonal process between the leader and the followers. The relationship between the leader and the followers decides how efficiently and effectively the targets of the organization would be met.
- *Attainment of common organizational goals*: The purpose of leadership is to guide the people in an organization to work towards the attainment of common organizational goals. The leader brings the people and their efforts together to achieve common goals.
- *Continuous process*: Leadership is a continuous process. A leader has to guide his employees every time and also monitor them in order to make sure that their efforts are going in the same direction and that they are not deviating from their goals.
- *Group process*: It is a group process that involves two or more people together interacting with each other. A leader cannot lead without the followers.
- *Dependent on the situation*: It is situation bound as it all depends

upon tackling the situations present. Thus, there is no single best style of leadership.

Importance of Leadership

- *Initiating Action:* Leadership starts from the very beginning, even before the work actually starts. A leader is a person who communicates the policies and plans to the subordinates to start the work.
- *Providing Motivation:* A leader motivates the employees by giving them financial and non-financial incentives and gets the work done efficiently. Motivation is the driving force in an individual's life.
- *Providing guidance:* A leader not only supervises the employees but also guides them in their work. He instructs the subordinates on how to perform their work effectively so that their efforts don't get wasted.
- *Creating confidence:* A leader acknowledges the efforts of the employees, explains to them their role clearly and guides them to achieve their goals. He also resolves the complaints and problems of the employees, thereby building confidence in them regarding the organization.
- *Building work environment:* A good leader should maintain personal contacts with the employees and should hear their problems and solve them. He always listens to the point of view of the employees and in case of disagreement persuades them to agree with him by giving suitable clarifications. In case of conflicts, he handles them carefully and does not allow it to adversely affect the entity. A positive and efficient work environment helps in stable growth of the organization.
- *Co-ordination:* A leader reconciles the personal interests of the employees with the organizational goals and achieves co-ordination in the entity.
- *Creating Successors:* A leader trains his subordinates in such a manner that they can succeed him in future easily in his absence. He creates more leaders.
- *Induces change:* A leader persuades, clarifies and inspires employees to accept any change in the organization without much resistance and discontentment. He makes sure that employees don't feel insecure about the changes.

INTERNSHIP

An internship is a period of work experience offered by an organization for a limited period of time Once confined to medical graduates, internship is used practice for a wide range of placements in businesses, non-profit organizations and government agencies. They are typically undertaken by students and graduates looking to gain relevant skills and experience in a particular field. Employers benefit from these placements because they often recruit employees from their best interns, who have known capabilities, thus saving time and money in the long run. Internships are usually arranged by third-party organizations that recruit interns on behalf of industry groups. Rules vary from country to country about when interns should be regarded as employees.

Internships for professional careers are similar in some ways. Similar to internships, apprenticeships transition students from vocational school into the workforce. The lack of standardization and oversight leaves the term "internship" open to broad interpretation. Interns may be high school students, college and university students, or post-graduate adults. These positions may be paid or unpaid and are temporary Many large corporations, particularly investment banks, have "insights" programs that serve as a pre-internship event numbering a day to a week, either in person or virtually.

Typically, an internship consists of an exchange of services for experience between the intern and the organization. Internships are used to determine whether the intern still has an interest in that field after the real-life experience. In addition, an internship can be used to build a professional network that can assist with letters of recommendation or lead to future employment opportunities. The benefit of bringing an intern into full-time employment is that they are already familiar with the company, therefore needing little to no training. Internships provide current college students with the ability to participate in a field of their choice to receive hands-on learning about a particular future career, preparing them for full-time work following graduation.

Importance of an Internship

An internship is important because it can present you with new skills and opportunities that you may not receive otherwise. Interns gain technical knowledge within the industry of their choice by working directly with professionals in that field. The importance of the Internship given as under:

- **Gain Competitive Advantage:** After completing your study programme, you will apply as a fresher when you look for your first job. You must remember that the recruiter will receive a sea of applications. For you to stand out from the crowd, an internship is essential as recruiters will prefer a candidate with first-hand experience. Your brief stint with any organisation on your resume can prove to be a turning point in your life.
- **Explore beyond your comfort zone:** You can experience your first presentation, meeting, cross-functional task, initial days of meeting the deadlines and more through an internship. You gain enriching insights during your training and officially become a part of a professional workspace. When you face new challenges, you will learn to adapt and become an effective problem-solver. You will be encouraged to push your boundaries and continuously evolve as a competent contender at work.
- **Find your passion**: Steve Jobs says, "The only way to do great work is to love what you do. If you haven't found it yet, keep looking. Don't settle". Did you know that according to National Centre for Education Statistics, 80% of students change their college majors? Similarly, internships, too, can help you explore opportunities to find the right fit for you. When you work, you can get a chance to evaluate your interests and find the perfect career path that you would like to take ahead.
- **Learn new skills:** When you work in a team, you learn essential life skills, including people management skills such as effective communication, team management, accountability, patience, and flexibility, to name a few. Employers these days emphasise on soft skills of the candidate during the hiring process. Adaptability, conflict resolution, critical thinking, and teamwork are some essential skills you can develop during your internship.

Advantages of Internship

- Allow to practice what you have learned in the classroom
- Familiarize with a working environment
- Help to build and expand professional network
- Make more marketable employers

Disadvantages of Internship

- Little or no Stipend: As an intern you will be earning a stipend which might not cover your basic needs.

- No Guarantee of a job: The ultimate goal is to be employed by the company you are interning at, but there is no guarantee this will happen.

INVOLVEMENT IN COMMUNITY

In the realm of Social Science Education, the significance of community involvement cannot be overstated. Understanding the dynamics of communities, their structures, cultures, and challenges is fundamental for students to grasp the complexities of society.

Why Community Involvement Matters:

- *Real-world Contextualization*: Community involvement provides students with tangible experiences that contextualize theoretical concepts learned in the classroom. By actively engaging with local communities, students can observe social phenomena firsthand, making abstract theories more relatable and understandable.
- *Cultivating Empathy and Cultural Competence*: Immersion in diverse communities fosters empathy and cultural competence among students. Through interactions with individuals from various backgrounds, students gain insights into different perspectives, values, and norms, promoting a deeper appreciation of cultural diversity and social inclusivity.
- *Promoting Active Citizenship*: Community involvement empowers students to become active participants in civic life. By collaborating with community members on social initiatives or addressing local issues, students develop critical thinking skills, problem-solving abilities, and a sense of responsibility towards their communities, laying the foundation for engaged citizenship.
- *Bridging Theory and Practice*: Engaging in community-based projects bridges the gap between theory and practice in social science education. Students apply theoretical frameworks to real-world scenarios, honing their analytical skills and understanding of social dynamics. This hands-on approach facilitates a deeper comprehension of complex social concepts and encourages critical reflection.

Incorporating Community Involvement in Pedagogical Practices:

- *Service-Learning Projects*: Designing service-learning projects that address community needs while aligning with curriculum objectives allows students to actively contribute to their communities while enhancing their academic learning. These projects can range from environmental conservation initiatives to advocacy campaigns for social justice issues.

- *Community Partnerships*: Establishing partnerships with local organizations, nonprofits, and governmental agencies enables educators to enrich classroom instruction through guest lectures, field trips, and collaborative projects. These partnerships provide students with access to resources, expertise, and opportunities for practical application of social science concepts.
- *Experiential Learning Opportunities*: Integrating experiential learning opportunities such as internships, volunteer work, or community-based research projects into the curriculum allows students to gain hands-on experience and develop transferable skills. These immersive experiences deepen students' understanding of societal structures and dynamics while fostering personal and professional growth.

Incorporating community involvement in social science education is essential for nurturing informed, empathetic, and civically engaged individuals. By embracing a pedagogy that integrates real-world experiences and community partnerships, educators can inspire students to become active agents of positive change in their communities and beyond. As we continue to advance methodology and pedagogical practices in social science education, let us recognize the transformative power of community involvement in shaping well-rounded and socially responsible citizens.

EXAMINATION AS A FEEDBACK MECHANISM

Examinations are often viewed solely as a means of assessing students' understanding and knowledge. However, they serve a much broader purpose beyond simply assigning grades. In the realm of social science education, examinations can be leveraged as powerful feedback mechanisms, providing valuable insights into students' learning processes, comprehension levels, and areas needing improvement. This content delves into the significance of examinations as feedback mechanisms within the context of social science education, highlighting their role in enhancing pedagogical practices and fostering student growth.

- **Understanding the Purpose of Examinations:** Examinations serve as critical checkpoints in the learning journey, enabling educators to evaluate students' grasp of key concepts, analytical skills, and critical thinking abilities. Beyond this evaluative function, examinations offer an invaluable opportunity for feedback exchange between educators and students. By analysing examination results, educators gain valuable insights into students' strengths, weaknesses, and learning preferences, which inform instructional strategies tailored to individual needs.

- **Feedback Loop in Social Science Education:** In the realm of social science education, where interdisciplinary perspectives and nuanced understanding are paramount, the feedback loop facilitated by examinations plays a pivotal role. Through assessments such as essays, case studies, and discussions, students engage with complex socio-cultural, economic, and political issues, applying theoretical frameworks to real-world contexts. Examination outcomes provide educators with a comprehensive overview of students' comprehension levels, enabling targeted interventions to address misconceptions and enhance conceptual understanding.
- **Enhancing Pedagogical Practices:** Examinations serve as catalysts for pedagogical innovation, prompting educators to reflect on instructional approaches and curriculum design. By analysing examination data, educators identify patterns in student performance, enabling them to adapt teaching strategies to cater to diverse learning styles and aptitudes. Additionally, examinations provide opportunities for formative assessment, allowing educators to provide timely feedback and scaffold students' learning experiences effectively.
- **Empowering Student Growth:** Central to the concept of examinations as feedback mechanisms is the empowerment of student growth and development. By providing constructive feedback based on examination outcomes, educators guide students towards self-reflection and metacognitive awareness. Through targeted interventions and personalized support, students are empowered to overcome challenges, deepen their understanding, and cultivate lifelong learning skills essential for success in the dynamic field of social sciences.

In short, examinations serve as invaluable feedback mechanisms in social science education, facilitating a continuous cycle of assessment, reflection, and improvement. By harnessing examination data, educators can refine instructional practices, tailor learning experiences, and empower students to thrive in an ever-evolving global landscape. Thus, integrating examinations as feedback mechanisms is essential in advancing the methodology and pedagogical practices of social science education, fostering a culture of excellence and innovation in teaching and learning.

OPEN BOOK EXAMINATION

Open book exam is an assessment method designed in such a way that allows students to refer to textbooks, class notes, or any other approved material while answering questions. It can also mean that students are provided with the question paper before writing the exam. It tends to ask students to analyse, synthesize, compare or evaluate information. They test whether you understand the main thing of the course and how it works. It requires you to understand the material properly and be able to apply or analyse information and content rather than just remember it. These exams provide students with a second learning opportunity to absorb and understand the course material. While reading through the textbook for answers, students will get more knowledge on the subject and can prepare for future examinations and professional development in a better way. To prepare for the open book exam, read and understand the test guidelines, know the test format, test yourself, study the class materials, plan your time, and carve out a quiet test-taking spot with minimal distractions. Many schools and colleges organize open book exams. While doing an open book exam you need to use your skills to analyse what is the perfect answer for the given question. Overall, it can be said that these exams are good to improve your skills.

Important features of open book exam: In an open-book test, students are allowed to use their textbooks and other resources to find the answers to questions. This type of testing is thought to be more effective in measuring a student's understanding of a subject, as well as their ability to find and use information effectively.

What are the main challenges of open book exam? If students are not guided well to give open-book exams, they may just copy what is in the textbook. And it will not serve the purpose for which the exams are held. Training a large number of evaluators in the new evaluation method is also a challenge.

Role of the teacher in open book exam: The teacher's role is viewed as facilitating the transfer of information from the textbook to the students' minds. What the student is expected to do is to understand this information, retain it, and retrieve it during the final examination.

Use of open book exam: Open book exam is an assessment method designed in such a way that allows students to refer to textbooks, class notes, or any other approved material while answering questions. It can also mean that students are provided with the question paper before writing the exam.

Advantages of Open Book Exam

- Open book experiments aid in the advancement of rational skills and real-world learning. This is extremely vital in a promptly expanding economy, where some kinds of businesses may go and new varieties of jobs may happen, necessitating skilling and re-skilling as part of one's vocation.
- For those who have a crisis recollecting passages, an open book exam is exceptionally effective as it is designed for civilizations who have a decent remembrance.
- Open book exams allow learners to relate what they've learned in class to real-life circumstances, whereas shut book exams force learners to memorize all they've studied without entirely understanding it.
- In an Open book exam, learners can scan the books. So, they don't have to plug in a lot of evidence.
- Learners get a second likelihood to obtain proficiency. Also, they can collect acceptable learning substances rather than recall them.
- It helps in remembering aspects for a longer period. Also, students find flexible ways to collect necessary information from different references.
- As they develop rational skills, learners will be encouraged to be rational and productive.
- Open-book exams can reform the strategy of pedagogy and can improve the mood of education.

Disadvantages of Open Book Exam

- Learners no longer study for exams as they are no extra concerned about declining in exams; this may decrease the students' memory conserving ability.
- Remembrance exercise is also significant, primarily for children. Open-book exams may discourage learners from memorizing even the fundamental aspects.
- As the experiment in open-book exams will be tough, it may put even more anxiety on learners.
- Culture speculates that learners inscribe answers from textbooks and therefore, these exams are very easy. But since problems are framed in real-life scenarios, questions are framed in such a way that students' conceptions must be understood before they resolve the problems.

- Suspicion of skipping the content will be abolished.
- It is impossible to judge whether all learners are equally equipped for an exam or not.
- Also, some books are very important and the library also has an insufficient number of books.
- The books and notes take a lot of opening. Also, the desk requires to be enormous to keep the books
- Sometimes learners take a lot of time uncovering some topics. Also, they stare at books fairly rather than countering their understanding and mastery.

ONLINE TESTS

An online exam (also called eExam) is a great way of conducting tests and other important exams with help of the internet. An online exam needs a device capable of accessing the internet such as a computer or a smartphone. This can be either done at an examination centre or at home.

Purpose of Online Examination

The objectives of online examination system or rather any other exam (purpose of online examination system) is to make sure that the student is thoroughly aware of the course curriculum and that the exam reflects the course content he/she has studied.

Importance of online examination

- Online Examination System is a computerized system that gives instant results and also saves time.
- It fully automates all the previous manual process of taking written exams.
- Our online examination system also allows assessments to be evaluated in less time.
- Through Remote Proctoring Multiple numbers of candidates can complete their examination at the same time and there is no requirement for physical faculty for monitoring due to the use of remote proctoring.
- The test takers can take the assessment or examination by logging into the online examination system during class or at home with the use of their own devices.
- They also get the opportunity to see their results and answers as

instant feedback about their knowledge or understanding of their chosen topics

Advantages of Online Examination System

- Online Examination System is a computerized system which gives instant results and also saves time.
- Fully automates the previous manual process of taking written exams.
- It is implemented by web based online examination software or through Intranet variance.
- It decreases the need of supervision during the exam is being examine or taken using web based Online Examination System
- Gives a high level of clarity as opposite of traditional method. Most of Online Examination System gives the result and instantly
- In high school, Online Examination System is able to reduce the workload of teachers by using automated test paper exams and marking schemes.
- Students can study independently for example at home or any place.
- The amount of time given at a particular question gives you the ability of "Quick Learning Quick Thinking".
- The data in Online Examination System is regenerated repeatedly so that students have access to new data.

Disadvantages of Online Exam

- The question and answers may be tricky and confusing as there are multiple choices for answers.
- Lack of interaction between the teacher and student.
- Network problems may arise in Online Examination System, test may be postponed or cancel.
- Group Projects, Collaborative Evaluations, and Vocational Examinations
- Not all examinations are simple question and answer.
- Some courses require evaluation of collaborative or group projects or evaluation through a vocational exam that can't be taken online.
- These types of exams require personal subjective evaluation, something which online examinations can't offer.

CONCLUSION

In Unit 6 of Social Science Education, we have explored a diverse array of assessment methods and strategies aimed at enhancing student learning and promoting quality education. From designing learner evaluations to implementing classroom assessment techniques, from utilizing portfolios and rubrics to fostering self-reflection and peer evaluation, this unit has provided a comprehensive toolkit for assessing student performance effectively. Through the examination of grading principles, the exploration of student progression, and the role of teachers in enhancing educational quality, we have gained insights into the multifaceted nature of assessment and its impact on student outcomes. Emphasizing the importance of innovation, leadership, and community involvement, we have underscored the integral role of educators in shaping the educational landscape and fostering a culture of continuous improvement.

In particular, the concept of examination as a feedback mechanism has emerged as a pivotal component of effective assessment practices. Whether through traditional examinations, open-book assessments, or online tests, examinations serve as invaluable tools for gauging student understanding, identifying areas for growth, and providing meaningful feedback to guide further learning. As we conclude Unit 6, it is evident that assessment is not merely a means of evaluating student performance but a dynamic process aimed at facilitating learning, fostering growth, and promoting excellence. By embracing innovative assessment methods, cultivating reflective practices, and leveraging examinations as feedback mechanisms, educators can empower students to thrive academically, intellectually, and socially. Together, let us continue to explore and implement best practices in assessment, ensuring that every student has the opportunity to reach their full potential and contribute meaningfully to society.

BIBLIOGRAPHY

1. Aggarwal J.C. (2003). *Teaching of Social Studies,* New Delhi: Vikas Publishing House
2. Aggarwal, J.C. (1993). *Teaching of Social Studies - A Practical Approach*; Second Revised Edition, Vikas Publishing House Pvt. Ltd., New Delhi.
3. Angelo, T.A. & Cross K.P. (1993). *Classroom Assessment Techniques: A Handbook for College Teachers*. San Francisco: Josey-Bass Publishers.
4. Aravind, G. (2005). *Nationalism and social reform in a colonial situation*. New Delhi: Gyan
5. Banerjee, A.C. & Sharma S.R. (1999). *Sociological and Philosophical issues in Education*. Jaipur: Book Enclave.
6. Belvedere, Carlos, & Merajver, Marta Ines. (2007). Phenomenology and the Social Sciences: a story with no beginning. *Sociedad (Buenos Aires)*, *2*(se) Retrieved September 21, 2021, from http://socialsciences.scielo.org/scielo.php?script=sci_arttext&pid=S0327-77122007000100001&lng=en&tlng=en
7. Bining A. C. & Bining D. H. (1952) *Teaching the Social Studies in Secondary School*, W. Y. McGraw-Hill Book Company.
8. Bloom, B.S. (Ed.). (1964). *Taxonomy of Educational Objectives*. New York: David McKay Company Inc.
9. Bossing, N.L. (1970). *Teaching in Secondary School,* New Delhi: Amerinal Publishing Co. Pvt.
10. Branard, M. C. (1953), *Principles and Practice of Geography Teaching,* London: University Tutorial Press.
11. Buch, M.B. (1969), *Improving Instruction in Civics,* New Delhi: NCERT.
12. Burrell, G. & Morgan, G. (1979). *Sociological Paradigm and Organizational Analysis*. London: Heinemann Educational.
13. Burton, W.H. (1953), *Principles and Practice of Geography Teaching,* London: University Tutorial Press.
14. Burton, W.H. (1972). *Principles of History Teaching,* London: Methuen.
15. Callahan, J.I. Dark, L.H. (1982), *Teaching in the Middle Secondary Schools Planning for Competence,* New York.
16. Chaudhary, K. P. (1975). *The Effective Teaching of History in India*, New Delhi: NCERT

17. Chauhan, S. S. (2008). *Innovations in Teaching Learning Process*. UP: Vikas Publishing
18. Clark, L.H. Stare, I.S. (1967), *Secondary School Teaching Methods,* London: University Tutorial Press.
19. Coulby, D. & Zambeta, G. (2005). *Globalization & Nationalism in Education*. New York: Routledge, Falmer.
20. Crossley, N., Prell, C., & Scott, J. (2009). Social Network Analysis: Introduction to Special Edition. *Methodological Innovations Online*, 4(1), 1–5. https://doi.org/10.1177/205979910900400101
21. Daisaku Ikeda on education for peace, retrieved on 21st September 2021 from https://www.peace-ed-campaign.org/daisaku-ikeda-on-education-for-peace-2/
22. Daisaku Ikeda, retrieved on 21st September 2021 from https://en.wikipedia.org/wiki/Daisaku_Ikeda
23. Dallmayr F.R. (1973) Phenomenology and Social Science: An Overview and Appraisal. In: Carr D., Casey E.S. (eds) *Explorations in Phenomenology. Selected Studies in Phenomenology and Existential Philosophy*, 4(1), Springer, Dordrecht. https://doi.org/10.1007/978-94-010-1999-6_5
24. Degrowth: A Simple Definition, retrieved on 21st September 2021 from https://youmatter.world/en/definition/degrowth-definition/
25. Dhamija, N. (1993). Multimedia Approaches in Teaching Social Studies, New Delhi: Harman Publishing House
26. Dhand, H. (2009). *Techniques of Teaching.* New Delhi: APH Publishing Corporation.
27. Dobkin, S.W. (1985). *A Handbook for the Teaching of Social Studies*. Massachusetts: Allyn and Bacon.
28. Duplass, J. A. (2009). *Teaching Elementary Social Studies*. New Delhi: Atlantic Publishers.
29. Fenton, E. (1967), *The New Social Studies,* New York: Ho Rinehart, Winston, Inc.
30. Gattone, C.F. (2020). *A Balanced Epistemological Orientation for the Social Sciences*, retrieved on 21st September 2021 from https://rowman.com/ISBN/9781793631442/A-Balanced-Epistemological-Orientation-for-the-Social-Sciences
31. Geoff, I. (1996) *Bloom's taxonomy of educational objectives.* The University of Queensland, Teaching and Educational Development Institute
32. Ghate, V. D. (1956). *Teaching of History*, Mumbai: OUP
33. Gontier, N. *Evolutionary Epistemology*, Internet Encyclopaedia of Philosophy, retrieved September 21, 2021, from https://iep.utm.edu/evo-epis/
34. Griffiths, M. (2008). *Epistemology of the Social Sciences*, retrieved on 21st September 2021 from https://www.skidmore.edu/sdm/documents/Michael-Griffiths-SDM-Proposal-Second-Version.pdf
35. Gupta, R. (2018). *The Methods of Teaching Social Studies.* Harman Publishing House
36. Haroon, S. & Nasleer, A. (2012). *Teaching of Social Science*. Delhi: Pearson-Dorling Kindersly.

37. Henryk, S. (2005). *Philosophy for a new Civilisation*. New Delhi: Gyan Books Pvt. Ltd.

38. http://www.buzzle.com/articles/importance-of-teaching-social-studies.html

39. http://www.non-plagiarized-termpapers.com/blog/importance-of-teaching-social-studies-in-our-schools/

40. http://www.socialstudies.org/positions/powerful

41. http://www.yourdictionary.com/library/reference/word-definitions/define-social-science.html

42. Jason, G. & Olivier, U. (2013). Daisaku Ikeda's philosophy of peace, education proposals, and Soka education: convergences and divergences in peace education, *Journal of Peace Education*, 10:3, 303-322, DOI: 10.1080/17400201.2013.848072

43. Jovanovic, D. (2015). "Important people in multimodality theory." In *Key Terms in Multimodality: Definitions, Issues, Discussions*, (edited by Norgaard, N), retrieved September 21, 2021, from www.sdu.dk/multimodalkeyterms

44. Joyce, B. & Weil. (2004). *Models of Teaching*. U.K: Prentice Hall of India.

45. Judith L. Pace, "*Why We Need to Save (and Strengthen) Social Studies*," Education Week (December 18, 2007).

46. Kenkel, W.F. (1980). *Society in Action: Introduction to Sociology*. New York: Harper and Row.

47. Khan, R. S. & Ahmad, I. (Eds) (1995), *Lesson Planning,* New Delhi: IASE, JMI.

48. Khan, S. U. (1998). *History Teaching-Problems*: Prospective and Prospect, New Delhi:

49. Kochar, S. K. (1963), *The Teaching of Social Studies,* Delhi: University Publishers.

50. Kochhar SK. (2003) *The Teaching of Social Studies*. New Delhi: Sterling Publishers (P) Ltd.

51. Kohli, A.S. (1996). *Teaching of Social Science*. New Delhi: Anmol Publication. Pvt. Ltd.

52. Kress, G. & Leeuwen, T.V. (2001). *Multimodal Discourse: The Modes and Media of Contemporary Communication.* Oxford UK: Oxford University Press

53. Lee, N. (Ed.) (1975), *Teaching Economics,* London: Heinenmann Educational Books.

54. Leon, A. & Leon, M. (2012). *Internet for Everyone*. New Delhi: Vikas Publishing House.

55. Leslie, W.T. & Bybee, W.R. (1996). *Teaching Secondary School Science*. New Jersey: Prentice Hall.

56. Lewis, E.M. (1960), *Teaching History in Secondary School,* Delhi: Sterling Publishers.

57. Luhmann, N. (1993). Deconstruction as second-order observing, *New Literary History*, 24(4), 763–782

58. Mangal S.K & Mangal U. (2008) *Teaching of Social Studies*. New Delhi: PHI Learning (P) Ltd.

59. Mangal, S. K., & Mangal, S. (2005). *Essentials of Educational Technology and Management.* PHI Learning
60. Martin, D.J. (2006). *Elementary Social Science Methods: A Constructive Approach*, Singapore: Wordsworth Publishing.
61. Mathur, S.S. (2008). *A Sociological Approach to Indian Education*. Agra: Vinod Pustak Mandir.
62. Max Weber's Social Action Theory, retrieved on 21st September 2021 from https://revisesociology.com/2017/01/26/max-webers-social-action-theory/
63. Michaelis, John U. (1969). Social Studies for Children in a Democracy. *British Journal of Educational Studies,* 17 (1):89-90.
64. Mofatt, M.R. (1955). *Social Studies Instruction,* New York: Prentice Hall.
65. Muhammad, F.N. (2018). Popper's Evolutionary Epistemology, *International Journal of Research*, 4(1), retrieved September 21, 2021, from https://theresearchers.asia/Papers/Vol-IV,%20Issue-I-2018/Popper%e2%80%99s%20Evolutionary%20Epistemology.pdf
66. Multimodality (Kress), https://www.learning-theories.com/multimodality-kress.html
67. Multimodality, retrieved September 21, 2021, from https://en.wikipedia.org/wiki/Multimodality
68. Nardelli, P.H.J. (2007). Construction-deconstruction-reconstruction framework: A methodology for interdisciplinary research, retrieved on 21st September 2021 from https://cpb-us-e1.wpmucdn.com/blogs.gwu.edu/dist/d/257/files/2017/02/Nardelli_WOSC17_v1-withbib-1izeo3c.pdf
69. National Focus Group (2006). *Position Paper on Teaching of Social Sciences (First Ed)* New Delhi: NCERT
70. NCERT (1974). *Teaching History in Secondary Schools*, New Delhi
71. NCERT (1988). *Guidelines and Syllabi for Secondary Stage (Class IX, X),* New Delhi: NCERT.
72. Noushad, P.P. & Kumar, S. (2006). *Teaching of Social Science*. Calicut: Scorpio Publishers
73. Pandey, H.N. *Conflict Theory of Georg Simmel*, Department of Sociological Studies, Central University of South Bihar, retrieved on 21st September 2021 from https://www.cusb.ac.in
74. Pandey, R.S. (1997). *East West Thoughts on Education.* Allahabad: Horizon Publishers.
75. Passi, B. K. (1976). *Becoming a better teacher*: Micro teaching approach. Press Publishing House Pvt Ltd.
76. Peter, M.H. (1994) *Social Studies for elementary School Children* (Developing Young Citizens) Meerut: Loyal Book Depot.
77. Philips, J. (2010). *Teaching History*. New Delhi: Sage Publishers.
78. Postpositivism, retrieved on 21st September 2021 from https://en.wikipedia.org/wiki/Postpositivism
79. Postpositivism, retrieved on 21st September 2021 from https://writingcommons.org/section/writing-studies/epistemology/postpositivists/

80. Quillen, I.J. & Hanna, L. A. (1943), *Education for Social Competence, Curriculum Sc Instruction in Secondary School Social Study.* Chicago: Scott, Foreman & Co.

81. Radhakrishnan, N. (2014). *Daisaku Ikeda.* Trivandrum: Ikeda Centre for Value Education.

82. Rekha, P. (2005). *Movements in Medieval India.* New Delhi: Gyan Books Pvt. Ltd.

83. Reuhela, S.P. (2009) *Teaching of Social Sciences.* Hyderabad: Neelkamal Publications.

84. Ronis, D. (2007). *Brain Compatible Assessments.* California: Corwin Press, Sage Publications.

85. Saxena N.R. et al. (2007) *Teaching of Social Science.* Meerut: R. Lal Book Depot.

86. Schultz, T.W. (1963). *The Economic Value of Education.* New York: Columbia University Press.

87. Shah, H. *NCFTE 2009*, Directorate of Distance Education, University of Kashmir, retrieved on 21st September 2021 from http://ddeku.edu.in/Files/2cfa4584-5afe-43ce-aa4b-ad936cc9d3be/Custom/6.NCFTE%202009.pdf

88. Sharma, R. A. (2008). *Technological Foundation of Education.* Meerut: R. Lall Books Depot.

89. Sharma, S.P. (2011). *Teaching of Social Studies.* New Delhi: Kanishka Publishers Distribution.

90. Shaver, J.P. (1992). *Epistemology and the education of social science teachers*, retrieved on 21st September 2021 from https://files.eric.ed.gov/fulltext/ED355143.pdf

91. Singh, Y.K. (2009). *Teaching of History: Modern methods.* New Delhi: APH Publishing Corp.

92. Sivarajan K, et al. (2008). *Social Science Education.* Calicut: Calicut University Central Co-Operative Stores.

93. Slev, E.B. (1950). *Teaching Social Studies in High School,* Boston: DC., Heath & Co.

94. Social development, retrieved on 21st September 2021 from https://www.giz.de/en/ourservices/social_development.html

95. Talla, M. (2012). *Curriculum Development Perspectives, Principles & Issues.* Delhi: Pearson Pvt. Ltd.

96. Trueman, C.N. (2015). *Anti Positivism,* The History Learning Site, retrieved on 21st September 2021 from https://www.historylearningsite.co.uk/sociology/research-methods-in-sociology/anti-positivism/

97. Turner, J.H. (2001). Positivism: Sociological, Editor(s): Neil J. Smelser, Paul B. Baltes, *International Encyclopaedia of the Social & Behavioural Sciences*, Pergamon, https://doi.org/10.1016/B0-08-043076-7/01941-0, retrieved on 21st September 2021 from https://www.sciencedirect.com/science/article/pii/B0080430767019410

98. UNESCO (1981). *Handbook for Teaching of Social Studies,* Paris: UNESCO.

99. Varma, O.P. & Vedanayagam, E.G. (2007). Geography Teaching, India: Sterling Publishers Private Limited.

100. Wesley, E. B. (1950). *Teaching Social Studies in High Schools*. United States: Heath.

101. What is social development? Government of New Brunswick, retrieved on 21st September 2021 from https://www2.gnb.ca/content/gnb/en/departments/esic/overview/content/what_is_social_development.html

102. Zevin, J. (1999). *Social Studies for the Twenty-first Century: Methods and Materials for Teaching in Middle and Secondary Schools*, 3rd Edition. (n.p.): Taylor & Francis.

APPENDICES

APPENDIX 1: MODEL QUESTION PAPER 1

Time: 2 hours; **Max. Marks: 50**

PART A: Answer any *Two* questions. Each question carries 10 marks; 2×10= 20 Marks

1. Critically examine various epistemological frameworks of Social Science Education.
2. Explain the impact of *human activities on environmental degradation*. Develop an instructional strategy mentioning specific instructional objectives, teaching-learning activities, and evaluation items to teach this topic.
3. Discuss the nature and scope of teaching Social Science as a core subject of the school curriculum. How would you avoid overloading of the syllabus that may result by correlating and combining individual subjects – like History, Geography and civics into a single component?
4. Discuss the possibilities and challenges of integrating ICTs in Social Science teaching.

PART B: Answer any *Four* questions. Each question carries 5 marks; 4x5= 20 Marks

5. "The qualification of a Social Science teacher educator is more personal than academic." Discuss.
6. Suggest various ways to improving professionalism of social science teachers.
7. Design a rubric on any Social Science topic of your choice.
8. Explain the significance of human rights education in the present global context.
9. Illustrate various techno-pedagogic skills required for a social science teacher educator.
10. Differentiate between integrated and interdisciplinary approaches to teaching Social Sciences.

PART C: Answer *All* questions. Each question carries 2 marks; 5x2= 10 Marks

11. Compare and contrast Paper-Pencil tests and Online examinations.
12. How you will develop the "dignity of labour" among your students?
13. List out a few scaffolding strategies in social science teaching.
14. How you will evaluate non-cognitive outcomes in Social Science?
15. Enlist few strategies for making Social Science Teachers as reflective practitioners.

APPENDIX 2: MODEL QUESTION PAPER 2

Time: 2 hours; **Max. Marks: 50**

PART A: Answer any two questions. Each question carries 10 marks; 2x10= 20 Marks

1. How do you substantiate the need of pedagogic analysis in the teaching of social sciences? Critically examine various pedagogical approaches generally applied in social science instruction?
2. "India has marked her specific place in the global digital learning map". Do you agree to this statement? Substantiate your arguments highlighting the effectiveness/ shortcomings of Indian digital initiatives?
3. Suppose, you are asked to design a well-knit module for the professional development of social science teacher educators. Sketch the modular blue print and develop the module considering the essential components.
4. Evaluate the significance of various assessment practices being used by the social science teachers and teacher educators?

PART B: Answer any four questions. Each question carries 5 marks; 4x5= 20 Marks

5. Elucidate the need for incorporating community living and social adaptation in the social science curriculum?
6. Give a brief account of various cognitive learning theories?
7. How are rubrics developed? Design a rubric on any topic of your choice?
8. Explain the significance of human rights education in the context of recent socio-cultural situation of India?
9. Briefly summarise the desirable techno-pedagogic skills of a social science teacher educator?
10. What are the basic tenets of Evolutionary Theory of Karl Popper? Do you find any association of the same with the Social Action principles of Max Weber?

PART C: Answer all questions. Each question carries 2 marks; 5x2= 10 Marks

11. Give the meaning of reflective teaching?
12. What do you mean by grade inflation?
13. List out a few scaffolding strategies (suggestive to the social science teacher educators)

14. How does growth differ from de-growth?
15. Define eco-habitation

APPENDIX 3: MULTIPLE CHOICE QUESTIONS

Correct answers are given in Bold; each question carries one mark

1. Who is belongs to humanistic school of thought?
   (a) Jean Piaget
   (b) Jerome Bruner
   (c) **Abraham Maslow**
   (d) BF Skinner
2. Who is the proponent of Micro Teaching?
   (a) DW Allen
   (b) John Dewey
   (c) Kilpatrick
   (d) Ned A Flander
3. Which university among the below mainly related to *Open and Distance Learning*?
   (a) JNU
   (b) **IGNOU**
   (c) University of Kerala
   (d) AMU
4. Which one is the indigenous MOOC platform in India?
   (a) Moodle
   (b) **SWAYAM**
   (c) Coursera
   (d) Edx
5. Herbert Thelen is associated which models of teaching?
   (a) Social Inquiry Model
   (b) Concept Attainment Model
   (c) Role Playing Model
   (d) Group Investigation Model
6. Max Weber considered administration as a
   (a) Process
   (b) Product
   (c) Bureaucracy
   (d) All of the above
7. There are only two sources of knowledge; logical reasoning and empirical experience is the view point of which school of philosophy
   (a) Logical positivism
   (b) Naturalism

(c) Pragmatism

(d) Realism

8. The origin of social stratification was considered as the conquest of one group by another. This was supported by

(a) Conflict theory

(b) Functionalist theory

(c) Interactionist theory

(d) All of the above

9. Japanese philosopher Daisaku Ikeda is associated with:

(a) Adult Education

(b) Special Education

(c) **Peace Education**

(d) Pre-Schooling

10. The school of philosophy that emphasized upon normative and social sciences than upon natural and physical sciences is

(a) Pragmatism

(b) Idealism

(c) Existentialism

(d) Marxism

11. Who advocated the creation of a classless society?

(a) Plato

(b) Comte

(c) Gandhi

(d) Karl Marx

12. A group of people living together by a common interests and purpose may be called as

(a) Community

(b) Family

(c) Religious institution

(d) Association

13. Values, attitudes, feeling, words etc. belong to the category of

(a) Material culture

(b) Non-material culture

(c) Both a & b

(d) None of the above

14. One of the most basic features of Indian culture is

(a) Faith in God

(b) Faith in ahimsa

(c) Faith in karma

(d) Faith in tolerance

15. Which of the following concepts is emphasized by Swami Vivekananda
    (a) Integral education
    (b) Man making education
    (c) Education for harmony
    (d) Citizenship education

APPENDIX 4: PRESCRIBED PRACTICUMS

1. Prepare an e-content based on any one of the social science subject areas of your choice.
2. Develop a meta-narrative about changing communities (observe, explain, witness, and elaborate the changes occurring in a particular community and develop thick descriptions)
3. Identify some archaeological materials in the locality and prepare a report on these items emphasizing the educational and historical significance.
4. Prepare a rubric for assessing the teacher trainees in teaching Social Science during their teaching practice.